B C L

D1304809

RESIDENTIAL SEGREGATION, THE STATE AND CONSTITUTIONAL CONFLICT IN AMERICAN URBAN AREAS

Special Publications of the Institute of British Geographers

Editorial Board

M. BLACKSELL, Department of Geography, University of Exeter
D. BRUNSDEN, Department of Geography, King's College, University of London
J. W. R. WHITEHAND, Department of Geography, University of Birmingham
M. WILLIAMS, School of Geography, University of Oxford

For a complete list of titles in this series, see end of book.

PREFACE

As they develop, and especially as they become densely populated, academic disciplines tend to fragment into specialized parts among which there is relatively little contact. This has been the case in human geography during recent decades. The various sub-disciplines – urban geography, economic geography, population geography, political geography, etc. – operate separately if not independently, with more contacts relating to technical (especially statistical) than to substantive issues. Within these sub-disciplines, too, there is separation; in urban geography, for example, the study of residential patterns in cities has very largely been divorced from that of the commercial pattern, and the study of elections has developed independently of that of mainstream political geography (see Taylor, 1978).

The main advantage of such sub-disciplinary specialism is that it promotes the study of topics in considerable depth and allows individuals to acquire substantial, if relatively narrow, expertise. The major disadvantage is that it involves the drawing of artificial bound-aries around blocks of subject matter, focusing attention away from potential links and leaving important problems untackled because they occupy the sub-disciplinary interstices. Such a disadvantage is particularly acute in a social science such as human geography for which a holistic perspective on society, its organization of space and its use of environment, is crucial. Specialism is unlikely to be removed, but it should not impede the integration necessary for complete understanding.

The topic of the present book clearly falls within the interstices of the sub-disciplinary specialisms. The element of spatial organization under consideration – residential segre-gation in American metropolitan areas – is generally considered part of urban geography, although aspects of it are also investigated under the separate head of social geography. But, as stressed here, the organization of space in residential areas has a strong political element, involving both political conflict in which the state, through its legal institutions, acts as arbiter and employer of the state apparatus to create particular morphologies.

Relative to much work in human geography, therefore, the study reported here covers a broad canvas, drawing not only on several geographical sub-disciplines but also on other social sciences including legal studies, political science and sociology. As an empirical exercise it is a case study, an investigation of how the local state apparatus has been used in the creation of a particular residential pattern in American urban areas, of how that use has been challenged in the country's courts, and of how the judiciary – especially the members of the Supreme Court – have arbitrated those challenges. More generally, it provides an example of how what appear to be general economic, social and political processes are influenced by particular environmental contexts and of how key individuals within those contexts – managers – may influence the detail of the consequences of the processes, if not the processes themselves.

The general processes operating in the United States are those of the capitalist mode of production. Associated with the economic system are a social structure characterized by class divisions and conflict and a political structure charged with maintaining conditions for successful capitalist operations (i.e. encouraging accumulation and providing legitimation; Johnston, 1982a). Similar systems and structures exist in all capitalist societies. But there are many dissimilarities in the detailed ways in which they operate. In Britain, for example, there is a large public housing sector, whereas in the United States there is a very small one; in

Britain, local government is much more constrained than its American counterpart; the United States has a written Constitution that protects certain individual rights and freedoms and allows individuals to sue those who abridge them, whereas in Britain there is no such document. None of these differences are fundamental to the general processes. The United States and Britain are both capitalist societies (both increasingly unsuccessful ones!). But the detailed nature of capitalism – how it should operate as an economic system, how its social conflicts should be contained, what particular functions should be performed by the state – has been interpreted somewhat differently in the two countries. The different interpretations accumulate, creating separate cultural contexts for capitalism that enable new interpretations but constrain others. Societies have been created with the same general goals – to support an increasing level of affluence through the purchase of labour power and the sale of its products. Pursuit of that goal varies from place to place, however, depending on the cultural context.

As a case study, therefore, this book identifies no general principles that have empirical relevance to other countries – or even, necessarily, to the United States at some time in the future. The details of the local state in America cannot be used as the basis for discussions of the local state elsewhere; nor can the decisions of the Supreme Court be translated to other contexts. There are, however, general methodological principles to be derived from this case study. These relate in particular to the nature of the state, to the texts which stipulate how the society should function, and to the individuals who interpret those texts. The case study indicates the necessity for a detailed study of these elements of a society in order to obtain an understanding of the empirical detail that comprises the spatial organization of a capitalist society.

The remainder of the book is in three parts. In Part One – *The Context* – the environment within which the case study is set is outlined. Distancing, it is argued in Chapter 1, is a general process in capitalist societies, whereby members of various socio-economic groupings (related to the class structure) seek for social and economic reasons to congregate together in particular residential areas and to segregate themselves from the members of, to them, undesirable groups. The result is an urban residential mosaic. The nature of this mosaic in the United States and its relationship to the process of distancing is outlined in Chapter 1.

Nearly every country has a system of local government which gives the residents of sub-national territories some autonomy in the control of certain aspects of their social environment. Countries vary in the degree of autonomy allowed to local governments, and in the extent to which territorial groups are allowed to manipulate this political organization of space to their own ends. The United States has a long tradition of local government, which includes separate political units in much of its suburban portions. Chapter 2 describes this system of local government, outlines the benefits that it offers to local populations, and illustrates how the political manipulation of space in suburbia has been used to advance the economic and social interests of particular groups in society. Thus distancing and the creation of an urban residential mosaic are general processes; in the United States, some of those who seek to benefit from those processes use the political environment to buttress their efforts.

Distancing comes about because of the class division of a capitalist society and the unequal allocation of income, wealth and other economic and social rewards among those classes. This unequal allocation of rewards, that is spent on consumption, generates conflict between the relative winners and relative losers, and as the unequal allocation is reflected in the spatial organization of society, so that spatial organization is part of the arena of conflict. The conflict itself takes a variety of forms, as illustrated in Chapter 3.

Because it has a written Constitution incorporating a Bill of Rights, the political environment of the United States provides the means by which certain types of conflict might be pursued and the arena within which arbitration can take place. Chapter 4 describes this environment, with particular emphasis on the relevant texts – notably the Fourteenth Amendment to the Constitution – and on the managers involved in the interpretation of those texts in the light of particular conflicts. Central to this are the Justices of the United States Supreme Court, whose decisions and opinions not only decide particular conflicts but also provide the precedents for other conflicts and decisions, that are determined in the lower federal courts and in the State courts. The Supreme Court's decisions are part of the environment within which American society, including its spatial organization, is reproduced.

Following this outline of the context for the case study, Part Two – *The Conflicts* – looks at the details of the individual conflicts. This involves discussion of individual cases, evaluation of the Court decisions and opinions, and conclusions about the impact of the Courts on the residential mosaic of American suburbia. Three sets of decisions are covered, each referring to the role of the local state in suburbia. Chapter 5 is concerned with land-use zoning, and with challenges to its constitutionality when it is employed to achieve particular social goals. In Chapter 6 the focus swings to the study of education in suburban areas, with special reference to racial segregation. And Chapter 7 – shorter, because of the small number of cases – looks at the provision of goods and services by the local state.

The general conclusion to be drawn from this review in Chapters 5–7 is that, with the partial exception of racial segregation in schools, the challenges have largely failed. The American Courts, led by the Supreme Court, have upheld the right – under the Constitution and federal and State law – of groups within society to use the local state in their manipulation of space for individual and community gain. Thus the conflict has been deflected to the legislative branch of the state, where new texts might be produced so that the challenges could succeed and the 'closed' suburbs could be opened-up to the less affluent and the non-whites. Chapter 8 discusses the attempts to create such new texts, the problems in their implementation, and the role of the Courts in this new round of challenges.

Part Three presents the conclusions to the study.

Throughout this manuscript, great care has been taken to distinguish between the concepts of state and government, and also between state and State. The concept of the state refers to the body of institutions within a civil society in which sovereignty rests; government, on the other hand, refers to a particular administration of all or part of the state apparatus. A State is one of the institutions that comprises the state apparatus in the United States; there are 50 States, plus the District of Columbia. Finally, the local state is that part of the state apparatus covering a part of the state territory only. The local state has no independent sovereign power. Local government is the administration of the local state.

Work on this book began in 1978, having been stimulated by reading the Supreme Court's decisions relating to reapportionment (see Chapter 8). It was advanced by 1979 by a visit to the United States, made possible by a period of study leave from the University of Sheffield and by a grant from the Nuffield Foundation. I am grateful to those two bodies, and also those who talked with me in America on these issues and made my visit an enjoyable one – notably Derek Thompson, Risa Palm, Bill Clark, Nick Entrikin, Allan Pred and Dick Walker. Since then, development of the work and my ideas has benefited from contacts with a number of workers – Gordon Clark, Kevin Cox and Mike Dear deserve special mention.

In preparing this book for publication, special thanks are due to the staffs of the Law Library and of the Inter-Library Loans section of the University of Sheffield for the good-natured handling of my many requests. I am grateful to Jeremy Whitehand and the Editorial Committee of the I.B.G. Special Publications Series, and to Academic Press, for their encouragement. A major debt is owed to Patrick Renshaw, for undertaking the onerous task of reading the full draft, while still in my handwriting, and making valuable comments on it. Finally, I am indebted once again to Joan Dunn for her secretarial skills.

March 1984   *R. J. Johnston*
Sheffield

CONTENTS

PART ONE

The context

ONE

The urban residential mosaic

There is a mosaic of residential districts of differing characteristics in all American urban areas. Some of those districts are peopled almost entirely by blacks; many are overwhelmingly white in their ethnic composition, but with people from different national backgrounds and birthplaces tending to live in separate areas. Many districts are dominated by single-family dwellings set in their own grounds; some are almost entirely composed of apartment blocks. In some districts, nearly every dwelling houses a family with young children; in others, children may be rare. And in some, the housing is very expensive and is occupied by (usually well-educated) people earning large incomes; in others, the housing is dilapidated and the residents are poor.

There are, then, several criteria which distinguish the various districts of the residential mosaic in American urban areas. Spatial separation of various groups one from the other is the norm, as a vast body of empirical research has indicated. Such separation does not occur randomly: as will be demonstrated here, it is the result of a combination of individual and collective decisions and reflects underlying economic (and hence social) forces within society. Members of particular groupings within society seek to congregate together, and thereby to segregate themselves from members of other groups. The present chapter outlines why this occurs; the remainder of the book looks at how it occurs.

Given the processes that produce residential separation, it could be that the spatial outcome is more or less random. That is, there need be no common features across all (or at least most) of urban America in exactly where particular groups are located. But this is not so. There is a considerable amount of spatial order in the detailed patterning of the American urban residential mosaic, as a great deal of research has shown. (This extensive literature is summarized in recent texts, such as Hartshorn (1980), Palm (1981) and Johnston (1982b).) In general terms, this research indicates that the higher income residents of an urban area tend to concentrate in particular sectors of it. These sectors are usually those with the most attractive physical environments, and within them the most affluent generally prefer to live some distance from the city centre. Thus the poor are concentrated in the inner residential districts, as are the blacks, although some inner-city districts have recently become very fashionable with certain affluent groups and have been "gentrified". Young families with children, apart from those that are relatively poor, tend to be concentrated in the outer zones of the built-up area.

Within the residential portions of American urban areas, then, there is a process of distancing in operation, whereby members of some groups within society seek to isolate themselves from those of other groups, creating their own niches in a complex urban ecology. Niches of particular types tend to be found in the same relative locations (relative, that is, to the city centre) in most urban areas. This book is about those niches, about why they are created and how, and about the resolution of conflicts which arise over their maintenance.

DISTANCING, CONGREGATION AND SEGREGATION

As suggested above, a great deal of research has been done which portrays the results of the distancing process. Most of this uses data from the United States Census and demonstrates, using the categories available from that source and the spatial units on which they are based, both the degree to which different groups live apart and where they are concentrated. Such work indicates that there are three separate – though far from independent – distancing processes going on, each producing a pattern of residential separation. (Rees (1979) presents the fullest analysis.)

The first of these processes is *socio-economic* in its character, and produces separation of groups according to occupational, educational and income criteria. If households are classified according to their incomes, and the homes of the members of various income groups are mapped, the results show that the greater the difference between the incomes of two households the smaller the probability that they are living in the same residential district. For most people, incomes are rewards for work. Certain occupations are paid more than others. In general, it is the white-collar, non-manual occupations which are best paid, especially those involving professional and managerial tasks. Blue-collar, manual work is generally less well paid, with skilled manual workers earning more than the semi-skilled, who in turn receive more than the unskilled. Thus, if occupations are arranged along a scale from professional and managerial at one end to unskilled manual at the other, then the greater the distance between two households on this scale, the smaller is the probability that they are living in the same district. And finally, because the non-manual occupations – especially those involving professional and managerial tasks – are in general restricted to the better-educated, this occupational-cum-income spatial separation also involves a separation of people according to their educational achievements.

This socio-economic separation is far from complete: few districts are entirely comprised of members of a certain occupational grouping only. In part this reflects on the boundaries of the census districts, which may not coincide precisely with the social boundaries on the ground. More importantly, it reflects the lack of perfect correlation between the three socio-economic criteria. Some unskilled manual workers are relatively well-paid, for example, and so can afford to occupy more expensive housing, in "better" residential areas, than their counterparts. And households are able to determine their relative priorities; some may choose to spend relatively high proportions of their incomes on housing in, to them, "desirable" residential districts, whereas others with the same incomes spend less, and live in relatively cheaper areas. But in general, there is a great deal of spatial separation of the various occupational/income/educational groups.

The second of these distancing processes is *ethnic*. Members of different ethnic groups tend to live apart from each other, and from the host society. The most apparent aspect of this ethnic distancing is the almost complete separation of black Americans, and also of other non-white groups (Chinese, Mexican–Americans, and Puerto Ricans, for example), from white society. The black ghetto, generally containing only black people, is a characteristic of nearly every American town and city and a black family living in what is otherwise an entirely white district is relatively rare (Rose, 1971.)

The United States has been populated by several large streams of immigrants, from many European countries and also from Asia and some parts of America. The members of these different streams have, in large part, moved to the urban areas, and there they have congregated into separate residential districts (Ward, 1971). Their homes tend to be isolated from those of native white Americans, and also from those of other immigrant groups. Over time, as the immigrants and their descendants are assimilated into American society, so some of them move out of those separate ethnic niches. But others remain – and may be joined by new migrants. The result is that the plural American society is reflected in its plurality of ethnic residential districts.

The final distancing process relates to *family life styles*. This has several facets. The first involves a division of households into those which occupy low density, generally single-family, housing, and those which occupy high-density apartment and tenement blocks. This is in part a division between families with children in the former and childless households in the latter, but is not entirely so because economic factors are also important (in that single-family, low density housing is, on average, relatively expensive). Apart from this general division between districts with many children and those with few, there is also considerable separation of families with different age profiles. There is a tendency for families with very young children to be concentrated in certain districts (usually those close to the edge of the built-up area), separated from those whose children are teenagers.

These, then, are the main distancing processes in operation in urban America. There are others, but they are either peculiar to certain places only or are closely related to one or more of the three already outlined. Religion, for example, is related to ethnicity. There is spatial distancing involving Jews, some of which overlaps various ethnic (i.e. birthplace) categories. In general, however, it is the three processes of distancing according to socio-economic, ethnic and life style criteria that bring about residential congregation and segregation in American urban areas.

A rationale for distancing

Why do these distancing processes operate, and why do the members of various groups within society live in separate residential areas? The simplest answer would seem to be choice, that people prefer to live among those who are like themselves, and to distance themselves from those who are not. Thus whites prefer to live apart from blacks, and vice versa, as do Italians and Irish; people without children prefer districts without many young people; high income people do not like to live among members of lower income groups, and so on. The residential mosaic is the result of the expression of preferences in a free market.

Why these preferences? One attempt to account for them uses the concept of externality (see Cox, 1973, 1979). This refers to the effect of the action of one person (or institution, including a firm) on another, over which the former has no control, and which is unpriced. An externality may be either positive (a good thing) or negative (bad). An example of the latter is the noise of aircraft using a runway; an example of the former may be a neighbourhood school with a high academic reputation.

Many externalities have a spatial morphology. With some, this refers to a particular area: the impact of the good neighbourhood school will only be felt in its catchment area, for example. For many, there is a gradient. The noise from the aircraft is more intrusive close to the runway than further away from it, for example, so that the force of the negative externality diminishes with distance from its source. As a consequence, the desirability of dwellings is likely to increase, all other things being equal, with distance from the source of the noise.

There are many sources of externalities within urban areas. Most of them are provided by certain types of land use, and many are public facilities. Thus, for example, Smith (1980) has shown that out of a list of 28 public facilities a sample of American urban residents wanted none of them on the same block as their own homes and only one – a park – on the next block. Only two others – a public library and an elementary school – were wanted for the resident's neighbourhood. Most of the others (such as a community health clinic, a shopping centre, a fire station, and a theatre) were wanted for somewhere in the town, but nine facilities (including prison, city dump, and a mental health centre) should be outside the town altogether. If such a perception of negative externalities is general across the entire urban population, then clearly there will be conflict over their locations. Nobody wants them on their blocks, or even within their neighbourhoods, but clearly they must be on some people's blocks and in many people's neighbourhoods: but whose? (Note that some facilities are negative externalities if they are too close, but positive ones if they are quite near. Most parents of young children want an elementary school within their home neighbourhood, but not next door to their own dwelling.)

That most public facilities are perceived as generators of at least local negative externalities means that the various groups within society will be in conflict to try and keep them out of their neighbourhoods. Such conflicts involve the state – usually its local arm – which is not only the provider of some of these sources but the facilitator for, and decision-maker regarding, many others. As the planning authority, the state influences the location of industrial, commercial and other facilities, many of which generate a variety of negative externalities – noise, pollution, traffic, etc. It also controls the routes of major transport arteries, which generate similar undesirable effects in their vicinity.

Why should this conflict over externalities come about, and how is it resolved? Clearly, if certain public facilities and land uses are considered undesirable, their location in a particular place will lead to a deterioration in the perceived environment there, and in the surrounding neighbourhood. This will make the area less attractive to live in, and as a consequence the values of properties there will decline. Thus those with investments in land and dwellings within an area will seek to prevent the incursion of negative externalities, because of the potential impact on their investments. Conflict over negative externalities is in part conflict over the built environment; it is also conflict over financial interests. To protect both, residents seek, through the institutions of the state, to ensure that their neighbourhoods are unaffected. Analyses of such urban politics suggest that the conflict is rather one-sided, and that the more affluent groups within society are best able to achieve the protection that they require (Saunders, 1980).

The contents of a neighbourhood comprise a range of facilities in addition to the housing. Some of these are provided by private businesses (in some cases, as with the telephone system and with TV in the USA, licensed and controlled by the state). Many are provided by the state. These are what are termed public goods (see Bennett, 1980). A pure public good is provided equally for all citizens within a territorial jurisdiction – national defence provides one of the best examples. These are relatively few, however. Most public goods fall into one of two categories (Johnston, 1981). Impure public goods are those that are unevenly available because they are provided at particular locations only. A park, for example, is probably used more by households living within a few hundred yards of it than by those living a mile or more away; thus those living close to the park gain more from its provision. Similarly, as many research studies have shown, access to medical facilities is positively correlated with their use and with health care. Overall, then, some neighbourhoods are better serviced than others because of superior access to impure public goods, and obtaining that access is part of the conflict involved in distancing.

The other type of public good is the pure good, impurely distributed. An education service may be provided for all, for example, but the quality of the education provided – the facilities, resources, teachers, etc. – may vary from one part of a jurisdiction to another. Again, obtaining a high level of service may be part of the distancing process.

Within any urban area, therefore, there is a geography of access to impure public goods and another of the distribution of impurely provided public goods. As Knox (1982) has shown, these geographies are closely correlated with aspects of the metropolitan population distribution. Part of the process of distancing involves creating neighbourhoods that not only exclude perceived negative externalities but also reap the benefits of access to desired public goods and services and high levels of provision of those goods and services that are impurely distributed.

The conflict over externalities refers not only to the built environment but also to the social environment. As the literature reviewed above has suggested, most urban residents apparently prefer to live among people similar to themselves. Members of other groups are perceived as (at least potential) negative externalities, people whose presence in a neighbourhood reduces its attractiveness, and therefore the price that others will pay to live there. Such negative externalities may be related to the general social milieu. Certain types of people will not be good neighbours, living the sort of life style that is consonant with the area's general characteristics and participating in a harmonious, consensus-based, local society. Even more so, to many people, their children's presence at local schools may depreciate the quality of the education provided, thereby reducing the desirability of the relevant catchment areas.

There is, then, a perceived neighbourhood effect in terms of the social composition of residential district populations: the presence of certain types is considered a positive externality, enhancing neighbourhood quality, whereas that of others is considered a negative influence (Timms, 1971). Many make residential location decisions in order to promote the positive externalities and minimize the negative, and once such decisions have been made and a milieu formed, they act to protect it. In American urban society, the clearest example of this is the desire to exclude blacks from almost all white residential areas. Blacks are perceived as undesirable neighbours because of a presumed influence on neighbourhood quality and because their children are believed to lower the quality of the schools that they attend; the result is that black movement into an area is associated with declining property values there. There are many other potential externality conflicts – between the various immigrant groups, for example (Boal, 1976), between the affluent and the poor, the middle-class and the manual workers, and between certain life styles (student flats versus family dwellings, etc.).

This conflict over the social environment is related to property values, therefore. And, like the conflict over the built environment, it frequently involves the state. In some cases this involves direct action, because the state is the decision-making agent. Public housing, for example, is built by a state body, whose decisions affect the characteristics of neighbourhoods, and the provision of a public education system is undertaken by the state. In other cases, the conflict involves the state as facilitator and arbitrator. Its jurisdiction over land-use planning, for example, influences the nature of the residential environment. Thus, as with the conflict over the built environment, groups come into conflict with and through the state over the social quality of their neighbourhoods. And, again, in general it is the more affluent and more powerful who appear best able to use the state to maintain the quality and value of their homes.

An alternative view

The thrust of the preceding discussion is that the residential mosaic is a result of the members of different groups seeking to live among some people but not others, thereby creating a desired social quality for their home districts, their schools and local life. They are also seeking to create a pleasant built environment, into which unpleasant land uses and users do not intrude. Both of these activities are reflected in property values: people will pay more to live in nice places, among nice people. Thus the social geography of American urban areas reflects private desires and is the result of a competitive bidding process in a free market; those with most money buy the "best" areas, and those with the least get the worst.

This interpretation has much to recommend it (Cox and Johnston, 1982), but it fails to tackle the important issues of why such conflict takes place. It does not ask, for example, why the various groups within society have separate identities, why the maintenance of those identities is crucial to the group members, why many people seek to change their group membership, why property values are so central to urban political conflict, and why the state is deeply involved in such conflict over residential areas.

The basic differentiating characteristics between American residential areas relate to socio-economic groupings and to race. The former are the major divisions of a capitalist society. These have now extended far beyond the original division into bourgeoisie and proletariat into a complex division of labour. The rewards of success in capitalist activity are very unevenly distributed between the various groups, as indicated above in the discussion of income variations. People seek, individually and collectively, to advance their interests in this distribution – to get a larger share of the rewards; this they do for themselves, for their group as a whole, and for their children. Thus capitalist society is a society in conflict, over the allocation of its rewards. (To some, there is also conflict over the basic structure of the society: they seek to create a different form, in which the inequalities are removed.)

Residential differentiation in urban areas reflects this conflict (Harvey, 1975a). A central element of it is differential access to education, which is seen as providing the passport for entry to various occupations, and hence to particular income levels. (In this sense, a capitalist society is a "positional society" (Hirsch, 1977). Only a certain proportion of the population can gain access to the most desirable occupations, hence access to those occupations is a source of conflict.) If all schools provided the same quality of education and equality of opportunity of access, i.e. entry to desired occupations was achieved on merit alone, then certain schools would not be considered better than others and there would be no conflict over catchment area residence. But this is not the case. Some schools are better able to attract good teachers than are others, because they are in pleasant environments, present few discipline and personal safety problems, and serve motivated and able children. And some schools have better resources, because the allocation of funds and facilities is undertaken by politicians, who may seek to benefit their home areas (and hence their own children, and those of their friends, relatives and neighbours). Furthermore, there is a widespread belief (and a certain amount of evidence to back it up) that a certain social composition in a school is more conducive to academic success (that composition is dominated by the children of non-manual workers). Hence, in a society in which educational success is a major key to occupational entry and career advancement, many parents will seek to manipulate the school system to the advantage of their children. (Some ethnic groups – such as the Jews – emphasize educational achievements more than others – such as the rich. This is in part a reflection of group economic status and in part a cultural difference. It bolsters the demand for inter-group residential distancing.) And if, as in the United States, schools predominantly serve their local neighbourhood, then parents will manipulate catchment composition. A "good education" means going to a "good school", which means living in a "good area".

The different socio-economic groupings in society have developed separate life styles; they form what Harvey calls "consumption classes". In part this reflects their different educational backgrounds, which inculcate different interests in a wide variety of subjects, from attitudes to the local environment (reflected in the upkeep of house and grounds, for example) and to the use of public space (whether children play on the street, for example), through to the nature of social interaction (dinner parties or drinking at taverns) and sporting and cultural interests. Associated with these life styles are particular moral codes and models of behaviour. Conformity to those codes is considered highly desirable, and those who do not conform are unattractive neighbours. Thus people wish to live among others similar to themselves not only because this provides an attractive local society (in which they may choose not to participate actively) but also because it ensures protection of their life style and its codes.

The neighbourhood is a major focus of child socialization. Parents seek to inculcate their own values in their children. They want these reinforced in the educational system, hence the care over choice of school. They also want them reinforced by their children's social acquaintances, hence the choice of a neighbourhood in which the relevant codes predominate and which will back up the mode of socialization being undertaken. In seeking to structure neighbourhood composition, therefore, people are seeking to manipulate their children – even to the extent of constraining their choice of potential spouse. Thus the divisions of capitalist society, which are economically based, take on a social form, and the manipulation of the residential mosaic is seen as a way of maintaining these divisions.

Capitalist society, as just indicated, has an economic base; it is built on the acquisition and accumulation of wealth. Private property rights are central to capitalist ideology, therefore, and in many capitalist societies these extend to the right to own one's own home; this is certainly the case in America. The home, therefore, is not merely a shelter and an environment for family life, set in a neighbourhood which promotes certain social norms, it is also an investment. The price people pay for a home reflects not only its *use value* – its suitability as a location for a certain life style – but also its *exchange value* – what others might be prepared to pay for it in order to live in that location (Marchand, 1982). The home-owners, in their actions regarding the neighbourhood and its present and potential externalities, are protecting not only their living space but also an investment, one that they hope will appreciate. The greater the number of negative externalities that intrude on an area, the greater the likelihood of property values there depreciating (at least in real terms). The owners then have a declining asset which may influence, for example, their ability to borrow money using the home as a security and the price that they will receive if they need to move (perhaps to a more expensive area).

Given that home-ownership is widespread in urban America, then much of the conflict over the built and social environments of residential areas is clearly related to residents' desires to protect, and if possible enhance, their investments. In this, they are not acting alone as individuals; the capitalist system as a whole is deeply implicated, as is the state. Most people cannot afford the price of a home, whose use value spreads over several decades and whose exchange value may be substantial. They must borrow, which they normally do now by raising a mortgage. The institutions which lend them the money want security – they do not want the exchange value to depreciate, or their investment will decline. Thus they are concerned not only to ensure that the people they lend to, and the homes that they lend on, are good risks, they also want to ensure that the district is a good risk too. They may not be prepared to lend in certain areas, because the outlook for exchange values is uncertain. They, too, are interested in the manipulation of spatial externalities and the maintenance of residential separation.

The production of housing is an investment also, and those involved (not only those who provide the homes themselves but also the many others who provide the environmental infrastructure) want to be sure that they will receive a substantial return, relative to what might be received if their capital was invested in other sectors (see Daly, 1982.) They want to be sure that people can pay high prices, so they want to be assured that potential customers will be able to raise large mortgages. And, like so many other sectors of capital, they would like their investments underwritten. And so they seek subsidies from the state, both for themselves and for the other institutions involved in the housing market (Harvey, 1975b). These are provided in a variety of ways, such as state guarantees for mortgages. Thus the state also participates in the creation and maintenance of exchange values. It is involved in ensuring the health of the capitalist system, on which its entire legitimation is based (Johnston, 1982a), which in America includes ensuring the health of the construction industry and the mortgage market. This health is dependent on high, and rising, exchange values, which are related to residential differentiation, hence the state is implicated in the creation and maintenance of such differentiation.

The reasons for residential differentiation of socio-economic groups lie in the nature of the capitalist system, therefore (and such differentiation basically developed as the United States evolved into an industrial capitalist society: Radford, 1981; Johnston, 1982b; Doucet, 1982). They need not, however, have taken the particular form that they did in America, as comparison with other industrialized countries will show. A high level of home-ownership is not necessary in an advanced capitalist society. Nor is extensive suburbanization, as outlined below.

Ethnic spatial separation within the residential mosaic is associated by some analysts with the socio-economic processes just outlined, whereas to others it is the consequence, at least in part, of a separate set of processes. According to the first view, members of various ethnic groups have been accommodated in spatially separate residential areas because they have occupied separate positions in the division of labour. Most immigrants to American cities have come in at the bottom of the socio-economic scale (see Ward, 1971). They have less skills than their counterparts in the host society, are least able to compete in the labour market, and as a result are concentrated in the unskilled, lowest-paid occupations: as a consequence, they are concentrated in the cheapest, poorest-quality housing also. As members of these groups improve their labour market competitiveness, relative to both some members of the host society and newer immigrants, so they are able to filter into better housing areas.

This labour market view of ethnic residential separation accounts for it in terms of position in a competitive market, therefore, with the implicit conclusion that as their competitive position improves so the separation of recent immigrants will decrease. This, it is claimed, has been the experience of migrants to the American city in the past, and should be the case for newer groups (e.g. blacks and Puerto Ricans) in the future. Against this view it is argued that the experience of older migrant groups does not necessarily indicate economic, social and spatial integration (Kantrowicz, 1981), that the current separation of blacks into ghettos is much more complete than could be accounted for by their socio-economic status alone (Taeuber, 1968), and that the United States has a long history of deep racial prejudice, especially against blacks (Woodward, 1955; Carroll and Noble, 1977), which shows little sign of diminishing. Thus the ghetto concentration of blacks – and to a lesser extent of other groups – reflects not just their lowly position in the labour market but also discrimination against them in the allocation of jobs and housing. As a result, they have reacted by withdrawing inside those ghettos, seeking security and reassurance among their fellows while at the same time campaigning to remove the prejudice and discrimination (Ley, 1974).

Ethnic residential separation reflects the operation of distancing processes additional to those that create socio-economic residential differentiation, therefore. These additional processes may, of course, be a product (not a necessary one) of capitalist society, whereby racial or similar factors are used to identify and maintain a seriously underprivileged proletarian group. Racism, according to this view, is not innate; it is created in a capitalist society in order to identify a permanent disadvantaged class entirely subservient to the power of those who lack the distinguishing characteristics. (Such a creation is not, of course, peculiar to capitalism.)

The final dimension of residential differentiation, according to life style, is largely a function of the operation of a capitalist housing market. In particular, the separation of the generations into different districts reflects the general orientation of both the providers of new housing and the mortgage agencies towards young families; the agencies, in particular, prefer the relative security of a loan on a new home that is likely to appreciate in value, relative to an older dwelling in a potentially declining district. Thus in general the newer the housing, particularly single family housing, the younger the occupants. Non-family housing, particularly apartment blocks, tends to be spatially concentrated because of the operations of the urban land market. In general, the closer a piece of land is to the city centre, the more expensive it is. To yield a profit to developers, therefore, it must be used intensively, which involves the provision of the forms of high density housing that are generally preferred by the non-family oriented and avoided by those with young children – for whom private open space is more important than accessibility.

With American towns and cities, therefore, choice of residential area reflects individual and group preferences, especially among the relatively affluent. But these preferences are not innate, they are created by the economic and social system into which Americans are born and over which they have relatively little control. Thus the desire for socio-economic distancing reflects the operation of the housing market and competition for advancement in a positional society. Associated with this is racism, which has been institutionalized in the society and in its mechanisms for allocating rewards. None of these distancing processes is necessary to the success of American capitalism. They were created as means of ensuring the continued reproduction of the system, and are now deeply engrained within it.

SUBURBANIZATION

The discussion in the previous section has concentrated on the nature and extent of residential differentiation, without any attention to its spatial morphology. As pointed out earlier, however, American cities have a characteristic zonal and sectoral spatial organization of their residential areas. In general, the affluent live in the outer zones and the poor, including the blacks and the other ghettoized immigrant groups, in the inner areas. Why is this; why the massive suburban sprawl and the apparent preference of Americans for low-density living?

A brief answer to this question could again be choice. But why do Americans prefer a particular organization of their living space, and compete for it so that only the more affluent can afford it? Again, such preferences are not innate, they are created. There has long been an anti-urban bias in American popular culture; the city is a necessary evil for (capitalist) progress but the countryside is the ideal living area (Palm, 1981; Chapter 2). This pro-rural ideology extends back to Jefferson, but it has been developed since.

Some of the arguments underlying the pro-rural sentiment, which encouraged suburban residential preferences among the affluent in particular, were related to the negative externalities of the rapidly-growing industrial cities. Health problems were rife as a consequence of population overcrowding, the poverty of the public utility systems, and the low incomes of many of the residents. And so those who could afford to do so were encouraged to escape to the suburbs, to more pleasant low-density environments – which offered social as well as physical advantages. This flight to the suburbs was encouraged by the developing intra-urban transport technology (Muller, 1981).

But why was suburbanization seen as the solution to the problem of an unpleasant environment by the affluent; why did they flee the problem rather than removing it by cleaning up the inner city areas? And why was transport technology developed to stimulate this flight? As Walker (1978) points out, the ability to afford commuting trips, the negative externalities of the inner cities, the fear of social unrest among the alienated immigrants, the high inner city land values, the high property taxes, and the rural ideal were all sufficient to propel the affluent towards the suburban solution and to seek the necessary means of transport to consummate the desired move. But such factors did not necessitate suburbanization even though this solution allowed successful distancing and "a place of refuge and a mystification of human relationships" (Walker, 1978, p. 198) via the family. Suburbanization was facilitated, indeed made possible by investors who perceived it as a profitable development and encouraged it in order to promote not only a "desirable" way of life, but also a successful form of large-scale investment. (Initially the focus was on the affluent; later it spread down to the middle-income groups (Checkoway, 1980).) Suburban land speculation has long been a characteristic of American urban areas (Walker, 1981). Investment has been directed towards the suburbs and away from inner city areas, private sector and state financial institutions have backed this, and the state has subsidized it by the provision of a public infrastructure (in particular a freeway system) which has facilitated the high level of mobility necessary in low-density suburban sprawl (Harvey, 1975b, 1978). In its turn, this encouragement for and subsidy of suburbanization has stimulated not only the construction industry and those linked to it but also the automobile industry and those producers of consumer goods which are bought in large quantities as new housing is occupied.

CONCLUSIONS

American urban society is a spatially separated society. Distancing processes operate to encourage the congregation of members of three types of groups – socio-economic, ethnic and life style. The day-to-day operation of these distancing processes involves the expression of preferences, some of which (mostly those of the economically more affluent and the politically more powerful) are realized. Those processes are necessary to the continuation of the late capitalist economic and social system, and its particular representation in the United States. The social and economic life chances of individuals are influenced by where they are socialized and educated, so that parents seek homes in neighbourhoods that are consonant in their characteristics with their personal requirements for child-raising. Further, household investment in the home requires protection of the financial stake, as does institutional support for that investment. Thus space is manipulated by a society. It is a means of reproducing itself in its particular form, and provides a vehicle whereby individuals can attempt to further their own and their children's life chances, relative to those of others.

Distancing and the manipulation of space and housing markets are common to all advanced capitalist societies, but the degree of congregation and segregation and the particular form that it takes varies from society to society (Cox (1978) notes, for example, that the neighbourhood school tradition in the United States encouraged greater congregation and segregation than did the – precomprehensivization – British post-11+ educational system). In the United States, suburbanization is a major element in the particular form that has developed there. As stressed here, suburbanization, in particular its extent in America, is not necessary to capitalism. But it is an excellent means of advancing the materialist goals that are capitalism's bulwark. As Ashton (1978, p. 85) expresses it:

> suburbs have become the most important vehicles of consumption in American society. ... For in capitalist society, consumption is recognized as an end in itself. The emphasis is on having certain traits or characteristics through *possession of certain commodities*. ... Nowhere is this alienated life style more developed than in suburbia. Goods must be consumed to "keep up with the Joneses"; personal worth and status are measured by the amount and type of possessions owned in relation to one's neighbours. Lawns, gardens, and "living" rooms are more for show than for recreation and pleasure.

Residential separation in American urban areas does result from choice, therefore, at least by some. But it is not a free choice – it is one that is created by the society of which individuals are members. Some can choose otherwise; some affluent Americans, for example, opt to live in relatively "undesirable" neighbourhoods and some whites seek to promote inter-racial housing. Many have little or no choice; the poor, especially the poor blacks, can afford to live only in those areas to which they are "assigned" by the remainder of the population, and by the institutions that manipulate space.

The situation that has been created, therefore, is one in which certain groups within society are seeking to protect their social and economic positions, and to advance the prospects for their children, by the manipulation of space. This involves conflict over space. It is not the fundamental conflict of a capitalist society over ownership of the means of production. It is a secondary conflict, over the benefits to be obtained from participation in the capitalist system. Those who are relatively successful are seeking to enjoy the fruits of their success, to maintain and advance their relative status: their relative position depends on achieving a certain type and quality of residential environment, within which the prospects for the next generation can be enhanced. Those relatively disadvantaged by the distancing processes want to improve their relative status within the system – not to overthrow it. They want to prevent the manipulation of space by the affluent whites, and to equalize inter-group life experiences and opportunities by creating a new spatial morphology. Their conflict is over how the city is constructed and reconstructed as a spatial organism; it is a political conflict, as depicted in the following chapters.

TWO

The local state in American suburbia

The term suburb was used several times in the previous chapter. As is usual in urban geographical writing, the usage was vague and no definition of suburb was offered. In general speech, suburb refers to an outer residential district of an urban area, and it is usually considered a desirable place relative to inner city residential districts. Muller (1981) has argued persuasively that this inexact definition of the suburb as the metropolitan bedroom is no longer satisfactory, because of the decentralization of employment and other land uses from inner areas to what he terms the "outer city".

In the United States, the relatively vague use of the term suburb is unnecessary because it has a precise, administrative meaning. In almost every urban area, the local state is divided between a number of authorities, some of them general-purpose bodies which provide a wide range of services and some of them single-purpose bodies responsible for one function only. The largest of these authorities is almost invariably the central city, a general purpose municipality responsible for the government of the inner portions of the urban area, including its central business district. Beyond it, and in many cases completely surrounding it, is a ring of separate authorities, each responsible for governance of a small proportion of the urban area: these authorities are independent of the central city, but not of the State legislature which is responsible for their existence.

Suburban America, then, is an administratively-defined portion of the metropolitan complex – "the ring-shaped territory that remains when the central city is subtracted from the metropolis" (Muller, 1981, p. xi). In most metropolitan areas, it is fragmented into a large number of independent, general-purpose authorities overlapped by a substantial number of single-purpose jurisdictions. The result is a maze of separate governments (Zimmerman, 1979): according to the 1977 Census of Governments, there were 25 869 separate units within the country's 272 Standard Metropolitan Statistical Areas (SMSAs). To many observers, this maze is inefficient and demands reform (see Hallman, 1977; Danielson *et al.*, 1977); to some, it offers a range of public environments from which residents can choose that most suited to their needs (Tiebout, 1956); and to others it is "an important institutional mechanism for creating and perpetuating inequalities" (Hill, 1974, p. 1557). The presentation in the present chapter follows the last of these arguments. After a brief description of the nature of the suburban governmental maze, it outlines the benefits that this maze offers to suburban residents and suggests its importance in the creation of residential differentiation and the promotion of social and economic inequalities.

THE LOCAL STATE SYSTEM

Four types of territorial local authority are relevant to this study of suburbia. (There is a fifth, the township, but its powers, where it exists, are in most places negligible: there were 4031 townships within SMSAs in 1977.) Apart from their territorial base, these types share two important characteristics: they have autonomy of action in certain defined areas of responsibility, and almost all have separate taxing powers. Together, these imply that local governments have a great deal of independence over revenue and expenditure, within the constraints on their action set by the State legislature. They are entirely independent of the Federal government.

The basic unit of local government in 48 of the 50 States is the *county* (the exceptions are Alaska and Louisiana where electoral districts and parishes respectively are county-equivalents): there were 3042 counties in 1977. Counties exhaust the entire State territory and provide the basic range of public services. In some States, the range of services offered varies with population size and density, with least in the most rural areas.

Within the counties, and in some places replacing them, are the basic units of urban local government, the *municipalities* (the term varies between States, and in some separate names are used for municipalities of different population sizes). There were 18 862 municipalities in the USA in 1977, including 6444 within the SMSAs.

The rationale for separate governmental units in urban places is that large, densely-peopled agglomerations require both different types of governmental services than do rural areas and a greater intensity of other services. Most municipalities have been created by incorporation, with the State legislature, or some body acting for it such as the elected County Boards of Supervisors in California, agreeing to the creation of the separate unit after receiving a petition from the residents of the defined area and assuring itself that incorporation is the wish of the majority of the residents there. Most States set a lower limit to the size of a municipality (usually only a few hundred residents) and assess the feelings of the population regarding the incorporation from the number of signatures on the petition, an election, or a referendum on the issue (Teaford, 1979, p. 7). These rules have generally been very liberally interpreted and, at least until recent decades, few State legislatures have been prepared to deny incorporation when it is clearly the wish of the residents of an area, even where it fails to meet the threshold requirements. Thus "municipal incorporation (especially around the turn of the century) became a right available to any aspiring community" (Teaford, 1979, pp. 7–8), and many communities availed themselves of this right.

Once established, a municipality may be expanded by the annexation of additional territory, either in the surrounding county (such land is often termed unincorporated county land) or in an adjacent municipality. The rules regarding annexation have varied substantially between the States. In some, such as Texas, there have been few restraints on the annexation of either land or of other municipalities, especially where the municipality doing the annexing is already large. But in most, the constraints have been considerable, especially with regard to the annexation of other municipalities. Increasingly, State legislatures have only been prepared to countenance annexations where they meet with the approval of a majority (in some cases two-thirds) of those affected, the residents of the areas to be annexed. Most States, too, only allow the annexation of contiguous areas.

The third type of local government is the *school district*, a special purpose authority established solely to provide education services, in most cases paid for out of locally-raised taxes and administered, within the constraints of State legislation, by locally-elected school boards. There were 15 174 of these districts in 1977, including 5220 in SMSAs; only Alaska, Hawaii, Maryland, North Carolina and Virginia do not have their public education provided by a mosaic of school districts. (In some States, all education is provided by "unified" school districts; in some there are separate districts for elementary and secondary education; in a few, all three are to be found.)

When public education was being introduced in the nineteenth century, from the outset it was perceived as a local service to be provided by the local state and administered by a local government. In some places, the function was added to that of existing municipalities; in others it was allocated to separate school boards serving the same territories as existing municipalities (usually the large cities). But in most areas, separate school boards were established to serve particular communities. The vast majority of these were in rural areas, serving small, often widely-dispersed populations. Many provided only a single school. In 1942, there were 108 579 school districts. Because of their small numbers, many were identified as inefficient and unable to provide a satisfactory education. Rural depopulation exacerbated the problems of many, and encouraged a consolidation programme – made easier by increased mobility. Thus the number of school districts has fallen by about 90 per cent in four decades, with most of the amalgamations being in the rural areas.

The relationship between school districts and municipalities is a complex one, especially when the annexation of territory is involved. In general, municipal boundary changes do not affect school district boundaries, producing unconformities. Exceptions to this occur in some States where a large municipality is also the school board; in these cases, municipal expansion is accompanied by school district expansion, replacing the existing educational administration in the annexed area.

The final type of local government is the ad hoc *special district*: there were 25 962 of these in 1977, including 9580 in SMSAs. Special districts are almost all single-purpose authorities, established in most cases to provide services which the general purpose local governments (counties and municipalities) either could not or would not. In some cases, the rationale for the special district is its fiscal independence of the other authorities which, either because of State restraints on taxing and borrowing levels or because the service is required for a certain portion of their territories only, are unable to raise the revenue to provide the needed service (Stetzer, 1975). In other cases, the demand for the service is not conterminous with the territory of one, or a group of, existing unit(s). In recent years, special districts have been created by consortia of municipalities and counties in order to qualify for Federal grants (which may require, for example, the existence of a regional planning authority). Within metropolitan areas, most special districts provide public services and utilities: the largest numbers are associated with fire protection, water supply, sewage removal, and control/ conservation of natural resources.

Local State and local government in suburbia

As already indicated there is a plethora of local state units in metropolitan America. In most SMSAs, these comprise one large unit – the central city – plus an aureole of suburban municipalities and school districts, and an overlapping set of special districts. Apart from the last-mentioned, most of these non-central city government units are small, as indicated in the data in Table 2·1. The situation in particular SMSAs is illustrated in Tables 2·2 and 2·3; maps for the Detroit SMSA are shown in Figs 2·1 and 2·2.

The degree of suburban political fragmentation is not uniform throughout the United States. Using data for 1972, Ziegler and Brunn (1980) have calculated the ratio of the number of government units per 100 000 population in each of 264 SMSAs. They report a range of values from 0·3 (Honolulu) to 274 (Johnstown, Pennsylvania: population 266 000). Almost all of the most fragmented SMSAs are in the north-eastern quadrant of the country (excluding the New England States); nearly all of the least fragmented are in New England, the Southern States (south of the Mason-Dixon line), and west of the Mississippi. This regional variation reflects differences in the ease and rate of central city annexation: Ziegler and Brunn list the 41 central cities annexing 10 square miles or more between 1970 and 1975, only one of which was in the north-east (Springfield, Illinois). Nevertheless, even in the south and west fragmentation is considerable (Table 2·2). Furthermore, such is the fragmentation that a 1962 study found that of the

TABLE 2·1. *Government units in SMSAs, 1977.*

(A) *Municipalities by population*

1000>	1000–2499	2500–4999	5000–9999	10 000–24 999	25 000–49 999	50 000<
1979	1262	915	719	744	374	391

(B) *School districts by number of schools*

0	1	2	3–9	10–19	20
35	1253	667	2653	732	481

(C) *School districts by number of pupils*

0	1–49	50–299	300–1199	1200–2999	3000–5999
35	105	492	1269	1562	1074

6000–11 999	12 000–24 999	25 000–49 999	50 000–99 999	100 000
721	357	132	49	25

(D) *Special districts*

Total 9580   with property-taxing power 5327

Source: US Department of Commerce, Bureau of the Census (1978). *1977 Census of Governments, Volume 1, Governmental Organization.* Washington D.C., Table 14.

TABLE 2.2. *Government units in individual SMSAs, 1977.*[a]

	Total (with property-taxing power)	Counties	Municipalities	Townships	School districts	Special districts
Chicago	1214 (1166)	6	261	113	315	419
Philadelphia	864 (570)	7	140	199	189	329
Pittsburgh	744 (433)	4	193	117	105	325
St Louis	615 (558)	8	194	61	113	239
Houston	488 (450)	6	86	0	53	343
Minneapolis–St Paul	406 (403)	10	175	101	67	53
Nassau–Suffolk	370 (370)	2	95	13	130	130
Dallas–Forth Worth	368 (336)	11	171	0	110	76
New York	362 (346)	4	106	38	135	79
Detroit	349 (327)	6	107	102	108	26

[a] The data are for the ten SMSAs with most units.
Source: US Department of Commerce, Bureau of the Census (1980). *1977 Census of Governments, Volume 1, Governmental Organization*. Washington D.C., Table 15.

TABLE 2·3. *The local government units of Detroit SMSA, 1977.*

(A) *Municipalities by population*

1000>	1000–2499	2500–4999	5000–9999
9	14	19	15

10 000–24 999	25 000–49 999	50 000
20	15	15

(B) *School districts by number of pupils*

1–49	50–299	300–1199	1200–2999	3000–5999
1	0	1	21	37

6000–11 999	12 000–24 999	25 000–49 999	50 000–99 999	100 000<
30	13	4	0	1

(C) *Special districts*

Total 26   with property-taxing power 4

Source: US Department of Commerce, Bureau of the Census (1980). *1977 Census of Governments, Volume 1, Governmental Organization.* Washington D.C., Table 15.

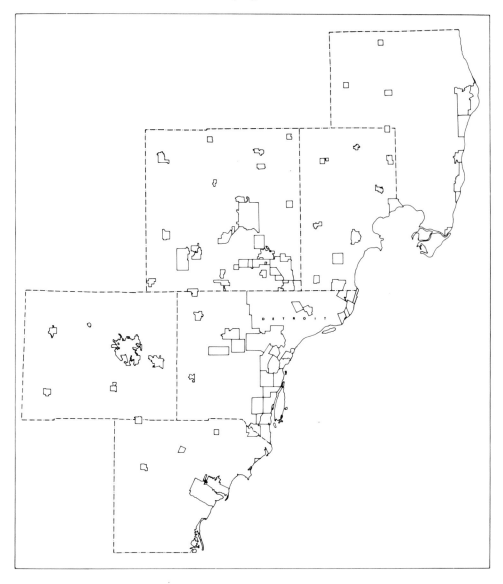

Figure 2·1. Municipalities in the Detroit SMSA.

6604 metropolitan school districts only 28 had boundaries conterminous with those of some other local government unit (Bossert, 1978, p. 296).

SUBURBAN ADMINISTRATIVE FRAGMENTATION AND RESIDENTIAL DIFFERENTIATION

Although the administrative fragmentation of suburbia is considered by some as an impediment to efficient government, it is clearly not so perceived by suburban residents; indeed, the majority of suburbanites report that they

Figure 2·2. The school districts of the Detroit SMSA.

are satisfied with their environments and with the quality of services provided (Marcus and Rodgers, 1975); and suburbs are the areas in which most
Americans would prefer to live (Campbell and Dollenmayer, 1975). This
satisfaction and attraction reflects the physical, social and economic
environments of suburbia, the exclusion from them of as many negative
externalities as possible, and the spatial organization which concentrates
the remaining externalities in particular parts of suburbia only.

The thesis developed in this section is that the organization of the local
state in the suburbs has assisted the creation of the desirable environments
and the spatial manipulation of the externalities. This is not to suggest that

jurisdictional fragmentation is a necessary means to those ends, but only to indicate that its availability has been capitalized on by those with interests in developing and maintaining a particular suburban morphology (Cox and Nartowicz, 1980). The special features of the fragmentation relevant to this thesis are "home rule" and "fiscal independence", which are closely related.

Home rule

Separate suburban municipalities are in no way obliged to participate in programmes that concern the metropolitan area as a whole, or indeed any district larger than their own territory. Under most State constitutions and legislation, those elected to municipal office are responsible only to their constituents, although they are, of course, required to act within the State law and to meet certain legal obligations.

One of the benefits of this independence concerns the nature of *political control*. By the end of the nineteenth century, there was much concern, especially among the more affluent urban residents, about the nature of urban politics, in particular its control by party machines. The machines were very efficiently organized by party bosses through a hierarchical structure that extended down to the ward bosses and the local precinct organizers and committeemen. The politicians operating at the various levels were responsible for "delivering the vote" to the party, which they did through a combination of dispensing patronage – thereby "buying" votes – and winning the support of community leaders, especially those of working-class and immigrant communities. At the same time, the upper level of the machine hierarchy negotiated with business interests, granting favours in return for others. In terms of political ideology, the parties dominated by the machines were essentially pragmatic. They existed to serve the interests of the bosses rather than any long-term goals of the community as a whole, and the coalition of ethnic voters and business support was put together simply to promote those interests. (For more detail, see Judd (1979, Ch. 3) and the references therein.)

The middle classes were far from enamoured with the machines and their politics, which they perceived as inefficient and against their own particular interests. By the end of the century, a National Municipal League had been established to campaign for reform of the local political process. In this it was encouraged by the success of businessmen at imposing a new form of "efficient" local government in certain cities, an imposition which in most cases involved winning voter support and State legislature approval: the first success came in the wake of a storm in Galveston, Texas, in 1901 and the need to reconstruct the city (Rice, 1977). In its campaign, the National Municipal League was supported by a variety of allies, including the Bureau of the Census (Fox, 1977).

The key to the campaign for Reform was that the management of municipalities and urban areas should be non-political. Running a town or community should be like running a business: the goal is efficiency. Thus the League's campaign focused on replacing the usual mayor-council structure by one in which at most a few people were responsible for the municipality's operations. A variety of forms was proposed, and some were eventually introduced, including: commission government, in which the municipality was run by an elected small board of commissioners, overseen by an elected manager, as an analogy with boards of directors (each member being responsible for a particular department) and chairmen/managing directors; and a city-manager scheme, in which the elected council appointed a single manager responsible for running all departments, who reported to the (small) council. In addition to such alterations to the structure, Reformers also sought to eliminate partisan activity and minority representation; this was done by banning parties from running candidates for office and replacing wards by at-large elections. At the same time, they sought to ensure democratic control and responsible government by introduction of the referendum, the initiative (a popularly-demanded referendum), and recall (a popularly-demanded by-election at which an elected member is required to defend certain actions).

The Reform movement had strong class overtones. It was designed to remove power from the party machines, the working-classes and the ethnic goups, and to put it in the hands of those who believed "that the city was a market place, not a complex social entity" (Judd, 1979, p. 111); the main beneficiaries of the transfer were those who had most power in the market place (and were fearful of mass democracy). Their success was founded on their ability to convince State legislatures to grant home rule to municipal governments. Achievement of this goal gave much greater independence to municipalities than had previously been the case.

Not every municipality in urban America has gone over to, or adopted on incorporation, some form of Reform government (between one-third and one-half currently do): in some of the smallest, it hardly seemed necessary. Nor has the success of the Reform movement been confined to the suburbs: some of the country's largest cities (Boston, Detroit, San Francisco and Seattle, for example) operate non-partisan, at-large elections. But it was the success of the Reform movement, and its achievement of a large degree of municipal independence from the State legislature, that permitted suburbanites to obtain certain advantages from incorporation.

One of the benefits of municipal autonomy in the control of neighbourhood character refers to the supply and distribution of public goods. As indicated in the previous chapter, the character of a neighbourhood is determined not only by its social composition and its land-use pattern but also by its public services. Since most of these are provided by the state, especially the local state, municipal autonomy provides for local control of the provision and allocation of services – and has been the basis of a great deal of analysis of inter- and intra-unit policies (Dye, 1969; Lineberry, 1977; Rich, 1982a,b).

The power to zone

The municipality in the United States is the land-use planning authority. It has control over the allocation of land to various uses, the spatial separation of externalities, and the overall morphology of its territory. This power, basically the power to zone, has been used not merely to organize land uses but also to control the social characteristics of many suburban municipalities.

Zoning originated in the United States in the City of New York (in 1916) where it was used to control the pattern of industrial development on Manhattan Island (Delafons, 1969; Tull, 1960). As such, it was being used for the ends with which zoning is usually associated – separating mutually incompatible land uses to benefit public welfare as a whole, even though in doing so it was infringing on the right of an individual to use his/her property as s/he wished. It was a means for abating nuisances. As its use spread, however, so its purposes expanded:

> The initial role of zoning in conflict mediation has grown to include the positive roles of promoting the general welfare through requiring actions that enhance the social, economic and physical environment. (Mann, 1976, p. 20)

Such enhancement embraces purposes including the conservation of property values, the protection of neigbourhood character, the preservation of natural resources and environments, the advancement of aesthetic interests, the provision of a transport infrastructure, the control of growth, and the advancement of certain fiscal policies.

The above purposes are adopted – implicitly if not explicitly – in the zoning policies developed by most of the large cities which seek to control land-use patterns in this way (only Houston of the country's largest cities does not operate a zoning scheme). But in the many small municipalities of suburbia, such goals are either irrelevant or have been replaced by others. There the "general welfare" refers not to the interests of a large, heterogeneous population, but to those of a small, relatively homogeneous group. They wish to protect those interests, and use the zoning power to that end.

Residents of suburbia, especially the more affluent, seek to exclude all negative externalities from their neighbourhoods. This involves not only preventing the introduction of physical nuisances – such as industrial estates and large shopping centres, both of which generate noise, traffic, and other pollution – but also social nuisances, the groups within society (basically the poor and the blacks) who are considered undesirable and potential "pollutants" of both the local social milieu and its key institution, the neighbourhood school. As Williams and his associates found in a survey of the residents of Philadelphian suburbs, a key objective of local government according to their respondents was "keeping undesirables out" (Williams *et al.*, 1965).

The mechanism for this policy is *exclusionary zoning* (for a full statement, see Danielson, 1976). Plans cannot be drawn up that say "poor people cannot live in this area", or "black people cannot live here" (though see p. 78), or "large families cannot live here" (see, however, p. 84). But the plan can be so phrased that poor people cannot afford to buy homes in an area, which in effect excludes most blacks also, and controls can also ensure that large families, especially large poor families, cannot move in either. Thus in suburbs that practice exclusionary zoning, there is little or no provision for either apartment buildings or mobile homes, both of which may be affordable to the poor. And in the single-family dwelling areas, zoning allows for low-density occupation only, by specifying minimum lot sizes, maximum building heights, and maximum percentages of the lot covered, for example. Such low-density zoning makes the land expensive, relative to the intensity with which it can be used; developers of medium- and low-cost housing will thus be dissuaded from using it, and thus the poor (and hence the blacks) will be excluded.

Exclusionary zoning policies seek to control the social characteristics of an area – either an entire municipality or some proportion of it – by preventing the construction of low-cost homes and by increasing the price of conventional single-family homes on large lots. The result of the latter is not always exactly as predicted, however; in a study of Charlotte, North Carolina, Jud (1980) has shown that whereas the price of housing in exclusively residential zones is greater than elsewhere, that of housing in zones with a minimum lot size of 16 000 square feet or more tends to be lower. Jud's analyses held constant the effects of neighbourhood income levels and building sizes, however, so that the costs of the large-lot properties were still relatively high. Wolch and Gabriel (1981), in an analysis of property values in the San Francisco Bay Area showed that, *ceteris paribus*:

(1) the higher the local tax rate (per dollar of assessed value), the lower the mean value of owner-occupied housing;

(2) the greater the percentage of school children in the area from minority groups, the lower the mean value of owner-occupied housing;

(3) the larger the expenditure per school child on education, the greater the mean value of owner-occupied housing;

(4) the larger the percentage of the area zoned for minimum lot size of one acre or more, the greater the mean value of owner-occupied housing; and

(5) a pro-growth attitude on behalf of the city council produces lower average values for owner-occupied housing.

For Chicago, Shlay and Rossi (1981a,b) showed that between 1960 and 1970, exclusionary zoning in the suburbs was associated with above average increases in median family income, slower growth in the number of non-

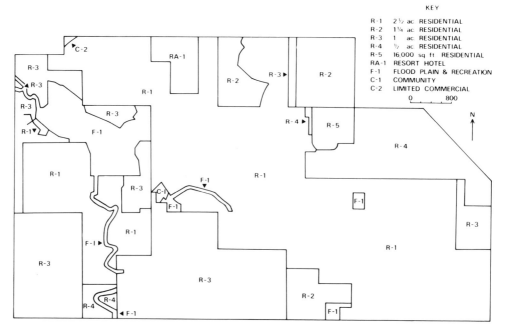

Figure 2·3. The zoning plan for the village of Cherry Hills, Denver-Boulder SMSA, Colorado.

white residents, and a well-above average growth in families – especially families without children.

Exclusionary zoning is widely practised in American suburban municipalities: examples of its implementation are provided in Figs 2·3 and 2·4. There are however, no national data available on its extent, nor even State-wide or metropolitan-wide data – with one major exception. Reliance must be placed on piecemeal and anecdotal evidence (such as provided in Danielson, 1976 and Miller, 1981). Only the work undertaken at the Center for Urban Policy Research at Rutgers University provides detailed material, referring to the entire State of New Jersey (which includes substantial proportions of suburban Philadelphia and New York) in the early 1970s (James and Hughes, 1973; Sagalyn and Sternlieb, 1973). This work shows that in the entire State 81·4 per cent of the developable land was zoned for residential use. Of this, only 6·23 per cent was zoned for multi-family homes (apartments) and 0·07 per cent for mobile homes. Over one-half was zoned for minimum lot sizes of 40 000–119 999 square feet and a further 11·53 per cent for lots of 3 acres or more. Similarly, on almost 90 per cent of the land, a minimum lot width of at least 50 feet was required; on 36·65 per cent, the minimum was 200 feet. (All of these data are taken from Sagalyn and Sternlieb (1973) which presents tabulations at the county level (see Table 2·4). Jones and Hughes (1973) present data at the municipal level.) The most exclusive counties are those in the north-east of the State on the

CITY OF EDGEWATER ZONING REGULATIONS

ZONING	MIN. LOT AREA	MIN. LOT WIDTH	MIN. FRONT YD.		MIN. SIDE YD.		MIN. REAR YD.		MAX. HEIGHT	MAX. LOT COVERAGE	LOT AREA GRD. FLOOR	LOT AREA UPPER STORY
			PRIN.	ACC.	PRIN.	ACC.	PRIN.	ACC.				
R – A	12,500	100	30	75	15	15	30	10	35			
R – B	9,000	75	30	60	10	10	20	5	35	35%		
R – 1	6,000	50	30	60	5	5	20	5	35	35%		
R – 2	9,000	75[a]	30	60	5	5	20	5	35		4,500	
R – 3	12,500	100[b]	30	60	15	15	20	5	35	50%	1,750	1,000
R – 4	200,000		1/2H		1/4H				85		1,400	
	300,000		1/2H		1/4H				110		1,000	
RC – 1	12,500	100	60		15				35	50%		
RC – 2	12,500	100	60		15				35	50%		
OTHERS	12,000	100							100	50%		

1. Corner lots shall be not less than 75 feet
2. Private garages may have the same front yard as the main building
3. Minimum side yard of corner lots shall be 30 feet

a. 25 feet frontage per ground floor unit

b. 20 feet frontage per ground floor unit

H = Overall height of principle building

Figure 2·4. Principal features of the zoning plan for the municipality of Edgewater, Denver-Boulder SMSA, Colorado.

TABLE 2·4 *Characteristics of zoning regulations for developable residential land in the counties of New Jersey, 1970.*

County	Per cent of residential land zoned for		Single family dwellings lots 40–119 999 sq. ft.	Lots 3 acres +	Minimum lot width 200 ft.	Minimum floor area 1600 sq. ft.
	Apartments	Mobile homes				
Bergen	0·61	–	54·79	–	29·77	15·7
Burlington	6·39	0·13	25·72	22·26	34·40	1·0
Camden	40·51	–	22·59	0·32	9·82	30·5
Essex	1·06	–	14·94	–	28·89	6·4
Gloucester	26·03	0·68	22·10	3·10	6·93	3·7
Hunterdon	0·25	–	66·43	30·45	78·58	0
Mercer	1·02	0·04	39·48	2·04	27·22	0
Middlesex	0·54	–	38·53	–	10·19	33·0
Monmouth	0·41	–	83·35	0·92	78·74	17·2
Morris	1·24	–	60·21	21·61	23·44	5·6
Ocean	7·03	–	63·99	–	9·19	0
Passaic	4·57	–	21·97	20·10	5·79	0
Somerset	–	–	60·82	24·64	44·80	2·2
Sussex	7·06	0·03	57·49	5·48	28·80	0·6
Union	7·00	–	22·40	–	–	7·1
Warner	5·90	–	53·40	2·44	20·67	–

Source: Tables in Sagalyn and Sternlieb (1973).

edge of New York's suburbia: in Hunterdon 96·68 per cent of the residential land is zoned at a minimum lot size of 40 000 square feet and in Somerset the percentage is 85·46.

Exclusionary zoning is not the true "cause" of residential differentiation in suburbia. It is the chosen mechanism to ensure social ends, and if it were not available, another would undoubtedly be found. As Rose (1979, p. 119) expresses it:

> zoning is not the cause of the inequity and the injustice. Zoning is merely a symptomatic manifestation of more fundamental social and economic inequities. The cause ... arises from the manifestations of racial and social prejudices within society.

Its impact is clear. Low-cost housing, at a price accessible to the relatively poor, is excluded from much of suburbia, thereby allowing the more affluent to isolate themselves in municipally-designed "tight little islands" (Sager, 1969).

Not every suburban municipality produces a zoning plan restricting residential development to very low densities and access to its territory to the extremely affluent. If they did, there would be an over-supply of such land, the price would fall, and the intent of the policy would fail. But most zone for, at the least, development to be occupied by medium-income people, at minimum densities of 1–2 homes per acre. And not every municipality zones out all non-residential uses; some may be allowed, to provide a local source of employment. More important, such development will provide needed property tax revenue (see below), so that the non-residential users subsidize the residential. (Indeed, the competition for such "subsidizing" non-residential uses is often very considerable: Herr, 1982.) But care is taken to minimize the negative externalities associated with any allowed industrial and commercial uses (see Miller (1981) on the contest for high value land in suburban Los Angeles).

The impact of zoning on the characteristics of a residential area extends from the neighbourhood milieu to the neighbourhood school. Since almost all schools serve a local catchment, by influencing the socio-economic characteristics of an area's population a zoning plan also influences the socio-economic composition of the local school, a much-desired feature among the affluent and middle-income America. Further, in the suburbs, although the municipal and school district boundaries rarely coincide, control over the nature of a municipality's population is likely to equate more or less with control over a school district's clientele.

Finally, the power to zone is associated in part with two other powers. The first is the power to decide whether or not public housing projects are built within a municipality. Clearly, such housing is considered a negative externality by the affluent (public housing in America is predominantly for the poor and has a high percentage of black occupants), so separate municipal government allows local populations to exclude such developments. Secondly, the local populations, through their elected representatives, have the power to distribute public facilities and resources across the municipal territory, to the advantage of some areas and the disadvantage of others. (The same power rests with the elected school boards, who can distribute resources to various schools in whatever proportion they desire – providing they meet any prescribed State minimum provision: Mandel, 1975; Harrison, 1982.)

The fiscal role

In the past, local governments in the United States have relied very heavily on local property taxes for their revenue. This reliance has been reduced in recent decades, as a consequence of the increased volume of federal grants, the increasing role of the State as a redistributive agent, and the introduction of non-property taxes and other sources of income (such as receipts from sales and licences). Nevertheless, the property tax remains the base on which much local government activity rests, and in 1972 it provided 36·7 per cent of all suburban revenues (MacManus, 1978).

The property tax is raised on the assessed (potential sales) value of a property, so that the geography of the metropolitan tax base is that of urban property values. Studies of the latter show that they tend to decline with distance from the central business district, the main suburban commercial and industrial nodes, and the major routeways. This is because non-residential uses generate much higher land values than do residential. Among the latter, as suggested above, the prime determinants of property values are related to density of occupation and resident characteristics. Thus in the single-family residential zones, property values are highest in the affluent areas.

Because residents' incomes and property values are correlated, higher income residential areas make relatively large contributions to municipal budgets. (This greater absolute expenditure does not necessarily mean that the rich pay more in relative terms. If property value differentials between rich and poor are less than income differentials, then in relative terms the poor may pay more of their incomes in taxes.) As a consequence, the relatively affluent perceive that by their larger contribution to the municipal budget they are subsidizing the provision of services for the poor.

Municipal (and school district) fragmentation allows the affluent who move to the suburbs, from which the poor are excluded, to escape from paying these apparent subsidies – at least through their property taxes. Since there is no metropolitan-wide taxation, they pay only to the municipality, school district and special districts within whose territory they reside. If those territories are relatively exclusive, and therefore homogeneous with regard to incomes, there is very little apparent subsidization (see White,

1975, for a detailed discussion). Thus the affluent are able to escape "fiscal responsibilities" towards the poor, who are trapped in central cities (plus some older, inner suburban municipalities) with low tax bases and who have to pay high tax rates for inferior services. Peterson (1976, pp. 76–77) shows that in 1971–1972 among the country's largest SMSAs the central city tax base – property value per capita – was almost always smaller than that of the suburbs; in some cases it was substantially so, as in Baltimore where in the central city it was $4019 and in the suburbs $9103. Yet the demands for many locally-provided services are frequently much higher in the central city – so that the demands on the poor are greatest and those on the rich least. In Baltimore, expenditure on police services in the central city was $65 per capita, whereas in the suburbs it was $21. And not only do the suburban affluent opt out of paying for central city services, in many cases they utilize them – either free or at a subsidy – whereas central city residents make relatively little use of suburban services. A study of Detroit in the late 1960s suggested that on average Detroit city residents subsidized their suburban neighbours to the extent of $80 per capita per year (for Detroit residents), with 6·5 per cent of the city's budget being used to provide services for the suburban free-riders (Neenan, 1972).

Because of their fiscal independence, separate suburban municipalities are able to decide what services, paid for out of the proceeds of local property taxes, are provided – and the amount of provision. They operate within constraints laid down by State governments. In Massachusetts, for example, a referendum was passed in 1980 limiting the property tax to 2 per cent of the market value. This limit applies to all municipalities, even those where it was opposed by a majority of the voters, and so is a constraint to local autonomy. Similar measures have been passed in other States – many of them stemming from the anti-tax movement made apparent by the success of Proposition 13 in California (Miller, 1981).

The benefits of a fragmented local government system in metropolitan America have been argued by Tiebout (1956) in a classic paper. He claimed that the nature of the American democratic system is such that citizens have no means of expressing their preferences for public goods, to which the tax system could be adjusted. But the availability of many municipalities in a metropolitan area means that

> The consumer-voter may be viewed as picking that community which best satisfies his preference pattern for public goods . . . the consumer-voter moves to that community whose local government best satisfies his set of preferences . . . . (Thus) the greater the number of communities and the greater the variance among them, the closer the consumer will come to fully realizing his preference position (p. 418).

According to this argument, consumers vote with their feet; metropolitan integration would deny them this opportunity, and if in any integration scheme any one former municipality suffers a deterioration of provision, relative to preferences (it may be an increase), then consumer sovereignty has been violated.

The benefits of this system, according to the Tiebout model, are illustrated in California, where the "Lakewood Plan" was developed in suburban Los Angeles as a means of holding down, and in some cases entirely removing, property taxes. Under this plan, created in 1954 for the newly-incorporated suburban municipality of Lakewood, the municipality is what is termed a "minimal city". It obtains its needed services (road maintenance, health services, law and order, building standards, etc.) by contracting with the surrounding county (from which it is seceding by the incorporation). Thus a separate municipal bureaucracy is not needed, so that

> the bureaucratic pressures for governmental expansion are clearly eliminated by contracting. Contracting for services guarantees that there will never be a homegrown bureaucracy pushing for new services and the expansion of old ones. (Miller, 1981, p. 85)

Because the county is a much larger unit, economies of scale in service provision are available, which would not be the case for a small municipality serving itself, and the costs are spread over a larger population. Under the Lakewood Plan, therefore, the populations of suburban municipalities can decide what services they want, and contract for them. They do not contribute to the costs of other services available from the county but which they have opted against. The municipal budget is held down, therefore. Indeed, with the availability of a 1 per cent sales tax to local governments in California, some municipalities incorporated to use the Lakewood Plan (26 in the seven years after Lakewood's incorporation in Los Angeles County alone), property taxes were unnecessary; income from other sources (including federal and State grants) was sufficient to cover all expenditure on the contracted-for services (see Miller, 1981, p. 76ff.). This was one of the main goals of suburban incorporation – "the most basic and pervasive common denominator for incorporation was the avoidance of high property taxation" (Miller, 1981, p. 82) – and one of its by-products was that the "minimal cities" suffered much less than older incorporations, which provide a wider range of services, following the budgetary cuts imposed after the passing of California's Proposition 13 in 1978 (which gained much support in the "minimal cities"). According to Miller, suburban incorporation is part of the low tax movement among the affluent.

The difficulty with Tiebout's argument is that it assumes that all consumer-voters are equally able to vote with their feet. But if, as G. L. Clark (1981b) argues, some are not able to express their preferences (because they are excluded from certain municipalities by the actions of those who have been successful) and some preferences are suppressed by central state constraints to local autonomy, then the Tiebout hypothesis is "both incomplete and overly simplistic" (p. 128). (See also Whiteman, 1983.)

One of the largest items in the total local government expenditure pattern is education, so the existence of separate suburban school districts produces major fiscal disparities in the costs of providing this service and, assuming some correlation between expenditure and the quality of the service, the standard of the education provided. Campbell and Dollenmayer (1975, p. 376) illustrate this with data for two New York suburban school districts. In Levittown, the property tax base was $16 200 per pupil, which at a property tax rate of $2·72 per $100 yielded a revenue of $410·31 per pupil. In Great Neck, the base was $64 600 per pupil, which at the same tax rate yielded $1684·07 per pupil – revenue from other sources, mainly State funds, reduced the differential from 4:1 to 2:1. Thus, since incomes were much greater in Great Neck, the relative tax burden was highest in Levittown, but the output in terms of expenditure per pupil was substantially lower there. The separation of rich and poor allowed the rich to get more for less, while the poor got less for more.

A major consequence of municipal and suburban fragmentation and of the accompanying residential differentiation is a system of substantial fiscal disparities. This leads to charges that exclusionary zoning as described above is to a considerable extent fiscal zoning, designed to eliminate from the suburban municipalities all land uses that it is believed will make greater demands on the local exchequer than they provide revenue (Zech, 1980; White, 1975). In particular, it is suggested that single-family homes make fewer demands on the local exchequer than do apartments. Windsor (1979; see also James and Windsor, 1976) has evaluated this hypothesis and found it wanting. He found that, per acre, multifamily apartment dwellings contribute more to the local budget than do single-family units, so that it is the residents of the latter who are the net beneficiaries, especially in the case of contributions to school district budgets, since they have more school children per dwelling unit than do residents of apartment blocks. The conclusion is that exclusionary zoning does not necessarily have fiscal benefits for the low-density residents compared to other strategies for the municipality. But this omits consideration of the fiscal benefits of being separated from the vast mass of the metropolitan area. Although some zoning for apartments in high income suburban municipalities may have net fiscal benefits rather than the perceived fiscal disadvantages for the existing residents, it would not contribute a social positive externality.

MUNICIPALITIES AND SUBURBIA

The discussion above has suggested that municipal fragmentation offers considerable advantages to suburban residents, especially affluent suburban residents, in their attempts to structure the morphology of the urban residential mosaic for their own social and economic ends. In particular, the zoning power allows them to influence the land-use and land-user characteristics of their neighbourhoods, thereby giving them the ability to determine, with a high degree of certainty, the composition of local social milieux and of local school catchments. At the same time, fiscal independence allows them to opt out of property tax contributions to the costs of providing services for the residents of the remainder of the metropolitan complex.

Suburban separateness is not necessarily cheap, and the residents of the "tight little islands" may pay relatively large sums absolutely, if not relatively, to live in their suburban fastnesses. In part this is because of high property values, enhanced if not created by the success of the exclusionary zoning processes. And in part it is because small municipalities may be relatively expensive to run, because they do not achieve significant economies of scale in service provision, assuming that they must provide some services, such as education. Additional to this, low density residential areas are expensive to service simply because of the amount of capital investment needed (in roads, water pipes, etc.) per household. But these high prices are worth paying, according to the residents, to obtain the desired positive externalities and to avoid the negative. A variety of strategies is used in many municipalities to try and reduce the costs; these include collaboration with neighbouring governments, purchase of services from private contractors, and purchase of services from a nearby county or city government. In all cases, but especially the last, the service may be more expensive than it would be if the small municipality were to merge with larger neighbours. The cost of not annexing is a relatively high price for some services; the benefits are the control over land use and schools, and the decision not to purchase some services at all.

The policy of separate incorporation and maintenance of the identity thus created is very largely a twentieth-century phenomenon. Teaford (1979) has outlined how many residents of suburban municipalities in the late nineteenth century voted for annexation with their central cities. The costs of providing services – even the inability to provide them in some cases – are cited as major reasons for the decisions to unite. And in nearly every case the central city was keen to accept the additional territory, for development there would extend its property tax base, as well as providing a general boost and greater political power for the city fathers.

The situation changed in the early twentieth century. The desire to unite with the central cities evaporated, and annexation slowed substantially; in many States, legislation made the latter much more difficult. Teaford (1979) suggests that this change of mind by suburbanites reflected the increased ability of small local units to provide their own basic services, the growing number of special districts to undertake the same tasks, the development of collaboration and service contracts, and the realization of the social benefits of separateness that come with the development of zoning schemes, the increasing social, economic and political problems of the central cities, and the issue of schooling. Expansion of the large central cities was virtually halted, particularly in the older metropolitan areas of the north-east where many became completely surrounded by suburban municipalities blocking their access to annexable unincorporated land. Only decisions to rescind suburban separateness could lead to central city expansion, and Teaford shows that such rare decisions were made only in relatively low status suburbs which were in fiscal difficulties.

Teaford's argument suggests that the entrenched suburban municipalities are the product of early twentieth-century decision-making by local residents who perceived increased benefits accruing from a policy of separateness rather than one of annexation. In part this was undoubtedly so (Cox and Nartowicz, 1980). But the decisions by residents were led, in many areas, by the decisions of non-residential land users to move to the independent suburbs, very largely for the fiscal benefits (Marcusen, 1978). Indeed, the municipal history of many suburban rings shows how a considerable number of incorporations were undertaken to promote business rather than residential interests (see, for example, Bigger and Kitchin (1952) and Miller (1981) on Los Angeles). A municipality zoned almost entirely for industries makes much less demands on the industrialists for taxes to pay for services to residents than does a large city with a range of land uses. Thus a separate "industrial municipality" offers substantial fiscal advantages, as illustrated in a number of metropolitan areas (see Nelson, 1952). The result, it is claimed (Gordon, 1978), is that the industrialists who perceived such benefits were able, because of their political clout, to ensure that the State legislature acted to protect municipal autonomy and to make annexation and city aggrandisement much more difficult. The affluent have benefited substantially from changing attitudes in State legislatures towards suburban political fragmentation, but it was industrialists who obtained those benefits for them.

Whatever the exact course of events, the outcome is clear. The suburban rings of most metropolitan areas are fragmented into large numbers of separate municipal, school district and special district territories. Certain characteristics of these units, especially the zoning power, have been used in the processes of distancing, creating a mosaic of socio-economic and ethnic separation into not only different residential areas but also different local government territories. Political fragmentation is useful to those who seek to avoid living among certain other groups, therefore. It also brings them certain fiscal advantages. Not surprisingly, such benefits are envied by others, and vigorously opposed by some.

THREE

Conflict over the residential mosaic

The previous two chapters have outlined the *raison d'être* for the urban residential mosaic in capitalist cities, the arguments for its particular morphology in the United States, and the critical role of the local state in the creation and maintenance of the present suburban situation. To some analysts, influenced by the social Darwinism that characterized the human ecology school of sociologists at Chicago (Robson, 1969), such a mosaic is a natural outcome of competition among unequals. This suggests a consensus model of society, in which individuals and groups accept their position within that society, plus the approved means (approved and controlled by the relatively powerful) for mobility between positions. In particular, with respect to the residential mosaic, it is accepted that some areas are "better" than others (i.e. have more, generally-agreed upon, positive externalities and fewer negative externalities), that access into these areas is governed by ability to pay, and that ability to pay is a function of occupational success, which in turn reflects educational success. One's place in society is earned, therefore, as is one's place in the residential mosaic. All have equality of opportunity in the contest for the "best" places; the losers are the less able, plus those who shun the opportunities available to them and fail to realize their own potentials.

This consensus model of society is opposed by a conflict model (Eyles, 1974), an outline of which was presented in Chapter 1. According to the latter, the driving force in society is class conflict, through which individuals and groups occupying particular positions in society seek both to define those positions against usurpers and to advance their situations by invading more favourable positions occupied by others. For such defences/attacks they mobilize whatever resources are available to them, using these to prevent the operation of the free market competition. Thus, for example, the public (i.e. state) school system is manipulated – largely through the manipulation of neighbourhood school catchment areas – to advance some children's educational chances, relative to those of others, by providing the former with a "better" education. In such manipulation, it is the rich who are usually the most powerful, and so the most successful (Saunders, 1980).

They protect their own positions by denying equality of opportunity to the less affluent. (If they deem it necessary, of course, they opt out of the public education system entirely.)

Manipulation of this type takes place in most spheres of life. To some who suffer from it, it is acceptable: they have assimilated a false ideology which presents the unequal contest as if it were equal, as if equality of opportunity were available and there was no manipulation of space to advance certain interests and to retard others. In accepting that ideology, they may apathetically accept their place within society and space, or they may choose to compete within the "unfair" rules, which competition is acceptable to the more powerful who control the contest in any case. But some accept neither the ideology nor the rules. They seek to change the system.

Both of the last two groups generate conflict within society. The first – those who choose to fight within it – create unease because of the threat that they might succeed, in one round at least if not in the whole contest. The second – those who seek change – are the most dangerous because they threaten the rules, not just to win the game. Thus the urban mosaic is the scene of continual conflict, most of it of the first type. This conflict involves individuals, ad hoc organizations, and permanent bodies; much of it is political action involving the state, especially the local arm of the state – local government.

NEIGHBOURHOOD CHANGE AND PROTECTION

The congregation of members of different groups into separate parts of a residential mosaic is presented by some commentators both as a means of avoiding social conflict and as a promoter of that which is to be avoided. Thus, according to Ley (1974), Boal (1976) and others, members of particular ethnic groups retreat into ghettos in order to avoid contact with either those who consider them inferior or those who are economically, socially, even physically threatening; Poole and Boal report considerable movement away from "mixed" Protestant/Roman Catholic residential districts of Belfast after the onset of the conflict in 1969, into protected ghettos (Poole and Boal, 1973). Once within such retreats, they are able – by a variety of techniques of social control, including occasional violence – to protect their communities, as illustrated in Suttle's (1967, 1972) work on Chicago. According to Sennett (1973), such behaviour reflects immaturity in society, with people withdrawing from those who are different from themselves rather than confronting the differences and, via mutual accommodation, promoting social harmony through awareness rather than ignorance. The need to retreat stimulates the need to defend, and thus promotes social conflict.

The concept of the ghetto and the conflict that surrounds it (both the concept and the boundaries of the ghetto itself) is typically applied to the segregated residential areas occupied by various ethnic groups; analyses such as Sennett's were stimulated by the American race riots of the late 1960s, which were related to the problems of prejudice, discrimination, segregation, and ghettoization. But, as Cox (1978, 1981), Harvey (1978b) and others have identified, similar processes operate throughout urban society. The degree of segregation may not be as great, the social milieux of the communities much less closely-knit (Bell and Newby, 1976), and the conflict more subdued (Robson, 1982), but there are differences of degree rather than of kind.

A major stimulant for conflict over residential districts is urban growth. As a city expands numerically, so competition for, and potentially conflict over, resources such as residential areas may be generated because there are supply : demand imbalances in particular areas. The classic portrayal of this was provided in the analyses of Chicago in the 1920s by Burgess and others (see Johnston, 1971). At that time, the major source of Chicago's growth was the flood of migrants, first from Southern Europe and later of blacks from the southern States of the USA. These people were constrained, by their lowly position in the labour market, to the worst housing in the inner city areas. But the amount of housing for them there was insufficient, even when occupied at much higher densities than previously, and they were forced to "invade" neighbouring districts. Such invasion may meet with resistance, but in general it was rapidly followed by succession, by the immigrants replacing the former residents, who in their turn were forced to invade other districts. Growth at the centre thus stimulated a ripple effect extending right to the edge of the built-up area, with groups being "forced out" of their home areas and needing to "invade" others in order to avoid incoming negative externalities and to recreate the desired positive externalities.

Invasion and succession sequences have been identified for many cities, and the processes involved have been the subject of much careful study (see Sinclair and Thompson, 1976). Later work has established that invasion by negative externalities need not be the cause of neighbourhood change; Hoyt, for example, pointed out that a desire for newly-created positive externalities may induce people to move from an area and to allow succession without *invasion*. And invasions may on occasion be successfully repelled, as illustrated by Hoyt's work on Chicago and by Firey's exposition of the continued high status of the Beacon Hill area overlooking Boston Common (this research is reviewed in Johnston, 1971). And neighbourhood change may be generated by a variety of other catalysts, most of which involve some form of land-use change and the introduction of negative externalities to an area.

The general thrust of the literature on the residential mosaic is that invasion and succession is the norm. Social Darwinism suggests the "survival of the fittest", so that outmovement is presented as the sensible reaction to neighbourhood change. This may be so with regard to major invasions, such as that of a black population, but many potential changes are resisted. The residential mosaic provides the arena for a great deal of, usually minor, conflicts over the manipulation of space, whether it be altering the boundaries of a school catchment area, building a new road through a district, changing the use of a piece of land, or a proposed development of low-income housing. As mapping exercises have shown (Ley and Mercer, 1980; Janelle and Millward, 1970), land-use changes are frequently contested through the formal mechanisms erected by the state, and community action is taken if feelings about a proposal are high (Robson, 1982). Furthermore, local residents not only protest against negative externalities, they also petition for positive ones (Burnett, 1981).

Protest

Most empirical analyses of community, or neighbourhood, action focus on protesting and petitioning as particular forms of behaviour. Such work either investigates an individual protest/petition/conflict or seeks to generalize about the nature of such activities.

A commonly adopted framework for making generalizations about local protest action over changes to the residential mosaic is a model developed by Hirschman (1970) for the study of organizational failure. According to this, an individual can choose between three possible responses to the failure of an organization to provide goods or services at the desired quality: *exit* involves finding an alternative source; *voice* involves seeking to change the quality of provision by protest; and *loyalty* involves acceptance of the poor quality. As some reviewers have suggested, the voice option is more powerful when exit is also available to the complainant; it is a sanction which might encourage an improvement of the service, whereas if the provider knows that loyalty in the end is certain, reaction to the voice may be much less prepared to yield (see the review by Hirschman, 1980).

Hirschman's model has been adapted by Dear and Long (1978) for the study of community responses to locational issues. In their presentation, *exit* is the decision to leave an area consequent on the introduction of (or the threat to introduce) a negative externality: it is what happens in the invasion and succession sequence. It may be, of course, that some groups do not have this option open to them; they cannot afford to move, or are constrained from doing so (as under apartheid in South Africa). *Resignation* is the equivalent of loyalty, and is usually what has to be adopted by those alienated from the political process, who see protest as a waste of time because they know that they will fail. *Voice* involves protest, either by the individual or, more commonly, by a coalition of those affected. Such a coalition involves the creation of a limited community (Bell and Newby, 1976). Dear and Long identify two further options. *Illegal action* involves a particular form of protest which may be violent – as in the "defence" of communal space; the

1936 building of the Cuttleslowe walls in Oxford (Collison, 1963) across a road in order to divide a middle class residential area from a public housing estate is often quoted as a classic example of such a non-violent response. Finally, the protesters may seek *formal participation* within the relevant institutions of the state, most usually the planning procedure.

This model may be used to provide a framework for the study of an individual conflict (as in Dear and Long's study) or it may be the source of hypotheses for a more general study. The latter was undertaken by Orbell and Uno (1972). Survey respondents were asked for their reaction to perceived neighbourhood problems, and their answers categorized into those considering only exit, those considering both options, and those considering neither. Classifying respondents by race and location they found that ghetto blacks and suburban whites favoured voice – i.e. they would fight change; the former because they had little option whereas inner city whites favoured exit. Such responses are typical of the problems discussed in the present book: whites have moved to, and defend, suburbia whereas blacks would like to move there, but cannot.

Somewhat similar work has been undertaken by Cox and McCarthy (1980, 1982; Cox, 1983) in a telephone survey of Columbus, Ohio residents. Respondents were classified as either activist or non-activist according to their degree of involvement in protest actions and local community organizations. Cross-classifications with variables such as home ownership, perception of neighbourhood problems, mobility intentions, and presence of young children in the household produced the findings that, *inter alia*:

(1) people who perceived problems in their home neighbourhoods were more likely to be activists than were those who did not;
(2) people who intended to leave an area were less likely to be activists than those who did not;
(3) home owners were more likely to be activists than were renters; and
(4) householders with children were more likely than those without children to be activists.

The first two of these findings are relatively unsurprising; people are more likely to be active when faced with a perceived threat than they are to be permanently involved with local issues, and those with strong ties to an area are more likely to be active there. The third finding suggests that those with an equity stake in an area's property and its exchange values are more likely to be active in its defence than are those who rent their homes and have no major investment to protect. And the fourth indicates the importance of the neighbourhood, with its local schools, for child socialization. Thus the activists are those who apparently have most to lose, economically and socially, from neighbourhood change. More detailed analyses, using multi-dimensional cross-classifications, produced further insights, showing, for example, that non-mobile activists are less concerned with property exchange values than are mobile "escapists" – those who wish to move, which involves realizing the exchange values (McCarthy, 1981).

In their evaluation of these findings, Cox and McCarthy (1982; see also McCarthy, 1981) indicate that it is false to identify community land-use conflicts as separate, individual events generated by disagreements between individual actors. They are, rather, to be seen as local issues that are particular manifestations of the general conflicts that characterize capitalist society, between capital and labour on the one hand and among classes on the other. The former type involve the search for accumulation coming into conflict with either a similar search by others or, more likely, a desire to protect the consumption levels of one segment of society. The latter types also involve conflict over consumption levels, often the consumption of publicly provided goods, and over the reproduction of class relations via education. These are, of course, the major conflicts within a capitalist society. Because they appear locally and affect only small portions of the population, they are defused considerably in the minds of actors and, in many cases, analysts. Community conflict and activism are manifestations of the central tensions over accumulation and consumption/reproduction under capitalism.

This is not to imply that the appearance of such local conflicts can be predicted, nor that whether or not a particular individual is an activist can be forecast with any degree of certainty. The individual residents of an area have freedom of choice. Similarly, some of those who generate local stress, especially developers seeking to alter the local built environment, have freedom to decide how and where to direct their activity. They are, in general, more powerful than the residents seeking to defend themselves, in part because of their greater resources (Johnston, 1982a), in part because of their ability to manipulate the agenda of the conflict (Robson, 1982), and in part because of their ability to obtain the support of the state. (The two main functions of the state in capitalist society – to facilitate capital accumulation and to promote the legitimation of the capitalist system – are contradictory, in that action directed towards one may harm the other. Thus any decision by actors within the state represents a balancing act between the two forces, determining which is the appropriate course of action at that time and place.)

Local conflicts, especially those over land uses, are manifestations of the general conflicts within society. Many involve state action. A very large proportion involve state mediation, in that the state has taken upon itself the power to plan and control the use of land. Those who operate that power, and who have "professionalized" planning in recent years, in general are sympathetic to capitalist goals, both generally and specifically (Knox and Cullen, 1981), and their work is oriented to the support of capitalist accumulation strategies (Simmie, 1981). Protest against such plans, and those involved in their preparation, brings local communities in conflict not just with a developer who is proposing something that they perceive as potentially a negative externality but with the entire logic of capitalism. Some, as has been shown here, are more likely to protest than others. And some protests are more likely to succeed (Saunders, 1980), which in most cases means that the proposed negative externality is relocated to an area where voice is less likely to be either substantial or successful. A major consequence of local land-use conflicts, then, is that those best able to articulate their protests ensure that those who are less able suffer most, if for no other reason than that developers will avoid potential trouble spots, where defence of their proposals may be expensive (in time and money). The morphology of the residential mosaic is maintained by the differential in quantity and quality of voice.

PROMOTING CHANGE

Virtually all of the discussion so far in this chapter has been concerned with conflict over proposed changes to parts of the residential mosaic. Voice has been examined as the strategy of protest against change. But what about protest for change – is voice relevant there too? As already noted, local action groups may petition a state body to obtain certain changes – the construction of community facilities, for example. These are usually minor, and involve small positive externalities over which there may be little conflict.

Some groups in society are seeking more than minor changes to the local economic and social infrastructure, however. They want fundamental changes in the various allocation processes that create and maintain the residential mosaic and its myriad positive and negative externalities. Thus, in the context of the present book, they want to end exclusionary zoning and to open up the suburbs to all groups (rich and poor, black and white) within urban society. They also want greater equality in the provision of basic services, notably education. They are not seeking to overthrow the capitalist system, which is the purpose of the urban social movements studied by Castells (1977), but to reform it, by reducing the inequalities of opportunity. Reorganization of the residential mosaic is only part of such a reform programme, but spatial changes are a necessary, though far from sufficient, part of much of that reform.

The major arena for the articulation of reform programmes is through politics, both local and national. The ideology of democracy is that concerns are voiced, that coalitions form around particular programmes, and that the electorate votes for its desired coalition which puts the relevant programme into action. The last part presents the biggest problems. When the reformers take control of the state apparatus they have to face the conflicting tasks of accumulation (advancing established capitalist interests) and legitimation (including putting their agreed programme into operation). If it is the national state that they have won control of, they face the power of multinational finance in the operation of policies; if it is the local state, they face the restraints on its actions erected by the national state (Johnston, 1982a). Thus reform programmes may be voted for, but only rarely are they fully implemented; in general, those that are implemented are ones that do not seriously threaten the accumulation strategies of established interests.

The exercise of voice via the democratic political system is the approved means of achieving reform; it rarely succeeds but the ideology surrounding it is so strong that, in the United States at least, the strategy remains the favoured one. (Meanwhile, established groups seeking to hinder reform use non-democratic, or corporatist, strategies – Jessop, 1978.) How has it been used to achieve the desired – by some – reforms in the morphology of the urban residential mosaic? One strategy available in the United States is to use voice in the judicial rather than the political arena (Johnston, 1982a). The Constitution of the United States provides a variety of grounds on which protests can be made, especially protests against actions by the state for the aim of the Constitution was to maximize individual liberties and to protect individual rights. It also provides a mechanism, the courts, for the consideration of these protests. The nature of those protests and of their consideration is the subject of the rest of this book.

CONCLUSIONS

The urban residential mosaic is the product of conflicts over positive and negative externalities. Such conflicts continue, as individuals and groups seek to change the mosaic, and thus the geography of the externalities. Many of those conflicts, directly or indirectly, are concerned with land use. Most are mediated through some arm of the state; many involve another arm of the state (including the local state) as one of the protagonists.

The majority of these conflicts are defensive actions, by groups seeking to protect the part of the residential mosaic in which they live from changes that are considered potentially detrimental. Some are aggressive, seeking to improve local environments. All of these relate to the situation at a particular place at a given time – although they are manifestations of general processes. In addition, there are aggressive actions that seek major reforms in the morphology of the residential mosaic. These, like the others, involve the strategy of voice, articulating demands and protests. But, reflecting the particular constitutional situation in the United States, they are probably articulated in the judicial rather than the political arena (even though the ultimate goal is political). They are usually specific, aimed at a particular local conflict because the judicial rules do not allow the discussion of general issues, only specific acts. But the aim is to achieve general reform through the precedent set by the decision in the local conflict.

Reform via legal action is a strategy that has been used a great deal in battles for economic and social change in the United States. The rest of this book looks at the use of that strategy in the search for reforms of the processes that produce and maintain the residential mosaic, especially those processes that involve state action.

FOUR

The state, conflict resolution and the Supreme Court: an introduction

Two types of conflicts over the urban residential mosaic were identified in the previous chapter. The first concerns defensive actions, by which individuals and groups potentially affected by some proposed change seek to prevent it from coming about. Their actions are usually both local and particular, concerned with unique events and having very little wider significance. The second concerns aggressive actions, by individuals and groups seeking to achieve reform not with regard to a particular issue but in terms of general policies and programmes. (A specific issue may be needed on which to fight the general thesis, as illustrated here. Decision-makers, such as judges, prefer to rule on specifics, thereby establishing precedents, rather than on generalized arguments supported by hypothetical examples.) Because they are demanding reform, those involved in the aggressive actions operate in separate arenas from those taking defensive positions. It is the former that are the focus of the remainder of this book.

These reformist programmes involve the state, in two ways. First, the state – or some element of it – is in most cases implicated in the activity. With regard to the residential mosaic, for example, it is the zoning and taxing powers of municipalities which are the concern of many of the reform programmes. Secondly, some element of the state is required to act as the umpire or arbiter in the conflict, to decide on the relative merits of the various cases and to introduce remedies where a grievance has been proved. The state, then, is crucially involved and implicated in the conflict over the residential mosaic. Before discussing its operations in the particular context of this book, its role within modern societies is first outlined.

THE STATE: AN INTRODUCTION

There are many popular theories of the state – considering what it is, what it does, and what it should do and why – alongside a substantial number of

academic presentations. These vary considerably in their content. Many are
only partial theories, in that they present accounts of what the state does –
often in particular circumstances – without considering why it exists and
has the functions that it does. Individual state actions, undertaken by those
working in and for it, are guided by the rationale for the state. To understand
the particulars, therefore, an appreciation of the general is required. This
suggests a three-level hierarchy of theories. At the top is the theory of the
state. Below it come the theories that account for the role of the state in
particular societies, whereas at the foot are the theories of action within the
state.

For the present purposes, a general theory of the state at the highest level
of the hierarchy is unnecessary. Before one can proceed to develop *theories of
state action*, however, it is necessary to provide a middle-level *theory of the
state in capitalist society*. Without the latter, the former are likely to be *ad hoc*
and relatively incoherent. One cannot understand why a certain action is
undertaken without first appreciating the context in which it is set.

The state performs many roles in advanced capitalist societies such as the
United States. Its roles vary from time to time, as well as place to place,
however, which suggests that a general, predictive theory of the state is an
impossible goal (Jessop, 1982). This is because the same ends can be sought
in a large variety of different ways. According to some theorists, such as
Clause Offe (see the review in Jessop, 1982, pp. 106–112), there are two basic
functions of the state in a capitalist system. The first is providing a conducive environment for *accumulation*. As indicated in Chapter 1, a capitalist
society is built on a materialist base and its continued existence depends on
the ability of investors to reap profits. The state aids and abets that search for
profits, thereby seeking to maintain the society's economic health. Part of
this aiding and abetting involves the second function, which is providing
legitimation for the capitalist system. Capitalism is built on inequality and
exploitation, which generate tensions between "haves" and "have-nots",
exploiters and exploited. The state seeks to relax these tensions, to convince
the relatively deprived that the system is beneficial to them and, when and
where necessary, to temper the demands of the exploiters, so that in their
search for greater profits they do not foment unrest which would damage or
even destroy the system.

Clearly there are many ways in which the state can perform these two
functions. Although it, or something like it, is almost certainly necessary for
the operation of a capitalist society, it need take no particular form. Thus in
Chapter 1 it was pointed out that suburbanization has become a major
element in the materialist dynamo of American society; it is a sufficient but
not a necessary means of advancing capitalist accumulation and was just one
of many possible routes to that goal that the state might have chosen to
promote. Similarly, in Chapter 2 it was argued that suburban municipal
fragmentation was a sufficient but not a necessary way of pursuing resi-

dential exclusivity. The particular form of the local state in America is conducive to that goal.

Given this general appreciation of the functions of the state, it is then possible to place analyses of how it operates in their proper context. Several theories of state action have been proposed (Johnston, 1982a). One, *instrumentalism*, suggests that the state machinery is the property of a single class in society (the bourgeoisie), which operates it to its own ends. At the national level, this is an undoubted over-simplification, which does not allow for the separate existence of the state and its large number of functionaries – who nevertheless, because of their need to promote accumulation and legitimation, act in the bourgeoisie's general interests. At the level of the local state, however, the instrumentalism theory has some validity. The discussion in Chapter 2 showed that many suburban municipal incorporations were undertaken to promote the interests of particular groups (almost invariably segments of the bourgeoisie). Many municipalities – and school and special districts – are the "property" of relatively small, homogeneous groups who use their legal powers to further their own goals and to distance themselves (socially and economically, as well as physically) from those of other groups.

In order to further its general functions and to promote the particular goals of its citizens, the state must be organized and operated. This is done by its employees, around whom the *managerialism* theory has developed. Managers act within guidelines, which include both general (professional) rules of behaviour and policies laid down by their employers – all managers, not only those employed by the state, operate in this way. Because of their training, skills, experience and full-time employment, the managers are often considerable influences on the development of policies as well as their implementation. To all of their activities, they bring their own values and attitudes. Because most are highly educated and come from particular social and economic backgrounds, these personal characteristics are widely shared (see Knox and Cullen, 1981). This means that, at a general level, managerial activity is predictable (it is usually "conservative"), although what one individual will do in a certain situation can rarely be foreseen with complete accuracy. Thus how the state operates depends in part on how the relevant managers interpret their roles in particular circumstances.

Most capitalist societies, and certainly that of America, are promoted by the majority of their citizens for their democracy. They argue that all decisions involving the state are made for the people, because they are made by individuals elected by, and accountable to, the people. This general theory of democratic state action has its academic counterpart in the theory of *pluralism*. This presents the state as the property of no particular group within society, but the arena for a – fair and unbiased – contest between opposing groups who wish to hold power (to set the policies which the managers operate) in order to advance particular programmes (see Dunleavy, 1980). To win that power, they must convince a majority of the enfranchised citizens of the merits of their programmes. There is no guarantee, even if they win once, that they will always obtain electoral support. Thus "control" of the state may shift over time.

The pluralist theory of state action is in part correct, for control of the state apparatus is indeed obtained by an electoral contest in many countries and that control does pass from one group to another. As a result, programmes and policies change. But only to a limited extent. If a programme threatens accumulation on any major scale, then those in control may find it necessary to alter their priorities in order to protect their power. Similarly, if they threaten legitimation, their control may be questioned. Capitalism is a relatively tolerant system, but only within defined limits (those in power may seek to replace capitalism, of course, but no popularly-elected government has yet achieved this).

Democracy, then, is not a sham, but it is constrained. Pluralism only operates within certain limits. To some analysts of advanced capitalist societies (see Jessop, 1982; Johnston, 1982a), however, the electoral process is a minor influence on how the state acts. The main influences on a government are major interest groups – large firms, trades unions, chambers of commerce, etc. – which lobby governments, legislators and managers outside the formal electoral system. According to this *corporatist* perspective, although the population at large may elect governments, it is the interest groups which are the main influences on policies.

None of these theories of state action provides a complete perspective on what is done, where and when. All provide useful insights in various situations. The remainder of this book is concerned with aggressive actions over aspects of the local state and the urban residential mosaic in the United States. In this, the instrumentalist perspective illuminates how and why suburban fragmentation operates; the managerialist perspective provides a basis for understanding the resolution of certain conflicts over that fragmentation and its consequences; and the pluralist perspective helps an appreciation of how the managers are selected and their guidelines are framed.

MANAGERS AND TEXTS

An organization as large and as complex as the modern state can only operate if rules and procedures are clearly specified and enacted. These rules and procedures take a variety of forms, including laws and directives from the elected government and operational guidelines for the managers. But these cannot cope with all eventualities. Nor can they be so precise that the correct course of action is obvious in every case. Managerial decision-making is usually necessary, and some freedom of action must be allowed. This occurs, for example, in the criminal justice system. Police officers must decide whether an offence has probably been committed, whether a particular individual has probably committed it, and whether an arrest should be made. If a suspect is arrested, law officers must decide whether a prosecution should be made, on what charge, and how the case should be conducted. Finally, judges (assisted by juries in many countries) must decide whether the offence has been proved and, if so, how it should be punished. In all of these stages, discretion is being exercised. This is done within the context of specific laws, which define the offences and the penalties for guilty parties, of guidelines which indicate the procedures that should be followed, and of legal precedents which suggest how the case should be judged.

The context within which the discretion is exercised can always be changed. Elected politicians can alter the laws defining offences and maximum/minimum penalties. Governments can suggest, in some cases direct, the police and legal officers to take a tough line on certain types of offence and offender, but a more relaxed position on others. And the managers themselves can alter what occurs; the judges, for example, can set new precedents in their decisions on particular cases which have consequences for a large number of others. Politicians and governments cannot overrule these managerial decisions except by changing either the law or the managers. Their degrees of freedom for doing both may be severely limited, and so the exercise of managerial discretion may, in effect, be the equivalent of law-making.

The operation of the state, then, involves the writing and interpretation of a series of *texts* by various groups of *managers*. Of prime importance in this process in democratic societies are the elected politicians, who are responsible for both preparing the texts and appointing the managers. Once the texts and the managers exist, control is removed somewhat from the politicians, and the managers take on a separate, though far from autonomous, existence. They act within the guidelines of the texts, but how they interpret their constrained role depends on their personal values and attitudes. In selecting the managers, the politicians attempt to obtain individuals who will operate the guidelines in a certain way and will exercise their discretion in particular directions, but unless they are prepared/able to change the texts and the managers once the selection has been made they are then in the hands of their appointees. Politicians initiate and oversee policies, but managers put them into effect (for a fuller presentation of this argument, see Johnston, 1983).

Of the many managers and texts that could be the focus of attention of a work on conflict over the residential mosaic in suburbia, the present book concentrates on the United States Supreme Court and the United States Constitution. The latter is the text, written in 1787 and amended on several occasions since. The Justices of the Supreme Court are the managers, who rule on cases that they agree to hear and which relate to that text. The decisions that they make and opinions that they pass set precedents, which are then interpreted by the justices on lower courts, and also by the Supreme Court Justices themselves when they hear further cases that are related to those already decided, but not precisely so. The remainder of this chapter outlines the nature of these managers, and the particular portion of the text relevant to the subject of suburban residential segregation.

THE SUPREME COURT

The Constitution of the United States divides the federal government into three separate arms – the Executive, the Legislature and the Judiciary. Members of the first two are elected (both, now, in popular elections with universal adult franchise). Members of the Judiciary are appointed by the Chief Executive (the President), whose nominees to the Supreme Court must be approved by a two-thirds majority of the Senate (Article II, Section 2).

Only the Supreme Court is mentioned in the Constitution (Article III, Section 1) which decrees that:

> The judicial power of the United States, shall be vested in one Supreme Court, and in such inferior courts as the Congress may from time to time ordain and establish.

The jurisdiction of the courts is also specified (Article III, Section 2.1):

> The judicial power shall extend to all cases, in law and equity, arising under this Constitution, the laws of the United States, and treaties made.

The position of the Justices is also spelled out, with provisions intended to ensure their impartiality and insulation from the claims of interest groups (Article III, Section 1):

> The Judges, both of the Supreme and Inferior Courts, shall hold their offices during good behaviour, and shall, at stated times, receive for their services, a compensation, which shall not be diminished during their continuance in office.

Justices, then, are appointed for life, or until they retire; they can only be removed in certain circumstances (Article II, Section 4):

> The President, Vice President and all civil officers of the United States, shall be removed from office on impeachment for, and conviction of, treason, bribery, or other crimes and misdemeanors.

A single court is clearly insufficient for the legal operations of a country as large as the United States, and a hierarchy of federal courts has been established (Fig. 4.1). For most criminal and civil cases, the lowest level of the hierarchy is the system of District Courts. Above these, decisions may be taken to the Courts of Appeals, and beyond them any party may seek leave to appeal to the Supreme Court, which is thus the final arbiter. (It is possible, under certain circumstances, to by-pass the lower courts.)

The Supreme Court operates under two jurisdictions (for discussion of

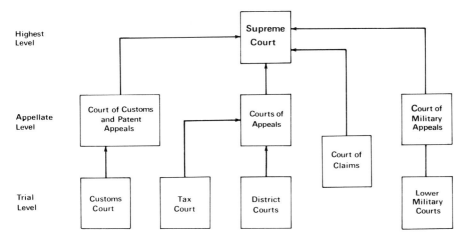

Figure 4·1. The hierarchy of federal courts in the United States. State courts also produce
cases that may be appealled to the higher federal courts.

these, see Baum, 1981). Its *original* jurisdiction, as specified in the Constitution, covers (Article III, Section 2.2)

> . . . all cases affecting ambassadors, other public ministers and consuls, and those in
> which a State shall be party.

With regard to disputes between States, a mandatory hearing is specified; for
cases involving a State, a dispute between a State and the federal government, and cases involving foreign diplomatic personnel, a hearing may be
granted at the discretion of the Supreme Court. Its main task concerns its
appellate jurisdiction. Hearings are mandatory in certain circumstances,
notably when an inferior court has found a federal law unconstitutional, and
also in those cases involving conflicts over State laws and the federal Constitution. For all other appeals from the inferior courts, the Supreme Court has
discretion over whether it will grant a hearing, as it does over appeals from
the highest courts in the State systems with regard to cases involving federal
law and Constitution.

Each State has its own Constitution, laws and courts. Each is bound by the
United States Constitution, with statements such as (Constitution of the
State of California, Article III, Section 1):

> The State of California is an inseparable part of the United States of America, and the
> United States Constitution is the supreme law of the land.

Many activities within individual States are covered by State laws only, so
that the State Supreme Court is the ultimate court of appeal. For cases
involving issues relating to the federal Constitution, however, appeals can
be made to the United States Supreme Court.

Most of the cases taken to the Supreme Court fall under its discretionary
rather than its mandatory jurisdiction. In the late 1970s, as many as 4000 per

year were being filed, a four-fold increase over the number at the end of the Second World War. In most cases (94 per cent of those filed in 1974; Baum, 1981, p. 81), the Court denies a hearing. For some, usually uncontroversial, it produces a written, unsigned opinion. For the remainder (about 200 a year) it calls for the relevant papers (i.e. it issues a writ of *certiorari*), conducts an oral hearing, and hands down a full written decision, signed by those Justices who support the judgement; each Justice in favour can submit a personal, concurring opinion, and those who disagree may submit a dissenting opinion.

The first task of the Justices is thus to decide which cases will be heard. This decision is taken in conference, after the Justices and their clerks have reviewed the pleas. To guide the decision, the Court has its own rule (Number 19) which outlines the criteria as:

> the existence of important legal issues that the Court has not yet decided, conflict among courts of appeals on a legal question, conflict between a lower court and the Supreme Court's prior decisions, and departure "from the accepted and usual course of judicial proceedings" in the courts below. (Baum, 1981, p. 86)

The aim is to select cases judgements on which will enhance "the certainty and consistency of the law". Nevertheless, terms such as "important legal issues" are vague and allow for considerable latitude in the selection of cases by the Justices. Who is on the Court, and what he is interested in,* can influence what the Court hears, therefore. As Baum (1981, p. 89) expresses it, "inevitably justices respond to petitions for hearing in part on the basis of their policy preferences" and their "evaluations of lower-court decisions are not random but are based largely on their ideological positions" (p. 90). A Justice may perhaps not vote for a hearing on a case if he believes that the final decision will be unfavourable to his opinions; he will prefer to keep the issue "on ice" until a more favourable time, and another relevant case.

A positive vote of four of the nine Justices is sufficient to have the writ of *certiorari* issued. Briefs must then be filed within 45 days, and a date for oral argument is arranged. Usually half-an-hour is allowed for argument by each side, and questioning by the Justices is usual. The court then proceeds to make its decision *in camera*, on which it presents a written opinion (the full procedure, as laid down in the rules, is given in Witt, 1979, pp. 932–945). Before making its decision, the Court may ask for further briefs, and in some cases further oral argument.

After oral argument (almost invariably on the following Friday) the Justices discuss the case *in camera*. Each Justice passes an opinion; argument may follow and then, unless a stay is requested, a preliminary vote is taken. If the Chief Justice is in the majority, he assigns one of the Justices to write the Court's opinion on the case; if he is in the minority, the senior Justice in the majority allocates that task. The relevant Justice then drafts an

---

* As no Justice, until the appointment of Justice O'Connor in 1981, was female, use of the male pronoun and adjective is used throughout.

opinion, which he circulates in order to get a majority of supporting signatures. Others may decide to assist, to write their own opinions, or to write dissents. The drafts circulate, comments are returned, re-drafting takes place, and eventually a majority of Justices is forged who not only accept the decision but support the opinion on which it is based. (In some cases, the two are distinct; a Justice may accept the decision but for his own separately-presented reasons.) Clearly much politicking goes on, especially with cases that at least some of the Justices see as important. Votes may be switched and deals may be done in order to increase the size of the majority. Eventually agreement is reached, the decision is announced, and the opinion is published. Most texts on the Supreme Court outline the process (see Hodder-Williams, 1980, Ch. 3) and for an attempt to illustrate the full details of what is overtly a secret set of proceedings, see Woodward and Armstrong (1979).

In many of its decisions, the Supreme Court must not only pass an opinion, it must also specify a remedy in order to right the observed wrong. The Court has no police power with which to enforce its remedy. It can only require compliance, which it generally does by passing oversight back to the relevant lower court. That court may disobey the Supreme Court, and earn its rebuke when further litigation is brought and the case is reviewed. More often, it is the guilty party which is reluctant (in civil rather than criminal cases) to act as required, thereby at least delaying implementation of the Court's decision. (This was certainly so in the 1950s with regard to one of the issues considered here, school desegregation.) The Executive and the Legislature, too, may be reluctant to support the Court (again, this was so with school desegregation: Peltason, 1971). Congress, for example, can speed-up implementation by the threat of withholding federal funds from recalcitrant authorities, as can the President, who is also influential in shaping public opinion. Despite its status, however, the Court may find its decisions having relatively little impact.

> When policymakers like a decision, they can be expected to carry it out. The Court's authority and its stock of sanctions provide an additional impetus for positive response to its decisions, but their force is limited . . . . But . . . it has little ability to control the implementation process. (Baum, 1981, pp. 198–199)

The text

The Justices of the Supreme Court are managers within the state, as defined above. Their jurisdiction is wide, and yet restrained, for they can only act when called upon to do so by petitioners. Three texts guide their decision-making; the United States Constitution and the Laws and Treaties of the United States, as passed by Congress and Signed by the President. These are linked, and the Court can be asked to decide whether a law is constitutional: the Court has found 105 Acts of Congress unconstitutional. Only one small area of their jurisdiction is considered here, however, although it has been responsible for an increasing proportion of the case-load in recent decades.

The Fourteenth Amendment to the United States Constitution was proposed on 13 June 1866, and ratified on 9 July 1868, having been approved, first by two-thirds of both Houses and then by the legislatures of three-quarters of the States (Article V of the Constitution sets these requirements). It comprises five, unrelated sections, the first of which reads:

> All persons born or naturalized in the United States, and subject to the jurisdiction thereof, are citizens of the United States and of the State wherein they reside. No State shall make or enforce any law which shall abridge the privileges or immunities of citizens of the United States; nor shall any State deprive any person of life, liberty, or property, without due process of law; nor deny to any person within its jurisdiction the equal protection of the laws.

This amendment was introduced after the Civil War. The Thirteenth Amendment abolished slavery, but did not counter the Supreme Court's earlier decision (in *Scott* v. *Sandford* 19 HOW 393, 1857, this is usually referred to as the *Dred Scott* case)* that blacks were not entitled to American citizenship. The first sentence of the section quoted above grants them that privilege. The second sentence was written to prevent States from removing the privilege, or aspects of it. Because of its wording, it is frequently known as either the "Equal Protection Clause" or the "Due Process Clause". (Due process is also covered in the Fifth Amendment.)

As written and enacted, the intent of the Fourteenth Amendment (Section 1) was limited. But its wording is, like most texts, relatively vague. Furthermore, it contains some important terms:

> The ideals of liberty and equality have animated revolutions, both armed and otherwise. Constitutional revolutions are not immune from such forces ... The first section of the fourteenth amendment may be seen as a shorthand endorsement of the two ideals – the due process clause has been a textual referent for the imposition of libertarian values, and the equal protection clause has served as the textual commitment to an evolving version of constitutional egalitarianism. (Lupu, 1979, p. 982)

Because of this, litigants have sought to use the Fourteenth Amendment in a great variety of ways, on a large number of separate issues, including freedom of contract, freedom of expression, freedom of political association, property rights, racial discrimination, the right to travel, and voting rights (see Kay, 1981; on the impact of the interpretation of the amendment in the economic geography of the United States, see G. L. Clark, 1981).

---

* The referencing system is that used by the Court, and by the major reprints of its decisions and opinions. The *italicized* portion names the litigants. Next come (1) the volume in which the opinion is found, (2) the edition of opinions, (3) the first page of the opinion, (4) the year in which the decision was announced. For most Supreme Court cases the volume is US. However, all references here are taken from the Lawyer's Edition, Second Series. In this book the Supreme Court reference only is given, but the page references for quotes are from the Lawyer's Edition. Thus the full reference for the case of *Hills* v. *Gautreaux* is 425 US 284 (1976), 47 L2d 792; it is in Volume 47 of the Lawyer's Edition, Second Series, starting on p. 792. Since the Lawyer's Edition also gives the Supreme Court reference, and is the most widely used, it is employed here.

How should Justices interpret the wording of texts such as the Fourteenth Amendment? This has been a major topic of debate within American jurisprudence, one on which the Justices themselves have taken sides. The debate can readily be polarized into two positions. On the one hand, there are those – often termed strict constructionists – who believe that the text should be interpreted *as was intended when it was framed*. Thus if, as Berger (1977) claims, the intention of the framers was simply to give, and then protect, citizenship to blacks, then this is all that the Amendment should be used for. Anything more involves the Justices changing the law, which is the proper task of the Legislature. On the other hand, there are those who claim that the Constitution is a "living document" that must be interpreted according to contemporary norms. There is no such thing as "fundamental values" (Ely, 1980, p. 43), so the Justices must act on what they see as the consensus of contemporary views. "Equal protection of the laws" may mean something different in 1968 than in 1868, therefore. The fundamental goals of the Supreme Court, according to Ely, should be to advance participation and to ensure representation, and these should guide its actions (see also Halpern and Lamb, 1982 and Gambitta *et al.*, 1981).

It is the use of the Fourteenth Amendment in the widening field of civil rights that has concerned many of the strict constructionists. In this, the Court has been required to interpret the meaning of the key phrases in the light of the claims and counter-claims before it. As Cox (1976) points out, the equal protection clause cannot be read as implying that all individuals must be treated equally. Classification, he argues, is an essential part of government which decides, for example, to give the vote to all people aged 18 and over but not to those who are younger. The Court must determine whether particular classifications, and the separate treatment involved, are *suspect*. The Fourteenth Amendment clearly suggests that classification on the basis of race is suspect, if members of one race are then discriminated against by the state. (Note that the Amendment is explicit on this point – only discrimination against certain classes *by the state* is outlawed.) But are there other suspect classifications covered by the Amendment? And what are the *fundamental rights* that the Amendment protects? If a classification is deemed suspect, does this cover discrimination in all fields of state activity? Or are certain state provisions – such as education, perhaps – fundamental rights, whereas others – e.g. health care – are not?

The answers to these questions are not explicit within the Constitution itself. Nor are there agreed-upon answers elsewhere. The Justices must interpret the Constitution as they see fit, within the context of the cases before them (which they, of course, have chosen to hear). As already indicated, how they should interpret it is a subject of major debate within American legal and political circles – including among the Justices themselves (see Berger, 1977; Ely, 1980; Polyviou, 1980). The values and attitudes of the Justices – or at least, of a majority of them – are crucial influences on what cases are heard and how they are decided. In many cases, especially those concerning aspects of civil rights, the evidence before them is not factual but circumstantial and subjective. Much of the evidence comes from the social sciences, and is usually far from precise (see W. A. V. Clark, 1981, 1982; Wolf, 1980), especially with reference to cases involving the Fourteenth Amendment – "the most judicially distended section of the Constitution" (Rosen, 1972, p. 19). Nor are the Justices skilled in the methodologies of the social sciences. Thus who they are, what they believe, and who they choose to listen to with sympathy are all critical to the Court's decisions, and the grounds on which they are based.

The members of the court

Civil rights activism is not new in the United States, but it increased markedly during the decades after the Second World War. Most of the issues relevant to suburban residential segregation have been raised – particularly in a legal context – during that period. Thus it is the composition of the Supreme Court over the last 40 years that is of interest here.

Because of their critical role in the interpretation of the American Constitution and laws, Supreme Court Justices occupy important political positions. All Presidential candidates, as part of their political philosophies and their offerings to the electorate, have views on legal and Constitutional issues and wish the courts to take a certain line on particular issues. They may indeed include reference to the Supreme Court in their campaigning – as Reagan did in 1980 with his promise (fulfilled in 1981) to appoint the first woman to the Court.

One of the clearest indications of political values and attitudes in the United States is political party, with Republicans generally more conservative (on a range of issues such as civil rights and the role of government in the economy) than Democrats. Thus almost all nominees for the Court have come from the same party as the President, for in this way the Chief Executive can influence the Court's composition and, hopefully, the approach of its majority (if not all of the Justices) to perceived key issues. Party affiliation alone is insufficient, however. Presidents must take into account a variety of criteria, such as regional representation, in nominating Justices – as well, of course, as ensuring that the individual nominee is qualified and acceptable (Hulbary and Walker, 1980).

The general thesis is that a President nominates Justices who are "in his own image" – they share his values and attitudes. Nixon made this clear in his campaign for the Presidency in 1968. In the preceding years, the Supreme Court had handed down a number of significant opinions regarding the nature of due process in law enforcement and criminal procedures. The rights of suspects and prisoners were substantially extended as a consequence (Witt, 1979, pp. 52–53, 523–580). This enraged the right-wing "law and order" lobby, and probably a majority of American voters. Nixon capitalized on this with attacks on the Court and with promises to nominate individuals who would halt this reform of American law by Court opinions rather than Congressional action.

> Like Nixon himself, the majority did not want reform so much as a return to old ways. A forward looking . . . Court represented the past; a backward looking Richard Nixon represented the future. The call was for managers, not leaders, men who would solve problems without delivering sermons. And so Nixon made the . . . Court a political issue in the 1968 campaign. (Simon, 1973, p. 289)

Whether or not a President achieves his goals depends on two factors largely outside his control. First, his nominee has to act in the way expected, for once approved by the Senate and on the Court it is extremely difficult for the President to influence his decisions if he chooses to be a maverick, or is converted by the existing Justices. (Note Andersen's (1982, p. 585) comment that "Any litigator knows that there is much that is accidental in the outcome of any lawsuit. Different motivations produce complaints. Different perspectives generate responses. Different tribunals with different compositions and different histories decide cases and write opinions. And throughout the accident of different factual and statutory settings produces additional variation".)

Secondly, and much more importantly, the President has to have the opportunity. Justices are appointed for life, and vacancies may not occur during a President's term (there were none in the period of Carter's Presidency, 1977–1980, for example). He may be able to obtain a vacancy, by offering a Justice another post, but the President basically can only influence the Court's composition substantially if either several vacancies occur or on the key issues the Court is fairly evenly divided and one or two nominations may be crucial. If neither occurs, the result may be considerable frustration for the President. One of the best examples of this came in the mid-1930s, when a conservative (strict constructionist) Court found several pieces of Roosevelt's New Deal legislation unconstitutional. The President responded in 1937 with a plan to increase the size of the Court. This was not approved by Congress, but in the following year there was a shift in the Court's decisions in favour of the administration. (Roosevelt added several new Justices at this period, some of whom were the nucleus of the "liberal Warren Court" of the 1950s.)

The membership of the Court since 1940 is shown in Fig. 4·2. In his later terms, Roosevelt made a number of nominations, producing a Court favourably inclined towards the liberal-intervention view of the state enacted under the New Deal. Studies of the Justices' voting records – whether they concerned or dissented from various opinions – have identified voting blocs, groups of Justices who tend to vote the same way on particular issues. According to Spaeth (1979), this allows a classification of Justices

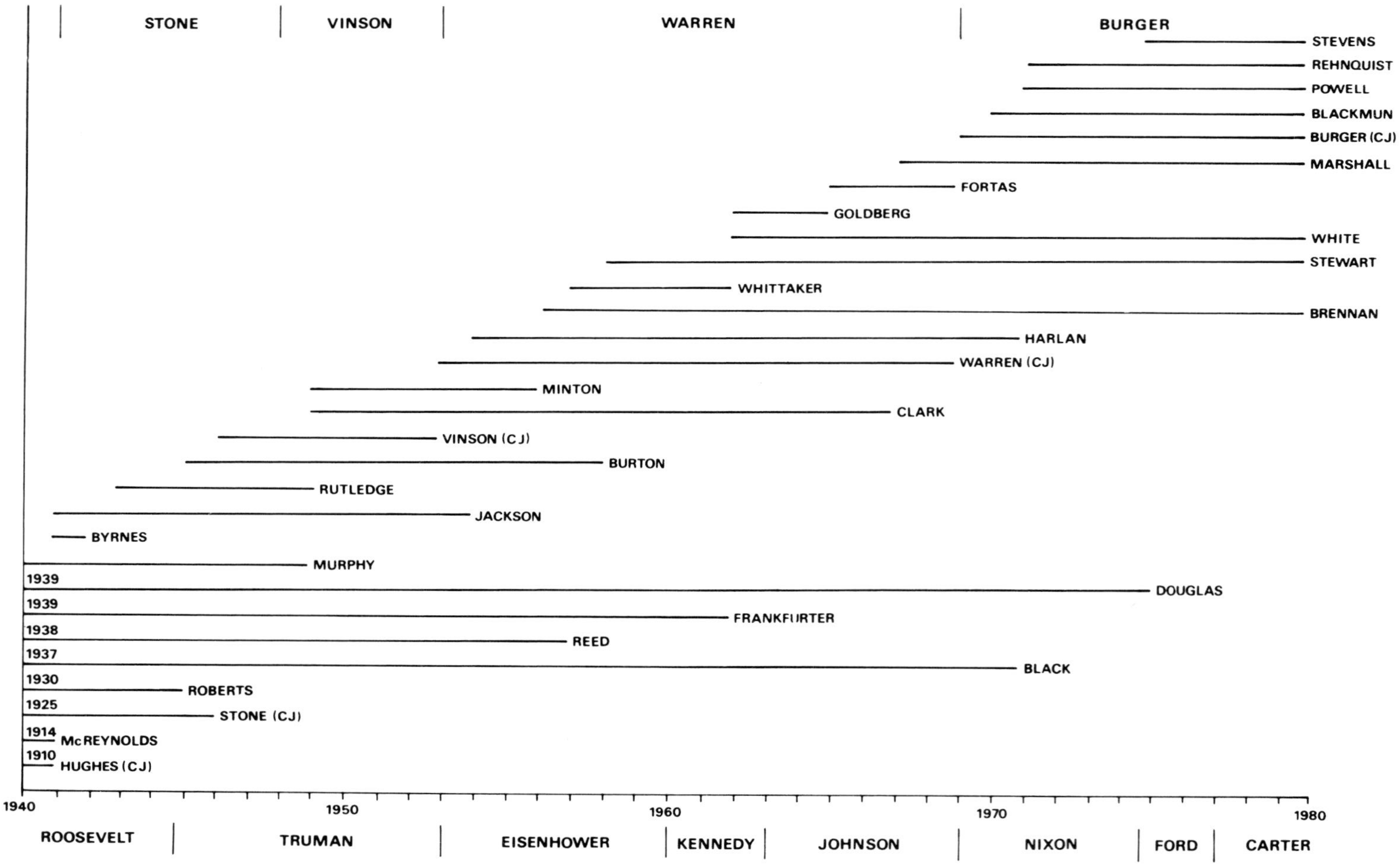

Figure 4·2. Membership of the United States Supreme Court since 1940.

TABLE 4·1. *Supreme Court Justice value systems.*

A. *Types of value systems*

Freedom	Equality	New dealism	Value system
+	+	+	Liberal
+	+	−	Civil libertarian
+	−	−	Individualist
+	−	+	Populist
−	+	−	Utopian collectivist
−	+	+	Benevolent authoritarian
−	−	+	New dealer
−	−	−	Conservative

B. *Ratings of Justices (1958–1977)*

Liberal – Douglas, Warren, Fortas, Goldberg, Brennan, Marshall
Populist – Black
New dealer – Clark
Conservative – Blackmun, Powell, Whittaker, Frankfurter, Burger,
  Harlan, Rehnquist
Moderate – Stevens, Stewart, White

Source: Spaeth (1979, pp. 133 and 135).
The typology in Part A is based on positive votes in cases on the three issue
positions. To produce the classification in Part B each Justice was scaled on
each value, with +1 for a positive vote on a relevant issue and −1 for a
negative vote. A score of ± 0·2 or greater placed a Justice in the relevant
category. The three moderates had no score of ± 0·2 or greater.

(Table 4·1) into eight value systems according to their voting on three sets of
issues – on freedom, equality and the New Deal. And how they vote can be
statistically predicted with some considerable success. Tate (1981)
accounted for 82 per cent of the variation in voting for civil rights; his
equations

> predict the most liberal score for the fictitious justice who is an experienced judge with
> prosecutorial experience, and who is a Democrat appointed from a non-southern state
> by Lyndon Johnson. Conversely, its most conservative score is predicted for the also
> fictitious justice who was a prosecutor without judicial experience, and who is a
> Republican (or Independent) appointed from the South by Harry Truman. (p. 362)

With regard to civil rights issues before the Court, and especially those of
relevance to the subject matter of this book, the number of "liberal" justices
is clearly crucial. To almost all observers of the Court, the key years in this
context are 1953 and 1969: in the first, Earl Warren succeeded as Chief
Justice, and in the second he was replaced by Warren Burger. Many refer to
the Court between 1953 and 1968 as the Warren Court, and from then on as
the Burger Court (Mendelson, 1972). In each, the Chief Justice sided with

the majority; under Warren this was largely liberal, whereas under Burger it has been conservative and strict constructionist. The Justices with whom Warren sat plus those who were appointed to join him by Eisenhower and, in particular, Kennedy and Johnson, were mostly either liberal, on Spaeth's classification, or moderate (i.e. did not fall consistently into any one category). One of them – Marshall, nominated by Johnson in 1967 as the first black on the Court – made a clear statement of his liberal position. With the Fourteenth Amendment, the nation was

> given the power to make certain that the fundamental rights of all individuals were respected . . . the task was left to us, the lawyers, judges, legislators, and citizens of the future. . . . What is essential now . . . is a new kind of activism, an activism in the pursuit of justice. (Marshall, 1968, p. 2)

The liberal majority was never large, especially on issues where race was not the suspect classification, however, and the Court that Burger joined in 1969 (after the retirement of the two liberals Warren and Fortas) was much more conservative; it was made more so by Nixon's three further appointments, plus that by Ford in 1975. Thus, as both Baum (1981) and Heck (1981) show, by the late 1970s there was only a small rump of civil liberties' activists on the Court (Marshall and Brennan, sometimes joined by Stevens, Powell and Stewart (Spaeth and Teger, 1982)).

THE STATE COURTS

Appointments to the federal judiciary, at all levels, are controlled by the Executive – with the Senate having a role in the appointments to the Supreme Court only. This power of patronage is substantially influenced by professional bodies – notably the American Bar Association. For the President, however, it provides opportunities not only to reward political allies but also to influence the course of judicial decision-making. The Supreme Court is the most important, but this hears a small minority only of cases.

Despite their power, the federal courts have jurisdiction over issues relating to the United States laws and Constitution only. State laws and Constitutions are interpreted by the State courts – except where federal issues are involved. Each State has its own court system. According to Article VI of the California Constitution, this system comprises:

> (1) for each county, subdivided into districts, a *Municipal Court* for each district with at least 40,000 residents and a *Justice Court* for each smaller district;
> (2) for each county, a *Superior Court*;
> (3) for each block of counties – defined as judicial districts – a *Court of Appeal*; and
> (4) a *State Supreme Court*.

These act as a hierarchy (with provisions for bypassing certain courts in particular circumstances). In addition, there is a *Judicial Council* – comprising members of the judiciary – which supervises the administration of justice, a *Commission on Judicial Appointments* which considers any Gubernatorial nominations, and a *Commission on Judicial Performance*.

Filling the judicial positions in California is an electoral task. Judges are elected by their relevant constituencies – for the Supreme Court by the State at-large, for the Courts of Appeal by the electorates of the Judicial Districts, and for other Courts by the voters of the relevant county or subdivision thereof. Those elected to the Supreme Court and the Courts of Appeal serve for 12 years, those elected to the lower courts for six. Any vacancies are filled by Gubernatorial nomination to the Commission on Judicial Appointments. To be eligible for election, candidates must have been members of the State Bar of California, for five years for Municipal Courts and ten years for all others.

Not every State has as detailed a system of courts as California (Florida and New York have 11 different types, however (Vines and Jacob, 1976)). Nor do all States elect their judges. Vines and Jacob (1976, p. 251) identify five different ways by which State judges are selected:

(1) partisan election, in which candidates may obtain party backing (16 States);
(2) nonpartisan election, in which formal political identification is forbidden (16 States);
(3) election by Legislature (5 States);
(4) appointment by Governor (8 States); and
(5) merit plan, under which the Governor selects from a slate of candidates presented by a nominating commission that usually has strong representation from the legal profession (12 States).

(Some States operate more than one plan, according to the type of Court, hence the sum of 57.) In the majority of cases, therefore, Judges are directly elected by the population, and thus their selection is likely to reflect popular ideology relating to the role of the law in contemporary society. In the remainder, they are political appointees, and again the choice is likely to be influenced by ideological considerations. As Vines and Jacob (1976, pp. 253, 265) express it:

all selection plans depend on state political processes. . . . State courts are not less political than state legislatures or state executive agencies, but they are usually less openly partisan . . . . Those who seek to influence state courts must do so through the procedures that select judges.

CONCLUSIONS

The concept of ideology has been contrasted with that of philosophy:

Philosophy denotes a carefully prepared and thought out set of values and ideas. Ideology on the other hand denotes values, attitudes, assumptions, "hidden inarticulate premises" that may not be well thought out and are usually disguised rather than spoken out loud. (McAuslan, 1980, p. xii)

In conflicts over civil rights issues, a variety of ideologies is involved: those of the participants to the dispute; those of the judges; and those of the framers of the text. Whereas the ideologies of the first two may be imperfectly articulated, those of the last group may be entirely hidden and can only be implied – inductively and ideologically – by research into their writings and other statements. With regard to planning issues, McAuslan (p. 2) identifies three ideologies: the law as the protector of private property; the law as the promoter of the public interest; and the law as the encouragement for public participation in decision-making. All of these are relevant to the issues discussed in the rest of this book.

The next three chapters explore in some detail the reactions of the courts, especially the Supreme Court, to a variety of issues relating to residential segregation and suburban municipal fragmentation. Each exploration illustrates how the ideological positions of the Justices have influenced their opinions on the various cases, and how their decisions have affected the shaping and reshaping of suburban America.

PART TWO

The conflicts

FIVE

The challenges to zoning

The basic purpose of suburban zoning was to keep Them where They belonged – Out. If They had already gotten In, then its purpose was to confine Them to limited areas. The exact identity of Them varied a bit about the country . . . . The advocates of exclusionary zoning justified it with euphemisms and technical jargon that sometimes even provoked protection of the environment . . . . It was racism with a progressive, technocratic veneer . . . zoning gave every promise of continuing to keep many suburbs closed to all but affluent acceptable whites. (Popper, 1981, pp. 54–55)

In Chapters 1 and 2, distancing was presented as a process undertaken for economic and social reasons in the creation and maintenance of class differences via residential congregation and segregation. Zoning was identified as a mechanism by which distancing processes could be strengthened, and suburban municipal autonomy as a means of gaining political control over the zoning mechanism. This control, and its impact on social, economic and racial residential patterns within American metropolitan areas, has been a focus of conflict in recent decades.

Part of this conflict has been centred on the courts, where litigation has been used as a means for attempting to "open up the suburbs". Some of this litigation has used the equal protection and due process clauses of the Fourteenth Amendment as its base. A small proportion of it has been dealt with by the Supreme Court, whose decisions and opinions will be considered here. To put those actions into context, it is necessary to begin with other decisions of the Supreme Court that are relevant to this issue.

On many legal issues, Supreme Court opinions set the precedents within which the lower federal courts and the State courts interpret other cases. That interpretation may lead to an appeal to the Supreme Court. But the latter body has been very reluctant to handle such appeals, because they deal with issues that are covered by State rather than federal texts. Thus a final section of the chapter looks at some of the opinions of State courts relating to zoning, and in particular its use to promote suburban residential segregation.

ZONING: ITS VALIDITY AND SCOPE

As a number of historians of land-use planning have indicated, zoning was introduced in several of the country's large cities in the early decades of the twentieth century in order to control nuisances; New York instituted height and lot coverage restrictions on part of Manhattan Island, for example, and San Francisco brought in zoning to stop the spread of Chinese laundries. These regulations were instituted under what is known as the police power of the States. According to the Tenth Amendment to the Constitution:

> The powers not delegated to the United States by the Constitution, nor prohibited by it to the States, are reserved to the States respectively, or to the people.

One of the powers reserved to the States, it was argued to and recognized by the Supreme Court, was the police power: "the power to govern its people, and to regulate the use of its land and its resources to ensure the public welfare" (Witt, 1979, p. 14).

In some States, it was believed that this police power extended to zoning, and in this they were backed by decisions of the State courts. The need for zoning was widely recognized, and in the early 1920s the federal government drafted a Standard State Zoning Enabling Act. This was enacted, in more or less the same form, by nearly every State Legislature with 35 doing so by 1930 (Anon, 1978). But was this Act and its implementation constitutional? The answer was given in the decision on a landmark case – *Village of Euclid* v. *Ambler Realty Co.*, 272 US 365, 1926.

Although the Supreme Court had previously upheld a zoning regulation – one which allowed the prohibition of brickmaking in certain parts of a city (*Hadacheck* v. *Los Angeles*, 239 US 394, 1915) – it was the *Euclid* decision which established whether zoning could be applied, without due process, to limit a property-owner's freedom to use his land as he wished. The case concerned the Village of Euclid, which is a suburb of Cleveland, Ohio. A zoning scheme was proposed in 1922 for the whole of the municipality – most of which was still farmland. One of the landowners affected was Ambler Realty Company, which had assembled properties close to the railroad tracks in anticipation of their development for industrial use. The assessed value of that land was $10 000 per acre. Most of this was then zoned for residential use, however, either single-family or apartment. As a result, the company claimed that the value of its land had been reduced to $2500 per acre and that this involved depriving it of its property rights without due process.

The District Court found in favour of Ambler, stating that the zoning ordinance violated both the Ohio Constitution and the Fourteenth Amendment to the United States Constitution. Ambler had been denied several hundred thousand dollars, because of a plan intended to preserve Euclid as a semi-rural retreat for the affluent. The municipality appealed, and the Supreme Court found in its favour. It was relatively uncertain in its statements as to whether the zoning ordinance did exceed the police power, and the majority opinion (the vote was 6 : 3; there was no dissenting opinion – *Village of Euclid* v. *Ambler Realty Co.*, 272 US 365, 1926) was that

> we are not prepared to say that the end in view was not sufficient to justify the general rule of the ordinance . . . . It cannot be said that the ordinance in this respect passes the bounds of reason and assumes the character of a merely arbitrary fact. (p. 311)*

Thus by zoning to segregate various land uses, the Board of Zoning was acting to reduce nuisances, and thereby to promote the general welfare, which overrides the interests of particular property owners. (One of the related issues, not relevant here, is the degree to which those who suffer "worsement" – a decline in property values – should be recompensed; those who reap "betterment" – an increase in values – as a result of zoning are not taxed: see Anon, 1978.)

Three aspects of the Supreme Court's opinion, written by Justice Sutherland, are of interest here. First, it indicates a belief in the autonomy of the local state. If a municipality has been established by the State legislature and its council is properly and democratically elected

> with powers of its own to govern itself as it sees fit within the limits of the organic law of its creation and the state and Federal Constitutions. (Then) its governing authorities, presumably representing a majority of the inhabitants and voicing their will (p. 311)

are proper exercises of the police power. This respect for municipal autonomy has continued since, in a variety of Supreme Court decisions; the Justices have not been prepared to impose remedies that are in the interests of a wider area (such as metropolitan Cleveland in this case), since "the village . . . is politically a separate municipality".

Secondly, there is the all-important issue of the reading of the Constitution. Justice Sutherland's words are far from the strict constructionist ideal:

> while the meaning of constitutional guarantees never varies, the scope of their application must expand or contract to meet the new and different conditions. (p. 310)

As the metropolis sprawls outwards and grows more complex in its spatial organization, so the police power must be extended to control this in the public interest. (Who defines the public interest became a major issue in the 1970s.)

Finally, there is an issue as to the extent of that police power and its exercise "so that the public welfare may be secure" (p. 309). What comprises the public welfare? Clearly this was an issue to be decided by the District Courts in the context of the *Euclid* decision and particular pieces of litigation. Justice Sutherland gave some indication of his understanding of the

---

* All page references, unless otherwise stated, are to the Lawyer's Edition.

power in his reference to "depriving children of the privilege of quiet and open spaces for play" (p. 313: see the discussion below – p. 84 – of the *Belle Terre* case). More importantly, Justice Sutherland extended the definition of the police powers regarding zoning in his opinion in the case of *Nectow* v. *Cambridge* (277 US 183, 1928). This concerned a zoning decision in the city of Cambridge, Massachusetts, whereby a piece of land adjacent to the railroad could not be used for business or industrial purposes. Because of its location, it was claimed that the zoning of the land for residential use only made it unsaleable, while not promoting the general welfare. The Court agreed:

> That the invasion of the property . . . was serious and highly injurious is clearly established; and, since a necessary basis for the support of that invasion is wanting, the action of the zoning authorities comes within the ban of the 14th Amendment and cannot be sustained. (p. 845)

Zoning ordinances, in other words, must be seen to promote the general welfare. If they do not, then they represent some arbitrary whim, which is denying individual property-owners their rights without due process, and without any compelling purpose (the public welfare) for doing so.

Developments based on Euclid and Nectow

The Supreme Court's decision in the *Euclid* case was "interpreted as a virtually absolute upholding of zoning ordinances as a valid exercise of the state's police power" (Listokin *et al.*, 1974, p. 22), with *Nectow* adding the constraint that zoning ordinances must be developed in the public good, with that being interpreted in the courts if necessary. This led to a rapid and widespread adoption of zoning.

Having ruled on the general principle, the Supreme Court refused to become involved further. It had established that zoning was constitutional, under certain conditions. Because zoning was undertaken by municipalities, and these were State creations outwith the purview of the United States Constitution, the oversight of the details of particular ordinances – and whether the conditions regarding arbitrary whims laid down in *Euclid* and *Nectow* were not – rested with the State courts. The Supreme Court declined to hear cases relating to particular issues, as outside its remit. It denied an appeal, for example, regarding a New Jersey decision in 1962 that upheld the exclusion of mobile homes (*Vickers* v. *Township Committee of Gloucester Township* 371 US 233 – the earlier, State Court hearings are reported in 181 A2d 129, 1962).

The Supreme Court's lead in *Euclid* undoubtedly resulted in the State Courts interpreting the police powers very widely. Thus in Massachusetts an ordinance specifying a minimum lot size of one acre was upheld (*Simon* v.

Town of Needham, 42 NE2d 516, 1942)* because of the advantages this carried:

> More freedom from noise and traffic might result. The danger from fire from outside sources might be reduced. A better opportunity for rest and relaxation might be afforded. Greater facilities to play on the premises and not in the street would be available.

(See also the opinions in: *Haneck* v. *County of Cook*, 146 NW2d 35, 1957; *Senior* v. *Zoning Commission of the Town of New Canaan*, 153 A2d 415, 1959; *Fisher* v. *Bedminster Township*, 93 A2d 378, 1952; *Board of Appeals of New Hanover* v. *Housing Appeals Committee*, 294 NE 393, 1962; Listokin *et al.*, 1974; Babcock and Bosselman, 1973.) Similarly, ordinances setting minimum floor areas were allowed (e.g. *Dundee Realty Co.* v. *City of Omaha*, 13 NW2d 634, 1944), as advancing public safety, local property values, and aesthetic considerations. The validity of the last of these (see Anon, 1978, pp. 1443–1462) was indicated by the Supreme Court in its unanimous opinion, handed down by Justice Douglas, on *Berman* v. *Parker*, 348 US 26, 1954. The District of Columbia Redevelopment Land Agency had been established "with the power to acquire land for the redevelopment of blighted territory . . . and the prevention, reduction, or elimination of blighting factors or causes of blight" (p. 29). A case was brought – under the due process clause of the Fifth Amendment which reads

> No person shall . . . be deprived of life, liberty, or property, without due process of law; nor shall private property be taken for public use without just compensation –

that the compulsory acquisition of a piece of commercial land was unconstitutional. Justice Douglas wrote that

> It is within the power of the legislature to determine that the community should be beautiful as well as healthy, spacious as well as clean, well-balanced as well as carefully controlled. (p. 33)

State Courts also limited the exercise of the zoning power, in line with the *Nectow* decision. In particular, they ruled (as in *Fasano* v. *Board of County Commissioners*, 264 Ore 574, 1973, and *Fleming* v. *City of Tacoma*, 81 Wash 2d 292, 1972)† that whereas general ordinances were proper use of the police power promoting the public welfare, allowing variances from such ordinances on particular pieces of land – especially if the interested parties were clearly identified – was not. Not all Justices agreed with the exercise of municipal autonomy to promote the "general interests" of a minority of the residents of a metropolitan area, however. In the case of *Vickers* v. *Township Committee of Gloucester Township*, 181 A2d 129, 1962, for example, Justice

---

* Citations other than that to US cover Courts other than the Supreme Court, as follows: Atlantic, California, North-Eastern, North-Western, Pacific, South-Eastern, South-Western publish some of the decisions of State courts, by regions; the Federal Reporter publishes the decisions of US Courts of Appeal; the Federal Supplement publishes some of the decisions of US District Courts.

† These citations refer to the volumes of State court decisions.

Hall wrote that the zoning power by municipalities does not condone

> the right to erect barricades on their boundaries through exclusion or too tight constriction of uses where the real purpose is to prevent feared disruption with a so-called chosen way of life. Nor does it encompass provisions designed to let in as new residents only certain kinds of people, or those who can afford to live in favored kinds of housing, or to keep down tax bills of present property owners.

At the time that he wrote, Justice Hall was in a majority for a short period; later, as will be shown below, he was not.

Finally, in the Oregon case – *Fasano v. Board of County Commissioners of Washington County*, 507 P2d 23, 1973 – oversight of reasoning was clearly assigned to the judiciary. The court agreed that the implementation of a comprehensive zoning plan was a legislative function properly carried out by the State Legislature or some delegated body (such as a municipality). But zoning changes, deciding whether they are "arbitrary or capricious", should be handled in the judicial arena. The standards for evaluation laid down (as reported in Freilich, 1981) were that: (1) a change must be in accordance with the comprehensive plan; (2) it must be proved that there is a public need for the change; (3) it must be proved that the need is best met by the proposed rezoning, rather than by the use of any other property (for which a rezoning may or may not be required); and (4) the burden of proof rests with the party seeking the change. This is taken as indicating that

> Courts . . . are becoming far less willing to uphold a regulation whose purpose or reasonableness cannot be established (Fox, 1981, pp. 87–88)

although later Supreme Court decisions (in the *James* and *Eastlake* cases – see p. 86 and p. 87) suggest otherwise with regard to the nation's highest court of appeal.

The limits to exclusionary zoning

The Supreme Court decisions of the 1920s, and the State court decisions (of which there were very many: Dolbeare, 1979) based on the precedents set, established an environment in which zoning flourished. It was used in small suburban municipalities to maintain and promote a certain economic and social milieu by its exclusionary nature. There were few apparent limits to this, for only explicit racial exclusion was apparently prohibited.

A limitation on the use of zoning to segregate blacks from whites was settled before the *Euclid* decision. The movement of blacks to urban areas, which gathered pace during the early decades of the twentieth century, increased the perceived threat to white residential areas. To counter this, for example, the City of Baltimore introduced a zoning ordinance in 1910 which designated each of its street blocks as either all-white or all-black (Rice, 1968, p. 181: there are clear parallels with the zoning in South Africa under apartheid – Johnston, 1980, pp. 171–179). The practice spread rapidly to other cities, and was validated by a State supreme court – *Hopkins* v. *City of Richmond*, 86 SE 139, 1915. (An ordinance adopted in Atlanta included the provision that a person of one colour on a mixed block could object to a person of another colour moving in next door. This was ruled as an invalid use of the police power: *Carey* v. *City of Atlanta*, 84 SE 456, 1915.)

The major challenge to this "racial segregation by explicit zoning" policy came in the City of Louisville, Kentucky; it was fought through the courts by the National Association for the Advancement of Colored People (NAACP), funded in 1909 and long in the forefront of the fight for black civil rights (Kellogg, 1967). Section 1 of Louisville's ordinance stated that it was

> unlawful for any colored person to move into and occupy as a residence . . . any house upon a block upon which a greater number of houses are occupied by white people than . . . by colored people

Section 2 stated the converse for whites moving into black areas, and Section 3 excluded domestic servants from these restrictions. To initiate the case, Warley agreed to buy a property from Buchanan, stating in a letter to him that

> It is understood that I am purchasing the above property for the purpose of having erected thereon which I propose to make my residence, and it is a distinct part of this agreement that I shall not be required to accept a deed to the above property or to pay for said property unless I have the right under the laws of the State of Kentucky and the City of Louisville to occupy said property as a residence. (quoted in Rice, 1968, p. 186)

Buchanan (a white) accepted the offer. Warley (a black, and local President of NAACP) refused to pay, because he would not have been able to live in the property. Buchanan sued Warley for breach of contract.

Buchanan's case (*Buchanan* v. *Warley*, 245 US 60, 1917) was not related to segregation per se.

> The right that the ordinance annulled was the civil right of a white man to dispose of his property if he saw fit to do so to a person of color, and of a colored person to make such disposition to a white person. (p. 163)

The legislation had been defended on the grounds that it

> tends to promote the public peace by preventing racial conflicts; that it tends to maintain racial purity; that it prevents the deterioration of property owned and occupied by white people, which deterioration, it is contended, is sure to follow the occupancy of adjacent premises by people of color. (p. 160)

The Supreme Court Justices were unanimous in their view that this was an improper use of the police power. Justice Day wrote that

> Property is more than the mere thing which a person owns. It is elementary that it includes the right to acquire, use, and dispose of it. The Constitution protects these essential attributes of property (p. 161) [and that] . . . We think that the attempt to prevent the alienation of the property in question to a person of color was not a legitimate exercise of the police power of the state and is in direct violation of the fundamental law enacted in the 14th amendment. (p. 164)

In this way, racial zoning was found unconstitutional, in a case concerned not with discrimination against blacks but rather with preventing a white from disposing of his property to whom he pleased. The decision was used by District Courts as a basis for outlawing other racial segregation laws, which were enacted even as late as 1949 (Williams, 1950).

This principle was extended by a later decision (*Hunter* v. *Erickson*, 393 US 385, 1969) on which Justice White wrote for a majority of eight. In 1964, the City of Akron passed a fair housing ordinance which forbade racial discrimination in the private property market. But then a new, retrospective ordinance was placed before the electorate in a referendum (secured by initiative) and passed. This stated that:

> Any ordinance enacted by the Council of the City of Akron which regulates the use, sale, advertisement . . . of any real property . . . on the basis of race, color, religion, national origin or ancestry must first be approved by a majority of the electors voting . . . before said ordinance shall be effective. Any such ordinance in effect at the time of the adoption shall cease to be effective until approved by the electors as provided herein.

This overruled the fair housing ordinance, introduced an explicitly racial classification, and prevented Mrs Hunter from obtaining a particular home. In reviewing Mrs Hunter's case, the Court ruled that

> insisting that a State may distribute legislative power as it desires and that the people may retain for themselves the power over certain subjects may generally be true, but these principles furnish no justification for a legislative structure which otherwise would violate the Fourteenth Amendment. Nor does the implementation of this change through popular referendum immunize it . . . . The sovereignty of the people is itself subject to those constitutional limitations which have been duly adopted and remain unrepealed. (p. 623)

Thus statutes explicitly invoking racial discrimination (see the opinion concurring with the majority by Justices Harlan and Stewart, pp. 624–625) are unconstitutional, however enacted. Note, however, the dissent of Justice Black:

> I protest . . . vigourously against use of the Equal Protection Clause to bar States from repealing laws that the Courts want the States to retain. (p. 625)

The majority favouring this extension of equal protection was slight, however. In an earlier case (*Reitman* v. *Mulkey*, 387 US 369, 1967) a majority of five Justices found invalid a section (26) of Article I of the Californian Constitution. This had been introduced by initiative and voted on in a referendum. It read that

> Neither the state nor any subdivision or agency thereof shall deny, limit or abridge, directly or indirectly, the right of any person, who is willing or desires to sell, lease or rent any part or all of his real property, to decline to sell, lease or rent such property to such person or persons as he, in his absolute discretion, chooses.

And Justice White, for the majority, found that it "was intended to authorize, and does authorize, racial discrimination in the housing market" (p. 838).

Justices Harlan, Black, Clark and Stewart believed it was neutral – "in such transactions private owners are now free to act in a discriminatory manner previously forbidden to them" (p. 842). A few years later, Justice Black – writing for the majority in *James* v. *Valtierra* – was able to limit similar discrimination implemented through the popular initiative and referendum.

Apart from zoning, racial segregation could also be advanced by agreements among property-owners not to sell, lease or rent to particular classes of owners. These agreements took the form of racial restrictive covenants. Such covenants were attached to the deeds of properties, and included statements indicating that a property would not be leased, rented or sold to non-Caucasians, and that future buyers would be subject to this constraint. They were widely used (Vose (1959, p. 5) reports them covering 5·5 square miles of St. Louis and 11 square miles of Chicago).

Racial restrictive covenants are examples of private discrimination, and do not involve the state. Thus an early attempt to outlaw them failed; the case referred to the District of Columbia, where 30 neighbours agreed a 21-year covenant. One of these (Corrigan) violated it. Buckley applied to the Court for the sale to be restrained. Corrigan applied for Buckley's motion to be dismissed, on the grounds that the Fourteenth Amendment prevented such covenants. The District Court and the Court of Appeal dismissed Corrigan's plea. The Supreme Court refused to hear it, but justified this with a brief opinion stating that (*Corrigan* v. *Buckley*, 271 US 323, 1926):

> the prohibitions of the Fourteenth Amendment have reference to state action exclusively and not to any action of private individuals. (p. 330)

If restrictive covenants involve the action of private individuals only, then they are not unconstitutional (this refers to the situation prior to the Fair Housing Act; see p. 157). But what if the state is involved in the enforcement of such covenants? Several cases in the District of Columbia had failed to break them (Vose, 1959, Ch. IV). Two more (*Hurd* v. *Hodge*, 334 US 24, 1948, and *Urciola* v. *Hodge*, 334 US 24, 1948) failed because the Fourteenth Amendment covers only the States, which do not include the District of Columbia. But concurrent decisions in two other cases (*Shelley* v. *Kraemer*, 334 US 1, 1948, referring to St. Louis, and *McGhee* v. *Sipes*, 334 US 1, 1948, referring to Detroit) found that state action related to the enforcement of racial restrictive covenants violated the Amendment.

The case of the Shelleys involved a Mrs Kraemer, whose parents had been among the original signatories of covenants covering a block (reproduced in Vose, 1959, pp. 113–114), suing her new black neighbours for violating that part of the covenant which stated

> that hereafter no part of said property or any portion thereof shall be, for said term of Fifty-years (the covenant was signed in 1911), occupied by any person not of the Caucasian race, it being intended hereby to restrict the use ... by people of the Negro or Mongolian Race.

Both the Circuit Court of St. Louis and the Missouri Supreme Court held that enforcement of this covenant involved no infringement of the Shelleys' constitutionally-guaranteed rights, for the Fourteenth Amendment "relates to a state action exclusively" (*Kraemer* v. *Shelley*, 198 SW2d 679, 1946, quoted in Vose, 1959, p. 118). The McGhee case involved a black family who had moved into a white residential area of Detroit covered by a restrictive covenant. Sipes asked the Courts that the McGhees be restrained

> from using or occupying their property or permitting its use or occupancy by any person except those of the Caucasian race. (Vose, 1959, p. 127)

This was granted by the Circuit Court of Wayne County, relying on State precedent that covered ownership but not occupancy of property. The appeal to the Michigan Supreme Court led to a unanimous decision in favour of Sipes, holding that the Fourteenth Amendment did not apply to the enforcement of private covenants.

On appeal to the Supreme Court, these judgements were overturned. In the majority opinion, Chief Justice Vinson indicated (in *Shelley* v. *Kraemer* and *McGhee* v. *Sipes*, 334 US 1, 1947) the nature of state participation, writing

> That the action of state courts and of judicial officers in their official capacities is to be regarded as action of the State within the meaning of the Fourteenth Amendment is a proposition which has long been established by decisions of this Court. (p. 1181)

The evidence led to the conclusion that

> We have no doubt that there has been state action in these cases in the full and complete sense of the phrase . . . (so) the States have denied petitioners the equal protection of the laws. (p. 1183)

The crucial issue with regard to the covenants, therefore, was not that their existence was unconstitutional. It was not, because they were entered into by private individuals. Any involvement of the state in their enforcement was unconstitutional, however.

The Supreme Court's ruling in the *Shelley* and *McGhee* cases was extended a few years later. The case of *Barrows* v. *Jackson* (346 US 249, 1953), covered not only the enforcement of a covenant but also a claim for damages as a consequence of its breach. The covenant covered a portion of Los Angeles. It was breached by Mrs Jackson who not only sold her home to blacks but also did not incorporate the restriction in the deed of sale. She was then sued by three neighbours, including the Barrows family, for damages, since her action, it was claimed, had led to a depreciation in the value of their property. The Los Angeles Superior Court and the District Court of Appeals ruled against the award, on the grounds that the *Shelley* and *Hurd* judgements precluded

> State courts from giving judicial recognition to and enforcement of race restriction covenants contained in private agreements, whether such judicial enforcement be by

way of injunction . . . or any other type of action in which the remedy is predicated upon a judicial holding, express or implied, that such a covenant is valid. (quoted in Vose, 1959, p. 234)

The Supreme Court of California refused a hearing, but the United States Supreme Court issued a writ of *certiorari*. It agreed with the lower court decisions. Justice Minton wrote (*Barrows* v. *Jackson*, 346 US 249, 1953) that

To compel the respondent to respond in damages would be for the State to punish her for her failure to perform her covenant. . . . The result of that sanction by the State would be to encourage the use of restrictive covenants . . . The action of a state court of law to sanction the validity of the covenant here involved would constitute state action. (p. 1586)

The Courts and zoning before Burger: A summary

Several conclusions can be drawn from the above cases, which cover Court decisions and opinions regarding zoning:

(1) That zoning is a valid exercise of the police power, as long as it is part of a general plan for the public welfare and not an arbitrary decision regarding one piece of land.

(2) That any involvement of the state (i.e. the States and their properly constituted local governments) in activities regarding the use of property that intentionally violates the rights of members of a racial group, is likely to be interpreted as a violation of the Fourteenth Amendment.

(3) That municipalities, constituted by State legislatures and run by elected councils, are to be regarded as representatives of the public interest and their decisions, as long as they do not violate constitutionally-protected rights, are to be respected.

(4) That protection of community character, aesthetic objections, and the promotion of health, safety and public welfare, are all proper uses of the zoning power.

(5) That constitutionally-protected rights cannot be denied to individuals and groups by the majority vote of the residents of an area.

These suggest that, except where explicit discrimination against blacks whose rights are protected in the Constitution are involved, the power to zone can be used by the residents of any municipality to promote their sectional interests.

THE BURGER COURT AND ZONING

Exclusionary zoning was long recognized as a major barrier to entry of blacks and other groups into many areas of suburban housing markets, where municipalities were benefiting from the powers enumerated above. But litigation was not a particularly attractive means of achieving change for a variety of reasons (see Danielson, 1976), although the developments in the field of civil rights and equal protection during the Warren Court era offered the hope of success. No relevant cases were heard by the Supreme Court until the 1970s, however, by which time the hopes were being dimmed. The decisions of the Burger Court did not favour those seeking to change the exclusive nature of much of suburbia.

Belle Terre: community protection via the environment

> Where to make a home, and with whom, are among the most important decisions individuals face. What takes place in the home – especially the raising of children – is important to society as a whole. The regulation of land use significantly affects the choices people make about home and family. (Anon, 1976, pp. 1568–1569)

The Village of Belle Terre is a small municipality, of about one square mile and containing some 700 upper-income residents, on Long Island in the State of New York. It is close to the Stony Brook campus of the State University (SUNY). As is common in such locations, students sought homes to rent in the surrounding residential areas, including Belle Terre. The residents of that municipality wished to exclude them, as a negative externality. They did this by zoning the village for single-family dwellings only, defining family in the relevant ordinance as

> One or more persons related by blood, adoption, or marriage, living and cooking together as a single housekeeping unit, exclusive of household servants. A number of persons but not exceeding two living and cooking together as a single housekeeping unit though not related by blood, adoption, or marriage shall be deemed to constitute a family.

To support this ordinance, the Village cited its aims of controlling population density, maintaining low rents, and the mitigation of traffic, noise and parking problems (Lamb and Lustig, 1979, p. 192).

One of the houses in Belle Terre was leased to six unrelated students. Their violation of the ordinance was pointed out to them, and three sued the Village, claiming that their right of freedom to travel was infringed, that social homogeneity was not a legitimate exercise of government police power, and that the fact of marriage was irrelevant to neighbours. The District Court upheld the ordinance, but the Court of Appeals reversed that decision, on the grounds that single-family zoning was irrelevant to the aims of the ordinance. The Supreme Court heard the case, and in a 7 : 2 majority decision (*Village of Belle Terre* v. *Boraas*, 416 US 1, 1974) upheld the ordinance.

Writing for the majority, Justice Douglas wrote of the "nuisance" caused by students to residential areas:

> The regimes of boarding houses, fraternity houses, and the like present urban problems. More people occupy a given space; more cars rather continuously pass by; more cars are parked; noise travels with crowds.

A quiet place where yards are wide, people few, and motor vehicles restricted are legitimate guidelines in a land-use project addressed to family needs . . . . The police power is not confined to elimination of filth, stench, and unhealthy places. It is ample to lay out zones where family values, youth values, and the blessings of quiet seclusion and clean air make the area a sanctuary for people. (p. 804)

These are environmental and aesthic issues, according to Douglas, not social ones; the Court was not condoning exclusionary zoning to create social homogeneity and display animosity to unmarried people – although the various issues are clearly linked. Justice Marshall disagreed, arguing that the majority were extending the police power too far:

Zoning officials properly concern themselves with the uses of land . . . . But zoning authorities cannot validly consider who those people are, what they believe, or how they choose to live, whether they are Negro or white, Catholic or Jew, Republican or Democrat, married or unmarried. (pp. 807–808)

To Marshall, the First Amendment provides for freedom of association – "Congress shall make no law . . . abridging . . . the right of the people peaceably to assemble" – and the Fourteenth Amendment guarantees freedom in the choice of associates. He claims, citing several precedents, and this includes what one does within the home and with whom:

The right to "establish a home" is an essential part of the liberty guaranteed by the Fourteenth Amendment. (p. 808)

Thus, according to Marshall, the Belle Terre ordinance goes well beyond any compelling state interest that is compatible with the police power:

It thus reaches beyond controls of the use of land and the density of population, and undertakes to regulate the way people choose to associate with each other within the privacy of their own homes. (p. 809)

But Marshall was in a small minority. The majority, represented by Douglas (who had strong environmental interests), were prepared to defer to properly-constituted local interests (Lamb and Lustig, 1979, p. 195). And they were later followed by the State courts, as in *Ybarra* v. *City of Town of Los Altos Hills* (503 F2d 250, 1974), which found that zoning out the poor, who could equally well live elsewhere, was justified to protect the rural environment.

There were limits, however, to the degree which the Court was prepared to allow such parochial concerns to be expressed. A single-family ordinance in East Cleveland had been used to jail a woman who lived with her son and two grandsons, the latter being cousins, not brothers (see Anon, 1978, p. 1570). The definition of single-family in this case was "no more than one married couple, their parents, and their dependent children, so long as no more than one child has dependent children of his or her own". In a 5:4 majority (*Moore* v. *City of East Cleveland*, 431 US 494, 1977) the Court invalidated such a detailed ordinance, arguing that it "sliced deeply into the family" and involved "intrusive regulation". (Note, however, Justice White's dissent (p. 519) in which he upholds the ordinance as being within "the normal goals of zoning regulation"; according to him, Mrs Moore could have lived with her extended family elsewhere than in East Cleveland, and so was not denied due process.)

Valtierra and Eastlake: Upholding local democracy

One of the elements in the opinion on *Hunter* v. *Erickson* (see p. 80) was that a vote by the local population in a referendum was invalid if the decision was itself unconstitutional. The Fourteenth Amendment could not be over-ridden by local opinion, however democratically expressed. But this did not mean that all local referenda decisions regarding zoning issues were con-sequently invalid. Where racial, religious or ethnic classifications are not involved, the Court has deferred "to the processes of direct democracy" (Slonim and Lowe, 1979, p. 197).

Following an initiative (see p. 28), the voters of California approved, on 7 November 1950, a proposed Article 34 of the State Constitution. This states that:

> No low rent housing project shall hereafter be developed, constructed, or acquired in any manner by any state public body, until a majority of the qualified electors of the city, town or county . . . in which it is proposed . . ., voting upon such issue, approve such project.

The purpose of this was clearly to prevent any low rent project (defined in the amendment as covering persons of low income unable to afford "decent, safe and sanitary dwellings, without overcrowding", without financial assistance) being constructed in a municipality without local majority support; it was an extra provision, supplementing the zoning power. The District Court found this unconstitutional, citing the *Hunter* precedent, but its finding was over-turned by the Supreme Court. The case for the District Court's action, as argued by the lawyers for the San Jose and San Mateo County housing authorities, was that the explicit discrimination in terms of wealth was implicitly racial discrimination, in that the majority of blacks were also poor.

The Supreme Court, in a 6:3 majority (*James* v. *Valtierra* and *Shaffer* v. *Valtierra*, 402 US 137, 1971) overturned the District Court on three grounds. First, it refused to accept that discrimination by income (or wealth) was unconstitutional under the Fourteenth Amendment. Writing for the majority, Justice Black argued that "a lawmaking procedure that 'dis-advantages' a particular group does not always deny equal protection"; if it did, then any group could bring suit, and this would produce unending litigation. As in the school district cases (see below, p. 130), the Court majority did not accept that wealth was a suspect classification, and that discrimination against groups on the grounds of wealth was unconsti-tutional. Nor, secondly, did they accept the implication that discrimination by wealth in effect meant discrimination by race:

the record here would not support any claim that a law seemingly neutral on its face is in fact aimed at a racial minority. (p. 682)

Intent to discriminate against racial groups was unconstitutional, but disproportionate impact of an action taken for other reasons was not: this was taken by other courts to mean that

there must be some showing that a policy or activity which has a racially discriminatory effect results from a prior pattern of discrimination or that such policies affect only racial minorities. (*Citizens Committee for Faraday Wood* v. *Lindsay*, 362 F Supp 651, 1973; quoted in Danielson, 1976, p. 182)

Finally, the Court majority stressed that the use of the referendum meant that local issues were being settled democratically:

Provisions for referendums demonstrate devotion to democracy, not to bias, discrimination, or prejudice. . . . This procedure ensures that all the people of a community will have a voice in a decision which may lead to large expenditures. . . . It gives them a voice in decisions that will affect the future development of their own community. (pp. 682–683)

Although the majority were in favour of referenda being used by local communities to support exclusionary zoning, Justice Marshall was not. He argued that discrimination by income is a suspect classification that should be found unconstitutional.

It is far too late in the day to contend that the Fourteenth Amendment prohibits only racial discrimination; and to me, singling out the poor to bear a burden not placed on any other class of citizens tramples the values that the Fourteenth Amendment was designed to protect. (p. 685)

But his desire to extend the meaning of the amendment reflected the Court under Warren in the 1960s, not the Court under Burger in the 1970s.

Marshall did not dissent five years later in a related case, although Justices Brennan, Powell and Stevens did. In the City of Eastlake, Ohio, the voters amended the City Charter in 1971, introducing a clause requiring that any land-use change agreed to by the City Council must subsequently be approved by 55 per cent of those voting in a referendum before it can be made effective. Forest City Enterprises had applied to build a high-rise housing development, on land for which a rezoning was required. The City Planning Commission and the City Council both approved the rezoning, but it was refused by the referendum. The company then sued, on the grounds that the referendum improperly delegated the power of the State (properly granted to the municipality) to the people, thereby denying due process.

The Ohio Supreme Court accepted the argument, ruling that the referendum provision introduced the arbitrary exercise of municipal power by delegating fundamental policy choices away from the responsible organ of government (Sager, 1978, p. 1409). But the Supreme Court overturned that decision (*City of Eastlake* v. *Forest City Enterprises Inc.*, 426 US 668, 1976) arguing (through the Chief Justice for the six-man majority) that

a referendum cannot . . . be characterised as a delegation of power. Under our constitutional assumptions, all power derives from the people, who can delegate it to representative instruments that they create (p. 137). . . . As a basic instrument of democratic
government, the referendum process does not, in itself, violate the Due Process Clause
of the Fourteenth Amendment when applied to a rezoning ordinance. (p. 141)

The majority did note, following the *Euclid* opinion, that

If the substantive result of the referendum is arbitrary and capricious, bearing no
relation to the police power, then the fact that the voters of Eastlake wish it so (p. 140)

would not justify such a result. The majority were clearly unwilling to
overturn the "democratic" decision in this case. The dissenters were not so
sure, arguing that whereas referenda may be valid for the approval of plans as
a whole, they were potentially arbitrary in cases of spot rezonings.

Arlington: The definition of intent

The majority decision in *Valtierra* was that intentional racial discrimination was unconstitutional, but that differential racial impact was not. This
opinion was bolstered in 1977.

Arlington Heights is an affluent Chicago suburb, of whose 67 000
residents in the mid-1970s only 27 were black. A non-profit developer,
Metropolitan Housing Development Corporation (MHDC), wished to build
a federally-subsidized high-density housing project there on land it had
obtained. To do this, it needed the zoning to be changed from single-family
to apartment. The residents opposed it, believing that blacks could well be
occupants of the development. Its application was denied, on the grounds
that the plan allowed apartments in "buffer zones" only, sited between
single-family and other uses. That plan had been applied consistently, and
the principle should not now be reversed, according to the Village Board of
Trustees. To support its decision, the Board pointed out that sufficient
vacant land was already zoned for apartments, and that there was currently an
11 per cent vacancy rate in existing apartments (Mandelker, 1977, p. 1222).

MHDC sued. The District Court upheld the Village Board's decision, but
this was reversed by the Court of Appeals. The case then went to the
Supreme Court (*Arlington Heights* v. *Metropolitan Housing Development
Corp.*, 429 US 252, 1977). In reaching its decision, the Court relied heavily
on a recent, non-zoning case (*Washington* v. *Davis*, 426 US 229, 1976) in
which it was claimed that because most black applicants failed a written test
when applying to join the DC Police Force, then the test was discriminatory.
The court ruled, as in *Valtierra*, that differential impact is insufficient
evidence of intent; "proof of a racially discriminatory motive, purpose,
or intent is required to find a violation of the fourteenth amendment"
(Mandelker, 1977, p. 1236). Citing *Washington*, Justice Powell for the
majority laid down guidelines as to acceptable evidence of intent to discriminate in rezoning cases, and found that in its continued application of

the buffer zone, racial discrimination had not been a motivating factor in the Arlington Board's decision. This opinion, according to Mandelker (1977, p. 1239)

> has foreclosed a finding of racially discriminatory intent in all but the most blatant cases. Unless a municipality has historically discriminated against zoning proposals for subsidized housing, or unless the municipality abruptly changes a zoning classification or otherwise acts affirmatively to frustrate the construction of a subsidized housing development, no opportunity for proving the existence of racially discriminatory intent appears present.

Justice Powell had concluded that

> Respondents simply failed to carry their burden of proving that discriminatory purpose was a motivating factor in the Village's decision. The Court of Appeals' further finding that the Village's decision carried a discriminatory "ultimate effect" is without independent constitutional significance. (p. 468)

The Constitution is concerned only with intent, and cannot be used to challenge the consequences of an action; other texts may, however, as indicated in a companion case (*Metropolitan Housing Development Corp.* v. *Village of Arlington Heights*, 558 F2d 1283, 1977 – see also p. 159).

Nor, it seems, was intent alone sufficient cause to find that a discriminatory act was unconstitutional. In the *Arlington Heights* opinion, Justice Powell referred to the recent opinion in *Mt. Healthy City School District Board of Education* v. *Doyle* (429 US 274, 1977) when the defendant was required to prove that the same decision would have resulted even if the impermissible reason (racial discrimination) had not been considered. In that case, relating to the dismissal of a teacher, the Court found that he was guilty of unprofessional conduct. He had also criticized his employer in a radio broadcast, and claimed that his dismissal violated his constitutionally-protected freedom of speech. Since he would have been dismissed for unprofessional conduct in any case the School Board had not acted unconstitutionally in dismissing him for his broadcast. And, in *Arlington Heights*, if exclusionary zoning could have been adopted for other reasons, the fact that it might also be racially motivated was inconsequential (see Miller, 1977, and von der Heyde, 1977).

Warth: preventing the challenges

The final case to be discussed in detail in this section is one which, according to one commentator, rests "on a thinly disguised premise that zoning decisions generally ought not to be made by the federal judiciary" (Sager, 1978, p. 1424).

Penfield is an affluent suburb of Rochester, New York, with a predominantly white population. It had enacted a low-density, exclusionary zoning ordinance which effectively precluded the development of low- and middle-income housing (because the densities would have been insufficient to ensure a profit). Five sets of plaintiffs challenged this ordinance, in a single case (Mann, 1976, p. 126):

(1) Four low-income, minority residents of Rochester, who claimed that the zoning's purpose and effect was to exclude low-income and minority residents from Penfield.

(2) Four Rochester taxpayers, who claimed that Rochester tax rates were high because Penfield prohibited low-income people.

(3) A non-profit organization (Metro-Act of Rochester) that exists to alert citizens to problems of social concern, and which claimed that Penfield residents were denied the opportunity of living in a racially-integrated community.

(4) The Rochester Home Builders Association, which claimed that Penfield's refusal to permit low- and moderate-income developments denied its members business opportunities and profits.

(5) Housing Council, a non-profit organization to advance the interests of low income people, which claimed that one of its member groups had been prohibited from building low-cost homes in Penfield.

The District Court dismissed their case on the grounds that they lacked standing to bring it. This decision was upheld by the Supreme Court.

According to the Court (*Warth* v. *Seldin*, 442 US 490, 1975), cases can only be brought (under Article III of the Constitution)

when the plaintiff himself has suffered "some threatened or actual injury resulting from the potentially illegal action" (p. 354) [and] when the asserted harm is a "generalized grievance" shared in substantially equal measure by all or a large class of citizens, that harm alone does not warrant exercise of jurisdiction. (p. 355)

Writing for the five-man majority, Justice Powell argued that

Without such limitations . . . the courts would be called upon to decide abstract questions of wide significance . . . the plaintiff . . . must allege a distinct and palpable injury to himself, even if it is an injury shared by a large class of other possible litigants. (pp. 355–356)

None of the plaintiffs could establish a "distinct and palpable injury". The five low-income majority residents had never lived in Penfield and, despite statements that they wished to, could produce no convincing argument that if the zoning were absent they would have been able to obtain homes there (p. 358). Regarding the five Rochester taxpayers, Justice Powell wrote that "pleadings must be something more than an ingenious academic exercise in the conceivable" (p. 360) and

No relationship, other than an incidental congruity of interest, is alleged to exist between the Rochester taxpayers and persons who have been excluded from living in Penfield. (p. 361)

Metro-Act's claim was dismissed because it was based not on an injury to the plaintiffs but on third parties who had been excluded. The Rochester Home Builders Association indentified no specific injury; nor did the Housing Council. In brief, although zoning is supposed to promote the general welfare, the Supreme Court would not allow a set of cases to be put which challenged its general, as against its specific, impacts (Mann, 1976, p. 128).

Justice Powell's opinion was written for a majority of five members of the Court. Justices Douglas and Brennan wrote dissenting opinions, with the latter being joined (i.e. supported) by Justices Marshall and White. Justice Douglas would have recognized standing for Metro-Act and the Housing Council, and noted that the

> zoning power is claimed to have been used here to foist an un-American community model on the people of this area. (p. 367)

Justice Brennan was extremely critical of the majority, whose opinion he claimed "can be explained only by an indefensible hostility to the claim on its merits" (p. 367). With regard to the case,

> the portrait which emerges from the allegations and affidavits is one of total, purposeful, intransigent exclusion of certain classes of people from the town. (p. 369)

By refusing standing, the Court was giving substantial protection to exclusionary zoning. In a key passage, Justice Brennan wrote that

> the Court turns the very success of the allegedly unconstitutional scheme into a barrier to a lawsuit seeking its invalidation . . . the Court tells the low-income minority and building company plaintiffs they will not be permitted to prove what they have alleged – that they could and would build and live in the town if changes were made in its zoning ordinance and its application – because they have not succeeded in breaching, before the suit was filed, the very barriers which are the subject of the suit. (p. 369)

But the argument had been lost within the Court; the poor could not gain equal protection, according to Brennan, and others could not sue on their behalf, because of the attitudes of the "suburban majority of the Nixon appointees" (Woodward and Armstrong, 1979, pp. 366–367).

The Burger Court decisions: A summary

The brief conclusion to be drawn from this review of zoning cases heard by the Burger Court is that unless an action was overtly and explicitly racially discriminatory, the majority has not been prepared to allow the use of the Fourteenth Amendment to overrule the exercise of local autonomy in the practice of exclusionary zoning. A minority of Justices continued to demand an interpretation of the Amendment that broadened its scope and the classes protected; but this attempt to continue the precedents set by the Warren Court was not heeded, especially by Nixon's conservative appointees. The message from the majority opinions to the suburbs was clear; as long as you are careful in how you draw up your plan, then go ahead. And, with *Warth*, added protection was offered in that it was made much more difficult to bring cases against exclusionary zoning – by being excluded, you were also prevented from complaining about being excluded. The Burger Court was not prepared to recognize the choice of where to live as a *fundamental right* protected by the Constitution, nor was it prepared to recognize groups other than racial minorities as *suspect classifications* against whom discrimination on a wide range of issues is illegal.

This series of Court decisions, seeming to reverse the pattern set by the Warren Court, has saddened a number of observers who believe that it has set back the cause of integration within American study. According to Pearlman (1978, p. 160):

> in view of the strong attitudes of the courts and the emerging militancy of the civil rights movement, it would not have been unreasonable to conclude that this judicial role would extend into other areas of segregation such as housing and restrictive zoning ordinances. This conclusion would have been incorrect.

The Burger majority has been antipathetic to claims of those injured by exclusionary zoning, according to Lamb and Lustig (1979), clothing this antipathy in a strict constructionist theory of the Court's functions – "the supposedly neutral tenets of judicial restraint" (p. 723). Its opinions have not only restricted fundamental rights and suspect classifications, but have also promoted the interests of small suburban municipalities:

> Perhaps the most legitimate criticisms of the Burger Court are its strong deference to local governments and its disinclination to consider the detrimental segregative effects that exclusionary zoning policies have on housing patterns surrounding metropolitan areas. The Court's conception of the general welfare has been narrowly construed to mean only the general welfare of the local community practicing exclusionary zoning. (Lamb and Lustig, 1979, p. 225)

The result is a policy of protecting the insular majorities in their tight little islands:

> the cases reflect the equation of the local zoning process with the joint exercise of the prerogatives of private ownership; the municipality is a club, which enjoys the mandatory and exclusive membership of its residents and landowners. (Sager, 1978, p. 1425)

OUTSIDE THE SUPREME COURT

Given this set of decisions during the 1970s, is exclusionary zoning now an established practice that is unchallengeable? Must the conflict over suburbia move to different institutional areas, or is there still the possibility of judicial resolution? Or will the challengers realize that residential congregation and segregation will undoubtedly continue, whatever the legal decisions on one particular mechanism for promoting distancing?

As noted above, the Supreme Court has very largely avoided cases concerned with zoning issues, except where important (to it) constitutional issues have been raised. It has indentified the practice as one properly overseen by the State courts, for municipalities are created by State Legislatures and controlled more by State Constitutions than by the federal Constitution. This situation is reflected in the number of times the Supreme Court has denied writs of *certiorari* for zoning cases indicating that they lie outside its jurisdiction. Thus those seeking to challenge zoning must use other channels. As Walsh (1976) has pointed out in a review of the *Warth* decision, in deciding to bring a case plaintiffs must choose whether to sue in the federal or the State courts, and whether to base their case on statutory or constitutional grounds. With "intelligent forum selection" (p. 254), she claims, many of the problems of standing and explicit racial discrimination created by the Supreme Court can be circumvented.

The many separate State Court systems make a comprehensive review of the progress of challenges to zoning outside the Supreme Court a massive task. This is outside the brief of the present book, whose particular focus is the Supreme Court. Nevertheless, since in many of the key cases that Court has, by refusing *certiorari*, in effect supported the State court rulings, a brief review of their main features is presented here.

Beyond the tight little island

The grounds for challenging exclusionary zoning in the State Courts are several (see Jorgensen, 1981), and there have been some successes. Mann (1976, p. 107) lists nineteen recent cases in ten different States, covering:

(1) Prohibition of mobile homes – in all three cases, this was ruled invalid.

(2) Exclusive single-family districts – in both cases, this zoning was upheld.

(3) Exclusion of multi-family housing districts from a municipality – this was found invalid in all four cases.

(4) Large-lot zoning – upheld in four States, ruled invalid in two others.

(5) Bedroom limitations (the number per dwelling unit) – upheld in three States, found invalid in one.

Clearly, there has been no consensus across all of the Courts. Nor, if successful, is the result always as desired. Mann (1976, p. 105) notes that after large-lot, single-family only districts were overruled in a Pennsylvania case, a developer built high-cost, luxury apartments on the land in question.

Two of the States where the Courts have apparently made the greatest inroads to exclusionary zoning, however practised, are New Jersey and Pennsylvania. Regarding *New Jersey*, early decisions in the 1950s upheld exclusionary provisions with respect to minimum lot size, minimum floor area of dwellings, apartments, the location of mobile homes and the exclusion of these (Muskowitz, 1977, pp. 225–226). But Justice Hall's dissent (quoted above, p. 78) in the case regarding mobile homes indicated at least some belief in the New Jersey Supreme Court that protection of tight little municipal islands was not necessarily in the general interest. This came through in a classic decision, which nevertheless did not lead to the major "tearing down of the exclusionary walls" that some hoped for.

Mount Laurel is a small township in the New Jersey suburbs of Philadelphia. A group of plaintiffs brought a case against the township government contesting the zoning ordinance. The plaintiffs included: residents of Mount Laurel, who were living in substandard housing and were unable to obtain better housing there, they claimed, because of the zoning ordinance; former residents who had been forced to leave Mount Laurel in order to obtain better housing, none of which was available to them there, at a price they could afford; people who wished to live in Mount Laurel, but could not do so; and civic associations representing minority group interests. Their case was that the zoning ordinance precluded the development of low- and moderate-cost housing of good standard. It was brought under the relevant New Jersey statute (quoted in Markowitz, 1977, p. 228) defining standing in such cases:

> Any person, whether residing within or without the municipality, whose right to use, acquire, or enjoy property is or may be affected by an action taken under the act to which this act is a supplement, or whose rights to use, acquire, or enjoy property under the act . . . or under any other law of this State or of the United States has been denied, violated or infringed by an action or a failure to act under the act to which this act is a supplement.

No evidence of a particular injury was required (hence the New Jersey situation differed from that described in *Warth*).

In the original case (*Southern Burlington County NAACP* v. *Township of Mt. Laurel*, 290 A2d 465, 1972) Judge Martino cited Justice Hall in the *Vickers* case (p. 78) that "courts must not be hesitant to strike down purely selfish and undemocratic enactments", and concluded

> that defendant municipality through its zoning ordinances has exhibited economic discrimination in that the poor have been deprived of adequate housing and the opportunity to secure the construction of subsidized housing, and has used federal, state, county and local finances and resources solely for the betterment of middle and upper-income persons. The zoning ordinance is, therefore declared invalid. (p. 473; quoted by Moskowitz, 1977, p. 233)

The township appealed, but the New Jersey Supreme Court, in a unanimous decision authored by Justice Hall (see Hall, 1977a, b), sustained Judge Martino's decision. The United States Supreme Court (423 US 808, 1975) then denied the township's appeal. Moskowitz (1977, p. 236) notes that the wording of Justice Hall's decision ensured this. It was based in Article I, paragraph 1 of the New Jersey Constitution which states that:

> All persons are by nature free and independent, and have certain natural and unalienable rights, among which are those of enjoying and defending life and liberty, of acquiring, possessing, and protecting property, and of pursuing and obtaining safety and happiness.

This, he argued, guaranteed "equal protection" to live where one wished, more so than did the Fourteenth Amendment.

Justice Hall based his decision on the belief that the exclusionary zoning was undertaken for fiscal motives. By excluding the poor, especially those with large families, exclusionary municipalities would keep their tax rates low:

> almost every one (i.e. municipality) acts solely on its own selfish and parochial interests and in effect builds a wall around itself to keep out those people or entities not adding favourably to the tax base, despite the location of the municipality or the demand for various kinds of housing. There has been no effective inter-municipal or area planning or land use regulation. (p. 723; in Moskowitz, 1977, p. 235)

But since the State itself has no right to restrict its citizens to live in certain areas only, then nor do its creations, the municipalities, have that right. Exclusionary zoning, he showed in a detailed analysis (see also the concurring opinion by Justice Pashman), in effect involves municipalities taking that right.

Having found in favour of the plaintiffs, the New Jersey Supreme Court was required to define a remedy. It approached this in a later case by asking a series of 18 questions (reprinted in Rose and Rothman, 1977, pp. 133–136). Fundamental to its approach and its *Mount Laurel* remedy was

> that every developing municipality has an obligation to provide the opportunity for the satisfaction of its fair share of the regional need for housing of persons of low and moderate income. This "opportunity" must be provided through non-exclusionary (or "inclusionary") land-use controls and other "necessary and advisable" actions. (Bisgaier, 1977, p. 140)

This remedy raised a number of questions, however; what are low and moderate incomes; how is need determined (see also p. 161); what is an appropriate region; how is fair share calculated; how is future need and fair share calculated; what is a developing municipality; and so on?

These questions could only be answered by the Court, as they were in a number of subsequent decisions. In *Taxpayers Association of Weymouth Township Inc* v. *Weymouth Township* (364 A2d 1016, 1976), a mobile home zone for the elderly was upheld, thereby excluding young married people with children. More importantly, in *Oakwood at Madison Inc* v. *Township of Madison* (371 A2d 1192, 1977), the New Jersey Supreme Court ruled on a case first heard in a lower court in 1971. Three issues were resolved (Rose, 1977a):

(1) An ordinance is exclusionary if its effect is to restrict certain groups from a municipality, even if no intent to achieve such restriction existed. This was contrary to the US Supreme Court decision in *Arlington Heights* (delivered only a few weeks earlier). A fair share allocation did not have to be calculated, however, but there must be a *bona fide* effort to meet regional needs, which should be overseen by the original trial court.

(2) The court did not need to define the relevant region, nor to calculate the fair shares for each municipality. It simply needed to weigh the relevant factors to determine what each municipality should do.

(3) The trial court was required to oversee the remedy – the rezoning – and to appoint experts to assist it in this. (In a dissent, Justice Pashman wanted the relevant regions defined, and the needs calculated and allocated to municipalities.)

This decision suggested some retreat from the judicial activism represented by *Mount Laurel*, and still left important questions unanswered. Perhaps the most crucial of these – what is a developing municipality? (Rose and Levin, 1977) – was answered in *Pasack Association* v. *Township of Washington*, 379 A2d 6, 1977. This made clear that the *Mount Laurel* decision did not apply to all New Jersey municipalities, but only to "developing municipalities" (of which Madison was archetypal according to the opinion in that case); these were defined negatively –

> They are not small, homogeneous communities with permanent characteristics already established, like the settled suburbs surrounding the cities in which planning and zoning may properly be geared around things as they are and as they pretty much will continue to be. (p. 14)

(This was taken from Hall's opinion (p. 140) in the *Vickers* case, and was italicized in the *Washington* opinion.)

Although upholding the fundamentals of the *Mount Laurel* decision, for developing municipalities, the majority in the *Washington* case clearly wished to draw back from any widespread use of the courts as regional planning agencies. Thus

> it would be a mistake to interpret *Mount Laurel* as a comprehensive displacement of sound and long established principles of judicial respect for local policy decisions in the planning field . . . . There is no *per se* principle in the State mandating zoning for multi-family housing by every municipality regardless of its circumstances with respect to degree or nature of development. (p. 11)

Municipal autonomy is to be respected and

> The judicial role . . . is limited to the assessment of a claim that the restrictions of the ordinance are patently arbitrary or unreasonable or violative of the statute, not that they do not match the plaintiffs or the court's conception of the requirements of the general welfare, whether within the town or the region. (p. 13)

This is close to the reasoning of the Supreme Court – except in the Warren era. It suggests no desire to extend either judicial power or regional planning, and was countered by a lengthy dissent from Justice Pashman (itself typical of the Supreme Court minority opinions of Marshall and others during the 1970s). He identified the majority decision as meaning that

> we can offer no hope that new advances will be made in our efforts against exclusionary

zoning . . . . Society as a whole suffers the failure to solve the economic and social problems which exclusionary zoning creates; we live daily with the failure of our democratic institutions to eradicate class distinctions. Inevitably, the dream of a pluralistic society begins to fade. (p. 31)

Previous Court decisions had granted to New Jersey citizens the rights of a thorough and efficient education, to acquire, own and dispose of real property, and of equal access to the State's resources. But

Today we make a mockery of these rights by perpetrating a ghetto system in which residents live in inferior and often degrading conditions. Unless and until we open up the suburbs to all citizens of the State on an equal basis, the cherished ideals of our constitutional rights will remain illusive and unattainable. (p. 31)

The *Mount Laurel* decision suggested to some commentators that the attack on exclusionary zoning was beginning to have effect and that the courts would be able to ensure the development of balanced communities in the suburbs (although some, such as Danielson (1970, p. 349), argued that the modifications to plans in the light of *Mount Laurel* would be minimal). The apparent retreat by the New Jersey Supreme Court in 1977 – by then lacking Justice Hall – meant, however, that "the status of suburban zoning is still very much in doubt and subject to conflicting judicial principles and statements" (Rose, 1977b, p. 251). New Jersey was apparently in the forefront, but

even in the most adventurous (State) . . . there has been a dance of substantive advance and retreat which indicates a good deal of uncertainty about the appropriate contours of the judicial presence in land use planning. (Sager, 1978, p. 1374)

And in another State, *Pennsylvania*, whose Supreme Court's rulings on exclusionary zoning have been widely quoted elsewhere, Moskowitz (1977, p. 185) concludes that

a careful analysis of the decisions reached by the Pennsylvania courts will reveal that the decisions are quite unclear, that the basis for the decisions is not carefully expressed and that the guidance they offer is illusory.

Policing the shoreline

Most of the discussion so far in this chapter has concerned the use of the zoning power to control the character of a municipality, by exclusionary means. An alternative procedure, becoming increasingly popular (Exline, 1978), is to control the rate of growth. Rapid growth is seen as a threat to certain suburban life-styles, so it is controlled by reductions on the number of new homes that can be built each year. (Alternatively, it could limit the number of connections to a public utility, such as water, sewage, or power: Wolfson, 1977.)

One of the pioneers of this growth management strategy was the semi-rural town of Petaluma, California, some 40 miles from downtown San

Fransisco. Its population grew rapidly through the 1960s and early 1970s, and in 1972 a growth management plan was instituted to

> establish control over the quality, distribution, and rate of growth of the city in the interest of:
> 1. Preserving the quality of the community;
> 2. Protecting the green open space from the city;
> 3. Insuring the adequacy of the city facilities and services within acceptable allocation of city and school tax funds;
> 4. Insuring a balance of housing types and values in the city which will acommodate a variety of families including families of moderate income and older families on limited fixed income;
> 5. Insuring the balanced development of the city east, north, and west of the central core. (quoted in Schwartz *et al.*, 1979, p. 7)

In enacting this plan, the limit was fixed at 500 new dwellings per annum (there were 880 permits issued in 1971).

The plan was challenged in the California Courts on the grounds that it infringed the citizen's right to travel. This freedom of access is guaranteed, according to some, by the Fourteenth Amendment, by Section 2 of Article IV ("The Citizens of each State shall be entitled to all Privileges and Immunities of Citizens in the several States") and by the so-called commerce clause (Section 10 of Article I). The District Court, citing the Pennsylvania exclusionary zoning cases, held that the plan was invalid, and that one municipality could not opt out of its share of regional growth – it was argued that the plan would limit Petaluma's growth to about one-third of market demand. The California Court of Appeals overruled this decision and found in favour of the plan. In *Construction Industry Association of Sonoma County* v. *City of Petaluma* (522 F2d 897, 1975) it argued (in part following the *Belle Terre* precedent) that the plan did not seek to exclude any particular income group or minority; indeed, it aimed to provide a "balanced community". The Court accepted that people wishing to live in Petaluma may not be able to (though it denied the plaintiff – a developer – the right to bring a case under the freedom of travel clause, since – as in *Warth* – it could not prove a particular injury to itself), but although "the Plan may frustrate some legitimate regional housing needs, the Plan is not arbitrary or unreasonable" (quoted in Moskowitz, 1977, p. 344). Whilst Petaluma existed as an autonomous unit, it had the right of self-management, and the Court concluded in a telling phrase that if the system were to be changed

> it is the state legislature's and not the federal court's role to intervene and adjust the system. (in Moskowitz, 1977, p. 345)

The Supreme Court refused to hear an appeal – 424 US 934, 1976 – and Petaluma was allowed "to preserve its small town character, its open spaces and low density of population, and to grow at an orderly and deliberate pace" (p. 909); as a result, house prices increased there substantially (Schwartz *et al.*, 1979).

The town of Ramapo, in the suburbs of New York, also introduced a growth management plan, in the late 1960s, with a zoning ordinance linked to the allocation of permits for connections to public utilities and services. This was challenged as an invalid interpretation of the New York enabling act under which municipalities carried out zoning. The lower court agreed, although accepting that rapid growth may put intolerable strains on a municipality's ability to provide needed services. The New York Court of Appeals overruled, holding – *Golden* v. *Town Planning Board of Ramapo*, 30 NY 2d 359, 1972 – that it had such power, and that its actions were to the benefit of developers because they ensured the provision of adequately capitalized services. Further, it ruled that the plan was not exclusionary as generally understood – "its purpose was not to prevent growth but to phase its occurrence" (Moskowitz, 1977, p. 349). It was accepted that such growth management strategies could have serious impacts on development in an entire region, but the majority opinion in both courts was that this was a legislative, not a judicial issue:

> The problems are indeed regional, and not local; and their solution lies within the province of the Legislature rather than within the more parochial vision of the town (District Court: Moskowitz, 1977, p. 347) . . . these problems cannot be solved by Ramapo or any single municipality, but depend upon the accommodation of widely disparate interests for their ultimate resolution. To that end, Statewide or regional control of planning would ensure that interests broader than that of the municipality underlie various land use policies. (Court of Appeals: quoted p. 345)

The majority of the Courts recognized a problem, therefore, but decided that the challenged ordinance "is not violative of the Federal and State Constitutions" (p. 305). Justice Breitel of the Court of Appeals dissented, although recognizing that

> Ramapo would preserve its nature, delightful as that might be, but the supervening question is whether it alone may decide this or whether it must be decided by the larger community represented by the Legislature. (p. 311)

He would set aside the ordinance and use the courts to develop regional planning. Not surprisingly, the Burger Supreme Court was not sympathetic, and denied *certiorari* (409 US 1003, 1972).

These two cases indicate that growth management has been interpreted as a valid exercise of municipal power, neither exclusionary nor infringing the rights to travel and to conduct interstate commerce. Elsewhere, municipalities have been allowed to impose population maxima as a means of promoting the public welfare there, although the means of achieving that goal may be unconstitutional (the case referred to Boca Raton, Florida in *Boca Villas Corp.* v. *Pence*, cited by Strong, 1981, p. 222). Such exercise of the right to plan in this way may not be in the wider public interest, but currently this is not an issue relevant to judicial decision-making. The judges in these cases have declined to extend the constitutional interpretation (if they had, the Supreme Court would undoubtedly have reviewed the cases) and have left the issue to the legislatures. Why it remains there, largely unaffected, is taken up later in this book.

Creating more islands

Although there was some initial expectation that the Pennsylvania and New Jersey court decisions would lead to a decline in exclusionary zoning, at least in developing areas not currently occupied by residential uses, this has not happened. The victories were at best hollow, and the general trend is that the use of the zoning power to advance parochial social and economic goals is supported, or at least not denied, by the courts (King, 1979). This would suggest that the incorporation of new municipalities would be a sensible project for those living in new suburban areas who wished to protect the character of their community.

The creation of new municipalities is approved by the Legislature in most States, though it may delegate that power to more local bodies (as in California; Miller, 1981). Some States have realized the problems generated by increased municipal fragmentation in the suburbs, and have sought to reduce them. In Virginia, for example, there was a moratorium between 1972 and 1976 preventing any new incorporations in counties adjoining cities, and nine States have permanent laws preventing this (Hallman, 1977, p. 29). But if such legislative action is absent, is there any other means by which new incorporations – or even annexations and other changes in boundaries – can be prevented? If people go to the courts, it seems that the only grounds on which they can win are, as in so much of the legal opinion reported here, related to intent to discriminate against minority groups (see also p. 91).

The earliest case heard in this context related to an attempt to disenfranchise the black voters of a town by redrawing its boundaries so that they no longer lived there. The town of Tuskegee, Alabama, had a population of about 6700 in the mid-1950s, about 80 per cent of them black. Most of the latter were not registered as voters, but increasing black political activity frightened the local whites who were determined to "run the Negro voters out of town or, rather . . . to run their residences out of town" (Taper, 1962, p. 14). This was done by changing the boundaries of the town from a square to a 28-sided figure, thereby removing about 80 per cent of the black residences but none of the white. The court case alleged racial discrimination; the defence was that it was a constitutionally valid act by the Alabama Legislature. The Supreme Court found that (*Gomillion* v. *Lightfoot*, 364 US 339, 1960):

> the inescapable human effect of this essay into geometry and geography is to despoil colored citizens, and only colored citizens, of their heretofore enjoyed voting rights. (p. 116)

They disagreed on why: Justice Frankfurter, writing for the majority, found that the Fifteenth Amendment ("The right of citizens . . . to vote shall not be denied or abridged . . . on account of race, color, or previous condition of servitude") had been contravened, whereas Justice Whittaker argued that the right to vote is not abridged by living in one place rather than another (the "removed" blacks could vote in Macon County) and that the Fourteenth Amendment was the text that had been contravened. The outcome was that Tuskegee's former boundaries were reinstated.

A further case, relating to the impact of the city's racial composition after annexation, was also brought under the Fifteenth Amendment. For a period of eight years, the Council of the City of Richmond, Virginia had been trying to annex territory in suburban Chesterfield and Henrico Counties, in order to find room for industrial and commercial expansion. Virginian State Law requires that the case for an annexation be heard by a special court which, if it agrees, fixes the new boundary and also the amount of compensation to be paid by the expanding city for the schools and utilities that it is obtaining from the county. The City of Richmond had rejected the court's award of compensation ($55m, in 1963) for its proposed annexation of part of Henrico County. It eventually sealed an agreement over its proposals regarding Chesterfield County in a compromise reached in 1969.

The case against the city was that its motivation to reach the compromise arrangement in 1969 was racial. By that time, the black population of Richmond comprised 51·5 per cent of the total, and three of the nine candidates elected to the City Council were members of a group that had wide appeal among black voters. It was alleged that the white councillors required a substantial annexation rapidly so as to dilute the black voting power, and that they conducted negotiations with the special court regarding the proposals for Chesterfield County from which the three members of the pro-black group were excluded. The land annexed contained 47 262 residents, of whom only 3 per cent were black: as a consequence Richmond's black population declined to 42 per cent of the total.

The District Court introduced an equivocal ruling on the annexation, but the Court of Appeals (in *Holt* v. *City of Richmond*, 459 F2d 1093, 1972) ruled by four votes to two in the City's favour. It found that

> For perfectly valid reasons, Richmond's elected representatives had sought annexation since 1961. Those reasons were compelling . . . . If some impermissible reasons crept into the minds of some members of Richmond's Council in 1969, that cannot negate all of the compelling reasons which led them and their predecessors in office to press on the same course in earlier years. (p. 1099)

Thus the annexation was for good reason, possible recent racialist motivation notwithstanding. (Note that the decision was delivered by the Chief Judge of the Fourth Circuit, Clement Haynsworth. His nomination to the Supreme Court by President Nixon in 1969 had been rejected by the Senate.)

In dissent, Judge Butzner showed how the 1969 compromise was intended to dilute the black vote, was reached with certain members of the Council excluded and by focusing largely on residential land contradicted the City's claim that it was seeking vacant land for business and industry. But the "dilution gerrymander" went through, because there were compelling reasons to ensure that the City of Richmond did "not become a city of the old, the poor, and the Black" (p. 1096). As a consequence, the State imposed a moratorium in 1972 on all annexations.

Finally, there is the case of the incorporation of the City of Black Jack, Missouri. This is considered important not so much for the decision as for the nature of the plaintiffs and the arguments. The case was brought by the Attorney-General (Mitchell), who sued the city for exclusionary zoning (a companion case involved a developer suing for damages). The equal protection clause was cited, but the foundation of the action was Title VIII (Fair Housing) of the Civil Rights Act of 1968 (see p. 157). Thus the Executive was involved in a case involving alleged racial discrimination, under the powers given it by the Act to bring an action against "any person or group of persons engaged in a practice that discriminated on the basis of race, color, religion or national origin" (quoted in Danielson, 1976, p. 231).

The area later to become the City of Black Jack was a 1700-acre tract in the unincorporated portion of St. Louis County. According to the 1965 County Plan, 67 of these acres were zoned for multi-family housing developments, and by 1970 15·2 acres had been developed, with 321 apartments. In 1969, the Inter-Religious Center for Urban Affairs decided to build an 11·9 acre development of 108 two-storey town houses – Park View Heights – within the remaining area zoned for such use. Federal funds were sought to subsidize this, and Department of Housing and Urban Development approval was given on 5 June, 1970. Meanwhile, members of the Black Jack Improvement Association had been warning local residents of the threat of not only the approved development but of a large number of similar subsidized projects (Danielson, 1976, p. 32). On 26 June, a petition signed by 1425 persons requested the incorporation of the City of Black Jack. Despite opposition within the State government, this petition was granted on 6 August. On 20 October, the city adopted a zoning ordinance which prevented the development of any more multi-family homes.

The Court of Appeals ruled that the effect of this "rezoning" would be a differential impact against blacks, many of whom could have afforded to live in Park View Heights if the project had gone ahead. In its opinion (*United States* v. *City of Black Jack, Missouri*, 508 F2d 1179, 1974) it first noted that Title VIII (Fair Housing) of the Civil Rights Act was constitutionally valid, under the Thirteenth Amendment which had been passed to remove all the penalities of slavery. The opinion of Justice Stewart in the case of *Jones* v. *Mayer* (392 US 409, 1968) was to the effect that

At the very least, the freedom that Congress is empowered to secure under the Thirteenth Amendment includes the freedom to buy whatever a white can buy, the right to live wherever a white can live . . . when racial discrimination herds men into ghettos and makes their ability to buy property turn on the color of their skin, then it too is a relic of slavery. (p. 1209)

Under the Civil Rights Act, the plaintiff need show only that an action has a differential impact on blacks, not that it was racially motivated. To counter such evidence, it must be shown that the discriminatory effect is a consequence of a "compelling government interest" in undertaking its police power. The case for the City of Black Jack focused on road and traffic control, preventing school overcrowding, and the devaluation of single-family properties. The Court of Appeals ruled that these were not "furthered by the zoning ordinance" (p. 1187) and ruled it invalid. In a separate decision in 1976 – following its earlier decision on *Park View Heights Corp* v. *City of Black Jack*, 467 F2d 1208, 1972 – the District Court awarded the developer $450 000 as damages; the development could not by then proceed because the federal funds were no longer available. The Supreme Court refused to become involved in any of the details of these cases and denied petitions for hearings – 442 US 1042, 1975; 443 US 884, 1975.

CONCLUSIONS

The purpose of the state, according to a theory underlying the American Constitution, is to promote the public welfare, if necessary overriding the rights of individuals in order to achieve its goals. But it must define those goals, and if necessary be prepared to defend them before the exacting scrutiny of the courts. These interpret whether the goals are valid, and whether the abrogation of individual rights enumerated in the Constitution can be justified in particular cases – which set precedents for many others.

The regulation of land use is a valid goal for the state to pursue, and State and municipal governments can properly restrict individuals' rights with regard to property in order to achieve their land-use goals. There is one main exception to this, the courts have determined. Any use of the zoning power with the intent of disadvantaging racial minority groups, especially blacks, is unconstitutional – in most cases because it denies them the equal protection they were accorded by the Fourteenth Amendment. Intentional disadvantages to other groups, and unintentional consequences for blacks, are not unconstitutional, however.

With this one major proviso, the zoning power can be used to pursue a variety of social, economic, fiscal and environmental goals, without fear of judicial restraint. Occasionally there has been some suggestion that the courts may substantially limit the power to zone out undesirable elements from an area. But little has ensued, and in general municipalities – to which most State legislatures have devolved the zoning power – have been free to define the public interest within their territories and to promote it by appropriate zoning strategies. Because most suburbs are divided into a large number of separate municipalities, this means not one definition of the public interest but many, which may conflict. The courts have recognized this, but in most cases have declined to intervene in what is seen as a legislative matter. Thus, as long as they do not explicitly and/or intentionally practice racial discrimination, suburban municipalities remain free to pursue the narrow sectional interests of their residents – which in the case of the higher income areas is to exclude those who might depreciate the social character of their milieu, its tax rates, and its schools. (Further, if compelling reasons can be found, the black vote can be diluted, according to the Richmond decision.) Zoning is a powerful tool for the protection of suburban interests.

SIX

The educational issue:
racial desegregation and school finance

In a meritocratic society, or one which is presented as meritocratic, educational success is widely perceived as the best means of ensuring good career prospects. If the educational system were the same everywhere and for all citizens, then presumably there would be equality of educational opportunity. The result should be that the most able children get the best jobs. But such equality of opportunity is not available. Nor is it likely to be, for those whose children appear to be at an advantage will not wish to yield their preferential position in the competition for the country's best jobs. The disadvantaged, of course, would like the situation to be changed, creating greater equality of opportunity. The present chapter deals with the struggle of one group to counter their disadvantage in the educational system, through the courts, and the relevance of this conflict to the understanding of the political geography of American metropolitan areas.

Parents seek to achieve structured inequality in educational provision, because they hope that this will advance their children's cause in the contest for college places and employment. Preferred is a school which has excellent modern facilities, a low student: staff ratio, no discipline problems, and an atmosphere which favours and fosters certain social and economic attitudes. Thus they do not want a "mixed" school, because this is thought to be both socially and educationally inferior. In particular, white parents, especially affluent white parents, do not want a school with a mixed racial composition. Black children are considered inferior in a variety of ways, and white parents wish to avoid any contact between their own children and such "undesirables".

One way for white parents to avoid this perceived problem of racial mixture is to send their children to private schools, which can control entry rigourously on whatever criteria they choose to apply. Racial or any other type of discrimination is not unconstitutional in such institutions, unless the state is involved. Many have chosen this option, with over ten per cent of children attending schools outside the public system (Adams and Brown,

1976). But the majority send their children to public schools, and it is the public system which some have manipulated and others seek to change.

With regard to racial separation within the public school system, three main ways have been used to ensure a minimal level of black-white mixture.

(1) The provision of separate school systems. Under this scheme, each school district (or comparable body) provides two entirely separate systems, one for blacks and the other for whites. In this way the races are entirely separated. Given such separation – which may be mandatory on the school district board through a ruling of the State legislature – the two races can be unequally treated in the provision of facilities, teaching and other resources.

(2) Use of residential separation of the racial groups plus careful definition of catchment areas to ensure that most blacks go to black-dominated schools and most whites to white-dominated schools. Again, given that racial separation is achieved, there can then be a maldistribution of resources.

(3) The creation or takeover of separate suburban school districts whose social and racial character can be closely controlled by use of the zoning mechanism. This has the added advantage, over the other two options, of not only providing a means of ensuring racial separation but also of allowing the suburban residents to opt out of any contribution, via property taxes, to the costs of educating those from whom they are distancing themselves.

All three of these have been widely used. The first, the so-called "separate but equal" provision, was employed throughout the southern States (in 17, plus the District of Columbia); it was the best available method given the large size of school districts in many of those States and the spatial mixing of the two racial groups at certain scales, especially in rural areas. The other two methods have been used in metropolitan areas. The first allows racial exclusion in the schools of large districts, notably the central cities. The second is clearly a suburban solution to the problem.

All three of these strategies have been challenged in the courts, mainly by the NAACP and similar bodies which are seeking to achieve racial mixture in the school systems of America. The (often explicit) argument for racial separation among whites, especially affluent whites, is that integration in the nation's schoolrooms would be harmful to white children – blacks in the same school, let alone the same classroom, would be major negative externalities. The counter-arguments of blacks are that integration would bring benefits to their children (which in the long term would be benefits to the whole of American society). Hooker (1978) suggests that their arguments incorporate three separate theories:

(1) that separation of blacks deprives them of the chance to observe and

learn from their "white superiors" and thus serves to maintain their imposed subordinate position within society;

(2) that separation of blacks inevitably means that their schools receive inferior financing and the provision of other resources compared to those occupied by whites, because of the relative powerlessness of blacks in the resource-allocation procedure; and

(3) separation implies, and seeks to ensure, inferiority.

Black advocates have sought, through the courts in particular, to prove the validity of these theories using social science evidence and to show that black children have been damaged in a variety of ways by their educational experience. This they succeeded in doing in some courtrooms – although the validity of some of the evidence that the judges accepted as facts has been doubted by other social scientists (see Rose, 1972; Wolf, 1980). But whether the remedies have achieved any noticeable gains for them is dubious, in part because of judicial restraint in suggesting remedies that will ensure that discrimination is removed (see, however, the essays in Hawley, 1981).

REMOVING "SEPARATE BUT EQUAL"

Of the challenges to the three strategies enumerated above, that against the "separate but equal" system has had by far the greatest success. Its relevance to the present book is only indirect, since it was not concerned with intra-metropolitan issues. It set the ethos for the whole range of challenges, however, because

> The factual finding of psychological harm caused by school segregation, documented by modern social science, constituted an empirical rejection of the separate-but-equal formula. (Rosen, 1972, p. 155)

Having accepted that racial separation was harmful, and that deliberate policies of racial discrimination (sending blacks to separate schools irrespective of equality of resource provision) were unconstitutional practices undertaken by States and their subordinate school boards, the courts then had to fashion remedies that would remove such discrimination.

For school education, the classic case was settled in 1954, in Chief Justice Warren's first written opinion, for a unanimous Supreme Court. But the groundwork leading to this decision was laid in a large number of other cases brought by the NAACP, and the Court in 1954 was able to refer back to Justice Harlan's dissent from the decision in *Plessy* v. *Ferguson*, 164 US 537, 1896 (which established the validity of "separate but equal" facilities in other spheres), when he wrote of "The arbitrary separation of citizens, on the basis of race . . . (and) The thin disguise of "equal" accommodations". (There are many books dealing with this major episode in American race relations: see, for example, Wasby *et al.*, 1977; Sitkoff, 1981). Even so, the

1954 case referred only to the one particular form of racial discrimination.

The provision of "separate but equal" educational systems in the South was apparently condoned in a Supreme Court opinion of 1896 which did not refer to education directly. In *Plessy* v. *Ferguson* (164 US 537, 1896) the court was dealing with a case of racial separation on the trains of Louisiana. A black was ejected from the "whites-only" carriage and was imprisoned for violating the relevant State law. He claimed that this was racial dicrimination and prolonged the "burdens of slavery" that were to be removed by the Thirteenth Amendment. The Supreme Court found, however, that if equal facilities were provided for blacks and whites, their enforced separation did not indicate unequal treatment and so was not unconstitutional under the Fourteenth Amendment. This ruling provided the basis for "separate but equal" provision on a wide range of facilities.

For education, the important element in the *Plessy* opinion was that schooling was offered as an example of "separate but equal":

> Establishment of separate schools for white and colored children has been held to be a valid exercise of the legislative power even by courts of States where the political rights of the colored race have been longest and most earnestly enforced. (p. 544)

This suggested that the Court did not see such a practice as unconstitutional, although it of course heard no arguments to that effect. Three years later it bolstered that view, and indicated that education was a State matter. The Board of Education in Richmond, Georgia, had closed its black schools as an economy measure. Blacks sued that this was unconstitutional, because the white schools were retained. But the Supreme Court dismissed their plea – in *Cumming* v. *Richmond (Ga.) County Board of Education*, 175 US 528, 1899 – because

> the education of the people in schools maintained by state taxation is a matter belonging to the respective States, and any interference on the part of the federal authority with the management of such schools cannot be justified except in the case of a clear and unmistakeable disregard of rights secured by the supreme law of the land. (p. 545)

And then in 1927, Mississippi's "separate but equal" system was not found unconstitutional when a Chinese girl questioned her assignment to the all-black school. Again, the Court – in *Gong Lum* v. *Rice*, 275 US 78, 1927 – "opted out" by ruling that the basis of her challenge:

> has been many times decided to be within the constitutional power of the state legislature to settle without intervention of the federal courts under the Federal Constitution. (p. 86)

The task of the NAACP, therefore, was to prove that "separate but equal" was in fact "separate and unequal" and so properly should be considered by the Supreme Court under the Fourteenth Amendment as unconstitutional discrimination by a State body. Higher education was tackled first, because inequality was substantial there and favourable decisions could establish valuable precedents. The first success concerned a black law student, who was denied entry to the all-white Law School at the University of Missouri. There was no all-black comparable school, but State law allowed the all-black College in Missouri to pay for him to attend law school in another State. The Supreme Court ruled that this was unconstitutional – in *Missouri Ex rel. Gaines* v. *Canada*, 305 US 337, 1938 – because each State was required to ensure equal protection, including equal educational provision, within its own jurisdiction. To counter the ruling, the State of Missouri established an all-black law school, "equal" to its all-white companion. In a later case (*Sipuel* v. *Board of Regents of the University of Oklahoma*, 323 US 631, 1948) the Court ruled that such a comparable institution must be established immediately to meet an applicant's need.

Given that a State is required to provide for black law students, what of the requirement that the facilities for blacks and whites be equal? Two crucial cases settled in 1950 suggested that such separate establishments could never be equal. In a Texas case (*Sweatt* v. *Painter*, 339 US 629, 1950) a black student refused to enrol at the all-black law school; the argument of his attorney, Thurgood Marshall (appointed a Supreme Court Justice in 1967) was that if it is segregated it must be unequal. The Court agreed with him, unanimously, and required that Sweatt be admitted to the University of Texas Law School, which – according to Chief Justice Vinson –

> possesses to a far greater degree those qualities which are incapable of measurement but which make for greatness in a law school . . . (such as) reputation of the faculty, experience of the administration, position and influence of the alumni, standing in the community, traditions and prestige (p. 634)

in addition to its better libraries. According to the Chief Justice, "it is difficult to believe that one who had a free choice between those law schools would consider the question close". The second case referred to a black student admitted as a graduate student at the all-white University of Oklahoma but required to occupy a designated separate area in classroom, library and cafeteria. The Court agreed, unanimously, that this was unconstitutional discrimination (*McLaurin* v. *Oklahoma State Regents for Higher Education*, 339 US 637, 1950).

The NAACP's strategy was to get the Supreme Court to overturn the precedent set in the *Plessy* opinion that separate but equal was not unconstitutional. Chief Justice Vinson was not prepared to do that, claiming that the *Sweatt* decision referred to the individual, not to all blacks. Nevertheless, the foundation had been laid and by the early 1950s the impact of the Court's rulings was

> to require a state to provide, within its borders, simultaneously, the same courses of study, educational facilities of the same size, quality, and variety, colleges of the same prestige, and faculties of the same reputation, for both whites and Negroes. In addition, inconvenience of location and cost of travelling could be considered, and segregation

within an institution was invalid. For all intents and purposes, then, separate but equal schools in higher education were operationally impossible. (Wasby *et al.*, 1977, p. 57)

The task was to extend this set of findings to pre-university education.

Brown v. *Board of Education*

This crucial step was achieved with the decision on five cases delivered by Chief Justice Warren on 17 May, 1954; the key case was that of *Brown* v. *Board of Education of Topeka* (347 US 483, 1954), which concerned a Topeka (Kansas) black child required to walk 20 blocks daily to an all-black school rather than attend an all-white establishment much closer to home. (Other cases ruled on simultaneously included *Briggs* v. *Elliott* (347 US 483, 1954), in which the Court was hearing an appeal on the failure of a South Carolina school board to equalize provision between its black and white schools under a District Court ruling.)

Preparation of the five cases, and presentation of the evidence, was a major task (reviewed in several places: see Kluger, 1976). Oral arguments were heard twice. The opinion was brief, unanimous, and clear (see Wasby *et al.*, 1977, pp. 92ff.). It ruled that the evidence on whether segregation in schools was intended to be covered by the Fourteenth Amendment was inconclusive. Education, it found, was probably the most important functional duty of State and local governments, because of its key role in preparing citizens. The key question was therefore:

> Does segregation of children in public schools solely on the basis of race, even though the physical facilities and other "tangible" factors may be equal, deprive the children of the minority group of equal educational opportunities?

The unanimous answer was that it does, leading to the conclusion that

> We conclude that in the field of public education the doctrine of "separate but equal" has no place. Separate educational facilities are inherently unequal. Therefore, we hold that the plaintiffs and others similarly situated for whom the actions have been brought are, by reason of the segregation complained of, deprived of the equal protection of the laws guaranteed by the Fourteenth Amendment.

The remedy: achieving desegregation

Having ruled on the claim that separate but equal educational systems (i.e. legal, or *de jure*, segregation of schools) are unconstitutional, the Court was then required to indicate a remedy. This would affect the 17 States with such laws (Delaware, Maryland, Virginia, West Virginia, Kentucky, Missouri, Tennessee, North Carolina, South Carolina, Georgia, Florida, Alabama, Mississippi, Louisiana, Arkansas, Oklahoma and Texas), the District of Columbia, plus the four (Arizona, Kansas, New Mexico, Wyoming) in which local school boards were allowed to operate *de jure* segregation if they wished (Lord, 1977). More hearings were held before the remedy was formulated, with all interested parties being invited to submit answers to a series of questions from the Court.

The remedy was laid down in a second opinion (*Brown* v. *Board of Education of Topeka*, 349 US 294, 1955), which is commonly termed *Brown II*. This is widely considered as relatively weak (Wasby *et al.*, 1977, pp. 122ff.). It decided that the oversight of desegregation should be a task for the District Courts, that a "prompt and reasonable" start to desegregation should be undertaken, and that the programme should be pursued with "all deliberate speed". Local difficulties were foreseen so that

> Once . . . a start has been made, the courts may find that additional time is necessary to carry out the ruling in an effective manner. (But) The burden rests upon the defendants to establish that such time is necessary in the public interest and is consistent with good faith compliance at the earliest practicable date.

Until final integration of the schools was achieved, the District Courts would retain their jurisdiction.

The slow course of desegregation in the South

The *Brown* decision was extremely unpopular in the Southern States, where it struck at the roots of a white supremacist social and economic system. There was determined opposition to the remedy, which in any case was imprecise and open to delaying tactics through the courts (see Peltason, 1971 and Bass, 1981, for descriptions of some of these). Many of the judges were themselves anti-integration and were beholden to constituencies determined to maintain segregated schools (see Chapter 4). Most importantly, the Court's ruling was not supported by either the Executive or a majority of Congress, and it was only in the 1960s – under Kennedy and, especially, Johnson – that legislative action was taken to promote desegregation:

> For half a decade after *Brown* there was no significant executive or legislature support for school desegregation, and progress was halting under judicial decree. From 1961 to 1969 integration progressed faster because the political branches gave varying measures of effective support in the area of education in addition to enacting legislation striking at discriminatory racial practices in such related fields as housing, employment, voting and public accommodations. After 1969 resistance became stiffer and compliance slowed while President Nixon pressed for legislation to deprive the courts of power to remedy past denials of Equal Protection. (Cox, 1976, pp. 90–91)

Thus, as Hodder-Williams (1979) makes clear, the Supreme Court is relatively powerless to impose its remedies if it lacks the support of public opinion and of elected representatives, although the impact of its words may not be negligible in the long term in promoting opinion change.

For several years after the *Brown* decision, the Supreme Court refused writs of *certiorari* on nearly all desegregation cases, leaving decision-making in the hands of the lower courts (Wasby *et al.* (1977) give a summary of relevant cases). The first case that it heard related to the notorious incidents in Little Rock Arkansas, where the State Governor – Orville Faubus – announced that integration of high schools would be inconsistent with the maintenance of law and order (Peltason, 1971). As a result of this reaction, the school board asked the District Court if it could postpone its integration plans. The judge agreed, and the NAACP appealed to the Supreme Court. There the Justices unanimously reiterated their previous position, and overruled claims that State governments were not bound to follow the rulings of a federal Court's interpretation of the Constitution. They argued (*Cooper* v. *Aaron*, 358 US 1, 1958) that

> State support of segregated schools through any arrangement, management, funds or property cannot be squared with the Amendment's command that no State shall deny to any person within its jurisdiction the equal protection of the laws . . . . The principles announced (in *Brown*) . . . and the obedience of the States to them, according to the command of the Constitution, are indispensable for the protection of the freedoms guaranteed by our fundamental charter for all of us.

Governor Faubus was unconvinced, and he and the Arkansas Legislature closed all Little Rock schools for a year. The local courts – with the Supreme Court affirming, *Faubus* v. *Aaron*, 361 US 197, 1959 – found this unconstitutional, and eventually the city's schools were slowly desegregated.

Apart from this blatant disregard of the Court's rulings, several other ploys were used to try and avoid the introduction of substantial desegregation. These included (Lord, 1977) State legislative acts claiming that the *Brown* decision did not apply (Mississippi) and abandonment of the public education system, replacing it with State grants to whites attending private schools (Virginia). Less aggressively, some school districts operated "freedom of choice" programmes assuming, rightly, that no whites would apply to go to what was previously an all-black school and that very few blacks would have the courage to apply to all-white schools. All of these tactics were eventually thwarted, only in the last case by the Supreme Court – in *Green* v. *County School Board of New Kent County, Virginia*, 391 US 430, 1968 and two other cases determined on the same day.

Gerrymandering again

In the previous chapter, the attempts of local communities to gerrymander against black residents of a municipality (making them ex-residents) was discussed (p. 100). The same tactics were employed with regard to school districts. If whites and blacks could be separated into different school districts by the creation of a new district, then integration within each district could be obtained and the schools would still be segregated. This procedure is not easily carried through in rural areas where the scale of black/white separation is local, but it was attempted in several places. The Supreme Court later ruled that it was unconstitutional in 1972.

Two cases were heard. The first was relatively straightforward, and drew a unanimous verdict (although there were two separate opinions delivered). Halifax County, North Carolina had a segregated, separate but equal, dual school system until 1965, when a desegregation plan was prepared for implementation in 1969. It covered 10 655 students at the latter date. In January 1969 a new school district within Halifax County was created, for the City of Scotland Neck; this was approved by local referendum. In the new district, of 695 students only, 57 per cent of the students were white, compared to 22 per cent in the entire county. According to the District Court that heard the case, this was creating a "refuge for white students" in Scotland Neck. The Court of Appeals disagreed but the Supreme Court ruled (in *United States* v. *Scotland Neck Board of Education*, 407 US 484, 1972) that such an action was deliberately intended to hinder the process of desegregation, and so was unconstitutional.

The second case was not as clear, and was decided on a 5 : 4 majority, with the dissenters (Burger, Blackman, Powell and Rehnquist) claiming that there was no evidence either of intent to hinder desegregation or of a consequence to that effect. Greenville County, Virginia – 34 per cent white in its schools – was required to desegregate its educational system. At about the same time, the city of Emporia seceded – properly, under Virginian legislation – and became independent of the county. The secession was largely over fiscal issues and initially Emporia was to remain within the Greenville County school system. In 1969, it decided to operate its own separate school system. This was challenged, and a majority on the Supreme Court (in *Wright* v. *Council of the City of Emporia*, 407 US 451, 1972) agreed that it was an unconstitutional action:

> We hold . . . that a new school district may not be created where its effect would be to impede the process of dismantling a dual system. (p. 66)

The minority of four disagreed, for the reasons specified above; the *Emporia* decision goes against the developing "conservative" tradition, as enunciated later in *Washington* v. *Davis* (see p. 88).

The import of these two decisions was that desegregation must occur within the pre-existing mosaic of school districts and that any attempt to gerrymander the boundaries to promote racial separation was unconstitutional. A strong minority disagreed with this, unless clear racial intent was proven, however, and indicated, through Chief Justice Burger in the Emporia dissent, their belief in the autonomy of local government units:

> To bar the city of Emporia from operating its own school system is to strip it of its most important governmental responsibility, and thus largely to deny its existence as an independent geographical identity. (p. 71)

Such a belief in local independence (already noted with regard to zoning, p. 96) was used by this group on the Court to reduce the impact of desegregation in a number of later decisions.

"Busing"

Taking pupils to school by bus is a major characteristic of American educational systems, especially in rural areas. It was a foundation upon which desegregation strategies could be built, but its use to integrate schools by transporting pupils to other than the most accessible school to their homes violated the tradition of attending the local school which is also deeply engrained in American education. Should busing be used to achieve racial balance in schools, then, even if it involved moving large numbers of pupils away from neighbourhood schools?

Some districts were using busing as part of their desegregation programme. Others were not, however, and as a consequence some schools remained segregated because of the nature of the local catchment. This was so in part of Mobile County, Alabama, where nine elementary schools in one corner of the school district were all-black. The Supreme Court ruled, unanimously, that in such a situation busing must be used. Writing for the Court (in *Davis* v. *Board of School Commissioners of Mobile County*, 402 US 33, 1971), Chief Justice Burger said that

> "neighbourhood school zoning" whether based strictly on home-to-school distance or on "unified geographic zones" is not the only constitutionally permitted remedy. (p. 581)

And in two other opinions handed down on the same day, the Court ruled (in *McDaniel* v. *Baressi*, 402 US 39, 1971) that busing was a proper remedy, and it found unconstitutional (in *North Carolina State Board of Education* v. *Swann*, 402 US 43, 1971) a State law outlawing busing. (Recent – 1981/1982 – Senate debates have led to attempted federal legislation outlawing busing: see also p. 129.)

It was the unanimous decision delivered in a fourth case on 20 April 1971 that had the most impact regarding busing, however. Charlotte-Mecklenburg County School district in North Carolina, the 43rd largest in the country, was undertaking a District Court overseen desegregation plan to achieve racial balance (29 per cent white; 71 per cent black) among its schools. This was proving difficult because of the 24 000 black students, 21 000 lived in the City of Charlotte. In his opinion, Chief Justice Burger approved of the goal of approximately the same racial balance in each school, recognized the problem of one-race schools because of residential segregation, required the school district to provide free transport for those voluntarily moving away from such schools, and agreed that white and black schools with non-contiguous catchments should be grouped so that pupil exchanges would ensure racial balance. Finally, with regard to busing as a means of operating these policies, he wrote (in *Swann* v. *Charlotte-Mecklenburg Board of Education*, 402 US 1, 1971) that we find no basis for holding that the local school authorities may not be required to employ bus transportation as one tool of school desegregation. Desegregation plans cannot be limited to the walk-in school. (p. 575)

(Note Woodward and Armstrong's (1979, p. 112) claim that Burger considered his ruling anti-busing.)

These four decisions both validated busing and insisted on it where necessary, as part of the Court's reiteration

that state-imposed segregation by race in public schools denies equal protection of the laws. At no time has the Court deviated in the slightest degree from that holding or its constitutional underpinning. (in *Swann*, p. 564)

Interestingly, the *Swann* judgement also referred to a number of other issues, that become significant in later cases (note that this opinion was that of a unanimous Court, in 1971 – before Rehnquist joined it). Thus, for example, Burger wrote that

The construction of new schools and the closing of old ones are two of the most important functions of local school authorities (p. 569) . . . [followed a little later by] . . . The location of schools may thus influence the patterns of residential development of a metropolitan area and have important impact on composition of inner-city neighbourhoods (p. 569) . . . [which led to the conclusion that] . . . it is the responsibility of local authorities and district courts to see to it that future school construction and abandonment are not used and do not serve to perpetuate or re-establish the dual system. (p. 570)

He also dealt with the problem of resegregation, whereby the impact of migration patterns can recreate racial imbalances (as it did in Charlotte-Mecklenburg: Lord, 1975; Lord and Catau, 1976, 1977, 1981). Thus

Neither school authorities nor district courts are constitutionally required to make year-by-year adjustments of the racial composition of student bodies once the affirmative duty to desegregate has been accomplished and racial discrimination through official action is eliminated from the system. This does not mean that federal courts are without power to deal with future problems; but in the absence of a showing that either the school authorities or some other agency of the state has deliberately attempted to fix or alter demographic patterns to affect the racial composition of the schools, further intervention by a district court should not be necessary. (p. 575)

On the later use of this opinion, see Woodward and Armstrong (1979).

DESEGREGATING THE NORTHERN CITIES

The discussion so far has been concerned with desegregating the separate but equal dual school systems in the South. By the end of the Warren Court, this had not been achieved but it had been advanced – in the decision on *Alexander* v. *Holmes Board of Education* (369 US 19, 1969), the Court had replaced its "all deliberate speed" standard of *Brown* with one requiring "immediate operation of unitary school systems". From then on, the focus turned to the northern cities, which were not *de jure* segregated with regard to schools but in which almost all schools were either all-black or all-white. For these, the segregation was largely *de facto* as a result of residential separation, and the NAACP and others seeking to remove it had to relate such segregation to explicit state actions. The decisions in some of the cases that they brought were guided by some of the opinions already referred to. All of the Supreme Court opinions on these issues were produced after the nomination of Chief Justice Burger, and reflect the growing strict constructionist majority of the 1970s, which was dedicated to the elimination of explicit and intentional racial discrimination, but no more.

Given that most blacks in American cities are concentrated into virtually exclusive inner-city ghettos, then operation of the neighbourhood school principle will almost certainly ensure that nearly all white pupils go to all-white schools while all black pupils go to all-black schools. To guarantee this outcome, a number of policies were applied to prevent any leakage across the ghetto boundaries, in both directions (see Wolf, 1981). These are illustrated with hypothetical examples here.

> (1) *School siting.* If a school is sited on or near to the edge of the ghetto, then on the neighbourhood principle it is likely to draw pupils from both black and white residential areas. To avoid this new schools and school extensions should be sited so that mixed catchment areas are not produced, and schools on the boundaries should be closed (Fig. 6·1).
>
> (2) *Gerrymandering of catchment area boundaries.* Whatever the location of the schools it should be possible to draw the catchment boundaries so as to maximize racial separation (Fig. 6·2; on a related issue of political control of quasi-independent school boards within a single district and the potential for gerrymandering board territories, see Jenkins and Shepherd, 1972).
>
> (3) *Optional zones in mixed catchments.* If racially mixed catchment areas exist (perhaps temporarily during neighbourhood change) give the residents a choice of schools. White parents will undoubtedly opt for all-white schools, and allocation accordingly will avoid integration (Fig. 6·3A).
>
> (4) Discrimination in *busing* to avoid overcrowding. In some parts of the city, the local school may be overcrowded whereas in others it is under-used (as in Boston for many years: Dentler and Scott, 1980). Busing may then be used to redistribute the load. It may be that the nearest underused school to an overcrowded all-black school is an all-white school; busing the black pupils to an underused all-black school further away will avoid the potential integration issue (Fig. 6·3B).

The aim of the pro-desegregation lobby was to prove that these practices were not only in existence but had been undertaken for discriminatory purposes.

No case was heard by the Supreme Court on these issues until the 1970s.

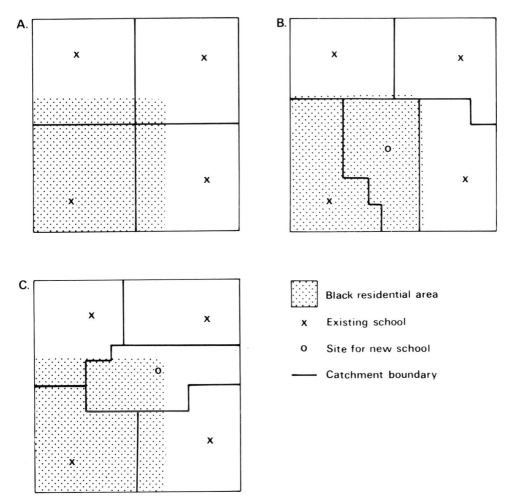

Figure 6·1. Promotion of *de facto* school segregation in part of a northern city by school siting decisions. (A) Pre-existing location of schools with catchment boundaries conforming to neighbourhood school principle; (B) location of a fifth school in the area, with catchment boundaries conforming to the neighbourhood school principle and promoting racial segregation; (C) location of a fifth school in the area with catchment boundaries conforming to the neighbourhood school principle and three schools with substantial racial mixing.

Previously, it had denied an appeal – in *Bell* v. *School, City of Gary*, 377 US 924, 1964 – of a lower court decision. In this, it had been argued that schools in Gary were racially segregated. The District Court found, however, that this resulted from a residential pattern that had developed after the school district and catchment area boundaries were defined. It had been claimed that, after *Brown I and II*, segregated schooling is incompatible with the Fourteenth Amendment. The District Court of the Court of Appeals disagreed, arguing that the Constitution does not require integration, it forbids discrimination. Thus (*Bell* v. *School, City of Gary, Indiana*, 324 F2d 209, 1963):

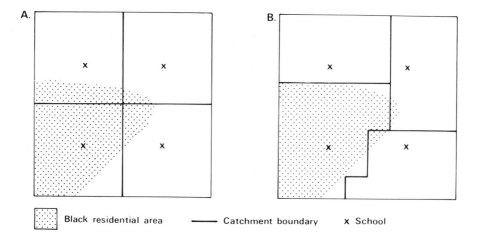

Black residential area   ——— Catchment boundary   x School

Figure 6·2. Promotion of *de facto* school segregation in part of a northern city by gerry-mandering catchment boundaries (B) rather than conforming to the neighbourhood school principle.

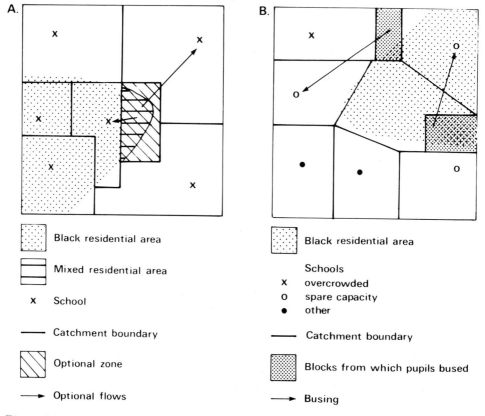

Black residential area

Mixed residential area

x   School

——— Catchment boundary

Optional zone

⟶ Optional flows

Black residential area

Schools
x   overcrowded
o   spare capacity
•   other

——— Catchment boundary

Blocks from which pupils bused

⟶ Busing

Figure 6·3. Promotion of *de facto* school segregation in part of a northern city by: (A) creating an optional zone in a mixed residential area and allowing parents to choose between a nearby all-black school and a more distant all-white school; and (B) discriminatory busing of pupils to schools with spare capacity that are not the closest to their homes.

> The School District boundaries in Gary were determined without any consideration of race or color . . . (and) were honestly and conscientiously constructed with no intention or purpose to segregate the races (p. 213)

which is not an unconstitutional act, simply because it has a particular impact on the racial composition of schools. The Supreme Court, by denying *certiorari*, clearly agreed.

The breakthrough for the opponents of *de facto* segregation in northern city school systems came with a case referring to Denver, Colorado. There it was shown that in the Park Hill area in the north-east of the city, as well as in the core of the city itself, the schools were virtually all-black (partly as a result of the election of a school board committed to retain the neighbourhood principle and not to use busing: Jackson, 1971). Park Hill was a mixed area, but its schools were all-black as a result, the parents of black pupils contended, of deliberate school board policies. The District Court agreed and ordered busing to remedy the segregation not only in Park Hill but also in the city core, where no evidence of segregation-by-intent in the schools was provided. The Court of Appeals agreed with the Park Hill busing, but not that for the city core.

The Supreme Court upheld both decisions of the District Court and required a desegregation plan for the whole school district (the City of Denver). Writing for the majority of seven (Justice White disqualified himself because he had practised in Denver), Justice Brennan first established that even if there were no *de jure* segregation, *de facto* segregation that is in part a consequence of state action is unconstitutional (*Keyes* v. *School District No. 1*, 413 US 89, 1973):

> where plaintiffs prove that the school authorities have carried out a systematic program of segregation affecting a substantial proportion of the students, schools, teachers and facilities . . . it is only common sense to conclude that there exists a predicate for a finding of the existence of a dual school system. (p. 559)

He then argued that this would have repercussions elsewhere within the district:

> common sense dictates the conclusion that racially inspired school board actions have an impact beyond the particular schools that are the subjects of these actions (p. 560)

so that if segregative intent has been proved in one part of the school district this

> creates a presumption that other segregated schooling within the system is not adventitious. (p. 561)

The consequence would then be a system-wide remedy, not one confined to the areas of proven segregation only. This is what the District Court was required to impose if it was satisfied that the school board had acted to promote segregated schools.

Only Rehnquist dissented, arguing that the occasional gerrymandering of attendance zones should not be equated with *de jure* segregation in the south. Justice Douglas, on the other hand, not only concurred with Brennan but argued that under the Fourteenth Amendment "there is no difference between de facto and de jure segregation" (p. 567: see Woodward and Armstrong, 1979).

The issue was revived in 1977, in a case referring to Dayton, Ohio. There schools were racially imbalanced, and optional attendance zones were used. The District Court – according to Rehnquist's opinion for the Supreme Court majority (seven; Marshall did not participate) – in *Dayton Board of Education* v. *Brinkman*, 433 US 406, 1977 – found

> no evidence of racial discrimination in the establishment or alteration of attendance boundaries or in the site selection and construction of new schools and school additions (p. 858)

and concluded that the optional attendance zones had no racial significance. Nevertheless, it required the Dayton system to be desegregated. The Supreme Court ruled that the "punishment did not fit the crime" and remanded the case to the District Court. It accepted that there had been some discrimination in the past, but needed evidence of its incremental effect and wanted a remedy fashioned which was relevant to the offence, and no more.

This decision suggested that the opinion of the Court was changing, as did another – *Austin Independent School Board* v. *United States*, 429 US 190, 1976 – which applied the *Washington* v. *Davis* criterion (see the discussion of Arlington Heights, p. 95) that a racially disproportionate impact was not in itself evidence of unconstitutional discriminatory action. Nevertheless, when the case came back to the Supreme Court in 1979 (it is known as *Dayton II*) a majority of five Justices upheld the *Keyes* principle. Writing for that majority, Justice White (in *Dayton Board of Education* v. *Brinkman*, 443 US 526, 1979) argued that

> Given intentially segregated schools in 1954 . . . the Court of Appeals was quite right in the holding that the Board was thereafter under a continuing duty to eradicate the effects of that system (p. 733)

and he upheld the requirement of a system-wide desegregation remedy, quoting *Keyes* that

> purposeful discrimination in a substantial part of a school system furnishes a sufficient basis for an inferential finding of a systemwide discriminatory intent. (p. 736)

Thus, if a school district has ever practised segregation on a substantial scale, it is required to eliminate the impact of that – at any time in the future while the consequences remain (Rehnquist, Powell and Burger (see below) disagreed).

In a companion decision to *Dayton II*, the Court decided (7 : 2) in favour of a similar remedy. The case referred to Columbus, Ohio, and Justice White (in *Columbus Board of Education* v. *Penick*, 443 US 449, 1979) wrote that we cannot fault the conclusion . . . that at the time of the trial there was systemwide segregation in the Colombus schools that was the result of recent and remote intentionally segregative actions of the Columbus Board (p. 680)

requiring a system-wide remedy. Chief Justice Burger agreed, pointing out that in *Columbus* there was evidence of post-1954 (i.e. post-*Brown*) segregation but that such evidence was absent in *Dayton*, hence his dissent in the latter. Powell dissented in both, arguing that

the federal judiciary should be limiting rather than expanding the extent to which courts are operating the public school system in our country. (p. 690)

The extent of the massive busing required (42 000 out of 96 000 students in the system) promised irreparable harm to education. Justice Rehnquist agreed, arguing that the systemwide remedy was

as complete and dramatic a displacement of local authority by the federal judiciary as is possible in our federal system. (p. 696; see also the discussion on p. 128)

Limiting the remedy I: resegregation

The Ohio cases discussed above suggest that even in the late 1970s a majority of the Court was prepared to tackle intentional segregation in city schools head on. But several earlier decisions indicated that they limited the remedy, so that segregation was unlikely to be removed totally.

The first of these cases concerned the issue of resegregation, caused by population shifts and referred to in Chief Justice Burger's opinion on *Swann* (p. 114). The school district concerned was that for Pasadena, California, which had adopted a desegregation plan in 1970 under the oversight of a District Court. In 1974, it applied to the Court to be released from any further need to act, having implemented a plan in which there was no school housing a majority of the minority race. The District Court refused, requiring annual readjustment of attendance zones to ensure that the "no majority" principle was ever breached.

The Supreme Court overturned the District Court decision. For the majority of six (Justice Stevens did not participate) Justice Rehnquist wrote (in *Pasadena Board of Education* v. *Spangler*, 427 US 424, 1976) that

There was . . . no showing . . . that those post-1971 changes in the racial mix of six Pasadena schools . . . were in any manner caused by segregative actions chargeable to the defendants (p. 608) . . . [but rather a] . . . quite normal pattern of human migration resulted in some change in the demographics of Pasadena's residential pattern, with resultant shifts in the racial make up of some of the schools. (p. 608)

Such normal patterns were outside the action of the Board, which had done what was required of it. Thus although earlier decisions had required all vestiges of past segregative action to be removed, this decision, in somewhat contradicting *Swann*, *Keyes*, *Dayton II*, and *Columbus* (Edelman, 1980) was limiting the scope of Court-ordered desegregation (Clotfelter, 1978). Once a

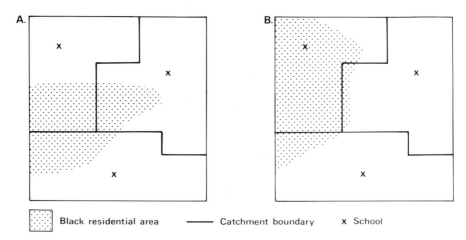

Figure 6·4. The process of resegregation. (A) catchment areas have been defined so that all schools have similar racial balances; (B) manipulation of the housing market so that black residential area is shifted, creating three segregated catchment areas.

new set of attendance zones had been instituted, the property-market could be manipulated (as Clotfelter, 1975a, b shows) and the rich at least could create a new segregated all-white school (Fig. 6·4) independent of state action. (A similar decision was reached on a New York case: *Parent Association of Andrew Jackson High School* v. *Ambach*, 598 F2d 705, 1979.)

Limiting the remedy II: metropolitan integration

If a school district is ordered to desegregate, and parents do not wish their children to attend integrated schools, one of the options available to them is to leave the district. They can do this either by enrolling their children in private schools, where the state is not involved and so segregation can occur, or they can move to another school district where, because of the racial composition of the population, desegregation is not an issue. Such an option is more likely to be available to affluent parents, who are less constrained in their residential choice than are their poorer counterparts. For those living in metropolitan areas (excluding those in some southern States where most school districts operate at the county scale), this avoidance strategy simply involves moving from one school district, usually the central city, to another, almost invariably suburban.

This central city to suburban movement to avoid school desegregation is widely known as "white flight". Its extent is a cause of much academic controversy (see, *inter alia*, Frey, 1979a, b; Spain, 1979; Taeuber *et al.*, 1981); Clark (1980, 1982, 1984) has provided an evaluation of particular judicial decisions and their relationship to later migration patterns. Whether or not any particular decision has stimulated white flight, however, or whether it has been generated by fears of desegregation, there is no doubt that one of the perceived benefits of suburban residence in most metro-politan areas has been avoidance of blacks in local schools.

Given that such avoidance has been a long-term process, which may or may not be accentuated by current judicial actions, it would seem that desegregation is unlikely to be achieved while the more affluent whites can escape its impact and leave the central city school districts dominated by blacks. Integration of the races in schools could only be achieved by amalgamation of school districts. This has been suggested in several places, and not suprisingly has been a focus of constitutional conflict.

The first case to come to the Supreme Court referred to Richmond, Virginia, in which the District Court ordered a consolidation of three school districts (one predominantly black and the other two predominantly white). The Court of Appeal overturned this as too drastic, and the Supreme Court upheld that decision. No opinion was written, however, and no precedent was set, because the Supreme Court was split 4 : 4 on the case, with Justice Powell having disqualified himself because he had previously served on one of the relevant school district boards. (On the case in the Supreme Court, see Woodward and Armstrong, 1979, pp. 266–268.)

The case concerned three school districts that for more than a century were coterminous with the City of Richmond and the Counties of Chesterfield and Henrico, respectively. Their boundaries were not, accord-ing to the US Court of Appeals (in *Bradley* v. *School Board of City of Richmond, Virginia*, 462 F2d 1058, 1972) drawn on racially-motivated grounds (though see p. 101). It was alleged that blacks were being "trapped" in Richmond, and therefore denied integrated schooling that would be available to them in the two counties. The Court thought some "trapping" may be occurring (e.g. in the construction of public housing; see also p. 127) but concluded that

> the root causes of the concentration of blacks in the inner cities of America are simply not known and that the district court could not realistically place on the counties the responsibility for the effect that inner city decay has had on the public schools of Richmond. (p. 1066)

Further, the Court concluded that it could not override the autonomy of the school districts which had been properly allocated by the Virginian Legislature. Thus

> One of the powers thus reserved to the states is the power to structure their internal government (p. 1068)

and if that power has not been exercised in an unconstitutional way it cannot be overruled by a federal Court. As a consequence,

> because it is not established that the racial composition of the schools in the City of Richmond and the counties is the result of invidious state action, we conclude there is no constitutional violation. (p. 1070)

The test of remedies involving city-suburban consolidation, presumably by cross-district busing, came with a Detroit case. There, it had been proven to the District Court Judge's satisfaction (though see Wolf, 1980, on the vagueness of the evidence, its poor presentation, and the level of judicial understanding) that the Detroit School Board, serving the entire central city, had been guilty of explicit discrimination on all four counts illustrated in Fig. 6·1–6·3. Having so decided, he was then persuaded that because more than 70 per cent of Detroit's students were black, the only realistic way of achieving desegregation was to consolidate all 54 school districts in the metropolitan area into a single busing scheme. This remedy was upheld by the Court of Appeals, and its legal validity was then contested before the Supreme Court. (Note that it was the concept of a metropolitan-wide remedy that was at issue, not any particular plan.)

The Supreme Court split 5:4, with the majority finding the proposed remedy unconstitutional, because it penalized innocent parties (the 53 suburban school districts which had not been found guilty of discriminatory actions) and because it overrode the autonomy of properly-constituted, independent school districts. Writing for the majority (in *Milliken* v. *Bradley*, 418 US 717, 1974) Chief Justice Burger noted that the District Court treated school district boundaries as "no more than arbitrary lines on a map drawn for political convenience" (p. 1089) and pointed out that the remedy, involving close judicial oversight, involved the District Court becoming the legislative authority and the school superintendent:

> This is a task which few, if any, judges are qualified to perform and one which would deprive the people of control of schools through their elected representatives. (p. 1090)

He recognized that school district boundaries may be drawn for ends that are unconstitutional (as at Emporia and Scotland Neck) but ruled that

> Before the boundaries of separate and autonomous school districts may be set aside by consolidating the separate units for remedial purposes or by imposing a cross-district remedy, it must first be shown that there has been a constitutional violation within one district that produces a significant segregative effect in another district. (p. 1091)

The evidence showed a constitutional violation by the Detroit school district only, so

> To approve the remedy . . . would impose on the outlying districts, not shown to have committed any constitutional violation, a wholly impermissible remedy not hinted at in *Brown I* and *II* or any holding of this Court. (pp. 1091–1092)

According to this ruling, the right to attend desegregated schools is not an absolute one; it is confined to the schools of the district in which one lives, and as long as all schools there have approximately the same racial balance (even, it seems, if that is 80–20) then the schools are properly integrated. As Burger expressed it, "The constitutional right of the Negro respondents residing in Detroit is to attend a unitary school system in that district"

(p. 1092). The fact of Detroit City being dominantly black is therefore irrelevant, particularly as Burger could identify no evidence that its boundaries were drawn to produce racial segregation in schools:

> The boundaries of the Detroit School District . . . were established over a century ago by neutral legislation when the city was incorporated; there is no evidence in the record . . . that either the original boundaries of the Detroit School District, or any other school district in Michigan, were established for the purpose of creating, maintaining or perpetuating segregation of races. (p. 1093)

This issue of the autonomy of the local state was important to the four who voted against the decision (Justices Brennan, Douglas, Marshall and White), who produced three separate dissenting opinions (two of them signed by all four). Thus according to Justice Douglas

> there can be no doubt that as a matter of Michigan law the State itself has the final say as to where and how school district lines should.be drawn (p. 1099)

so that if they have been drawn to promote segregation, then the State is ultimately responsible and thus is constitutionally invalid under the Fourteenth Amendment. He concluded that "Michigan by one device or another has over the years created black school districts and white school districts" (p. 1101), an unconstitutional situation requiring a drastic remedy. But the Court majority according to Justice White had overthrown such an effective remedy because it would cause "undue administrative inconvenience to the State" (p. 1102). Justice Marshall agreed, noting that Michigan boundaries had been altered for other reasons, and should be removed to ensure desegregation. If Detroit has acted unconstitutionally, then the State of Michigan is responsible; however, as Justice White observed

> the state of Michigan, the entity at which the Fourteenth Amendment is directed, has successfully insulated itself from the duty to provide effective desegregation remedies by vesting sufficient powers over its public schools in its local school districts. (p. 1102)

The same was likely to be found in other States, so that the hopes for effective desegregation were confounded by this majority verdict in favour of local autonomy. As with exclusionary zoning, the tight little suburban islands seemed to be well protected (see also the dissent by Judge Winter in *Bradley* v. *School Board of City of Richmond, Virginia*, 462 F2d 1058, 1972).

This conclusion did not apply everywhere, however, and in 1975 the Supreme Court, by not hearing a case, affirmed a lower court decision requiring a metropolitan-wide remedy. (Justice Rehnquist, supported by Powell and Burger, dissented and in the dismissal of the writ provided a written opinion arguing that the lower courts should not have heard the case – *Buchanan* v. *Evans*, 425 US 963, 1975.) The case concerned Wilmington, Delaware (see Raffel, 1977), and the District Court found (in *Evans* v. *Buchanan*, 379 FSupp 1218, 1974) that despite 20 years of work and litigation, the schools had never been desegregated; by 1974, 83 per cent of its students were black. The District Court Judge was unsure whether the constitutional requirement to desegregate could be met

> within the existing boundaries of the Wilmington School District . . . (and required) alternate desegregation plans (a) within the present boundaries of Wilmington School District, and (b) incorporating other areas of New Castle County. (p. 1224)

In concurring, Judge Gibbons went further and argued that Delaware's Educational Advancement Act, 1968, that established the City of Wilmington School District, was unconstitutional. Citing the *Emporia* and *Scotland Neck* Judgements (p. 113), he argued that

> just as a state-imposed limitation on the responsible school board's authority for pupil placement must be disregarded, so also a state-imposed limitation on the responsible school board's geographic area of responsibility must be disregarded, if either limitation has the effect of preventing the elimination of all vestiges of state-imposed segregation. A gerrymander of school district lines in a state where a dual system flourished will be judged by its effects on desegregation and not by whatever nonracial motivations were behind it. (p. 1227)

Judge Gibbons provided substantial evidence that the impact of the 1968 Act (14 years post-*Brown*) was to promote racial segregation in schools, and concluded that this was in violation of the requirement of the State of Delaware that it eliminated *de jure* segregation "root and branch". On similar cases, see Manley (1978). Redwine (1981) argues that an Atlanta case should have been decided in the same way as that for Richmond, but it was not, and the Supreme Court (in *Armour* v. *Nix*, 422 US 332, 1975) affirmed that decision.

The Wilmington case clearly refers to special circumstances and it is the Supreme Court opinion in *Milliken* that sets the general precedent with regard to metropolitan integration as a remedy to problems of ensuring desegregation (see also *Cunningham* v. *Grayson*, 541 F2d 538, 1976; Manley, 1978). However, according to Redwine (1981), the situation is far from clear, and – as in the Wilmington case – later Supreme Court decisions not to issue writs of *certiorari* suggest preparedness to accept metropolitan remedies in some situations. Further, the decision in another case indicated that – as in the earlier case relating to *Emporia* – local government boundaries could not be manipulated to avoid desegregation.

In 1969, the Indiana State Legislature approved the creation of Uni-Gov, a metropolitan local government combining the former city of Indianapolis with suburban areas in surrounding Marion County. The school districts were not similarly consolidated, however, leaving the great majority (95 per cent) in the territory of the Indianapolis Public School District, covering the jurisdiction of the former city. A case alleging discrimination within that district (IPS) was brought and proven, and the District Court required a metropolitan-wide remedy. Ruling one month after the Supreme Court's *Milliken* decision, the Court of Appeals altered the remedy. In a retrial, however, the District Court found that the failure to consolidate school districts when Uni-Gov was formed was an unconstitutional discriminatory act, and this decision was upheld in the Court of Appeals. The Supreme Court referred the case back, largely on an issue relating to housing (see below, and Heinz, 1977; Miller, 1977). In *United States* v. *Board of School Commissioners of City of Indianapolis, Indiana* (541 F2d 1211, 1976), the Court of Appeals noted that the Marion County suburbs were only prepared to accept Uni-Gov when school district annexation was excluded from the Act. Thus, although

> the most substantial reason advanced against the consolidation of the schools in Marion County when it was under consideration in 1959 was that a consolidated school district would be large, with consequent loss of citizen participation, and that it would increase taxes. These considerations, although not racially motivated, cannot justify legislation that has an obvious racial segregative impact. Administrative convenience cannot be a justification for violating the Equal Protection Clause. (pp. 1220–1221)

It was, therefore, prepared to rule that the State had directly created a segregated school situation:

> The Indiana Legislature acted directly in passing Uni-Gov, thereby creating the existing situation which confines black students within IPS. (p. 1221)

As part of their case, those suing for an inter-district remedy claimed that Uni-Gov, through the Housing Authority of the City of Indianapolis (HACI), had contributed to segregation by its policy on the location of public housing projects. Despite having jurisdiction outside the former City of Indianapolis, HACI constructed all its public housing projects within the IPS district. The claim was, therefore, that the housing authority was creating residential, and hence school, segregation. The Court agreed:

> By locating its projects within IPS and in many cases near all-black neighbourhoods, the Housing Authority significantly contributed to the disparity in residential and school populations between the inner city and the suburbs (p. 1223)

and it upheld the District Court's remedy that the HACI should build no more public housing within the IPS district. Of course, as Heins (1977, p. 664) notes, this requirement will not necessarily promote school desegregation:

> The court . . . imposed only a negative injunction which would have prevented exacerbation of residential segregation by the housing authority, but would not likely have helped in integrating Marion County schools.

Thus the effect of the decision on residential and educational segregation is likely to be slight. As with the case of *Warth* (see p. 89), it may be that the wrong basis for a challenge was chosen, and that the conservatism of the Courts in using the Equal Protection Clause should have been realized (Heins, 1977, p. 690; see also the discussion of cases relating to public housing in Chicago: p. 161).

The Court's decision and opinion in *Milliken*, and its general stance against inter-district remedies, have protected the position of those involved in "white flight" to the suburbs in order to avoid the perceived threat of integrated schools. As yet, those "trapped" in the large (inner city, except in the South) multi-racial school districts have received little succour from the Court with regard to the creation of integrated schools by busing. A minority on the Supreme Court has indicated considerable disquiet on this issue, however, which may be a preface to future decisions (presumably when the composition of the Court has changed). The case refers to the Dallas school district. This is divided into six subdistricts. In four of them, racial balance in the schools had been satisfactorily achieved, but in the other two (one largely white, the other almost entirely black) integrated schooling had proved difficult to create, because of their spatial isolation from the rest of the city. The Court of Appeal (in *Tasby* v. *Estes*, 572 F2d 1010, 1978) was not prepared to accept this argument, and remanded the case to the District Court for the formulation of a new plan and justification for any one-race schools that may be created.

The plan produced to meet the Court of Appeal's objections necessarily required extensive busing. This was appealed to the Supreme Court, where a writ of *certiorari* was dismissed. Three of the Justices dissented from this decision, and took the unusual step of issuing a dissenting *per curiam* opinion – authored by Justice Powell and supported by Justices Rehnquist and Stewart. They noted (in *Estes* v. *Metropolitan Branches of Dallas NAACP*, 444 US 537, 1980) that

> It is increasingly evident that use of the busing remedy to achieve racial balance can conflict with the goals of equal educational opportunity and quality schools. In all too many cities, well-intentioned court decrees have had the primary effect of stimulating resegregation. (p. 627)

Dallas, they believed, could be on the way to an entirely constitutional "separate but equal" system again. In 1971, the school district's enrolment of 163 000 included 69 per cent "Anglos"; by 1980, the percentage was 33·5, of a total enrolment down to 133 000. In one subdistrict, 1000 Anglos on the roll were due to be bused according to the new plan; because of white flight since its publication, there were by 1980 fewer than 50 of these still enrolled. Clearly, they argued, a major cause of school segregation was residential segregation – "which results largely from demographic and economic conditions over which school authorities have no control" (p. 631). But Court decrees requiring desegregation were stimulating such residential segregation (see also O'Donnell, 1980, on the inequitable impact of the desegregation remedy in Buffalo).

To Justices Powell, Rehnquist and Stewart, busing is not a sensible remedy in metropolitan school districts. One of the key decisions requiring busing (*Green* v. *County School Board of New Kent County, Va.*, 391 US 430, 1968) was, they claimed, framed in language . . . suitable to the small rural county before the Court in that case. . . . But it makes no sense to apply that statement to the Dallas Independent School District or any major metropolitan district. (p. 631)

Because most metropolitan areas comprise several school districts, the search for integration in one of those merely encourages white flight, erodes the district tax base, and denies those "trapped" there any chance of multi-racial schooling and community life. Thus

> Out of zeal to remedy one evil, courts may encourage or set the stage for other evils. By acting against one-race schools, courts may produce one-race school systems. (p. 634)

The remedy, to some, is to prevent one-race school systems by finding the State guilty of promoting segregated schooling via a multiplicity of school districts within a metropolitan area. But to others, the remedy is to withdraw from the position established by the Courts since *Brown I*. Thus Justices Powell, Rehnquist and Stewart not only condemn busing, they also argue that

> There can be no legitimate claim that "racial balance" in the public schools is constitutionally required. (p. 632)

Clearly, the more conservative elements on the Courts are seeking relevant cases with which to attack the busing remedy. In this, they are in tune with public opinion, as reflected in the US Senate at the time. In March 1982 this passed a bill that would prohibit federal courts from ordering students to be bused more than five miles, or 15 minutes journey time, from their homes (*The Times*, 5 February 1982; 4 March 1982). This has not yet been approved by the House. It indicates, however, growing support for the stance against integrated schooling for the autonomy of local school districts. The Supreme Court, it seems, may once again be in the vanguard of public opinion – reversing its actions of three decades ago.

INTER-DISTRICT DIFFERENTIALS

The separate suburban school districts have two major benefits for their residents, racial and fiscal. Regarding the first, the *Milliken* decision has allowed its retention; suburban school districts in most situations do not have to be consolidated with central city districts so that desegregation can be achieved on a metropolitan-wide basis. On the second, the benefits are two-fold: the suburban residents do not have to contribute to the costs of educating central city poor children, because school districts are financed by local property taxes; the suburban residents can provide a heavily-financed educational system, at relatively low costs to themselves, as a consequence. As a result the poor, notably, but not especially, the ethnic poor in the inner cities, get a lower equality education, assuming that expenditure and quality can be equated. Is this unconstitutional? The federal and (some) State courts disagree on the answer.

The Supreme Court says no

In San Antonio, Texas, there are several school districts. One of these, Edgewood, covers the inner city area that houses many Spanish-speakers. In 1971, property there was assessed as $5960 per pupil in its School system, and it spent $356 per pupil per year. In nearby Alamo Heights, on the other hand, assessed values were $49 000 and, at a much lower tax rate, expenditure was $594 per pupil. This differential was the basis of a case claiming that the Texan school system treats people unequally. The poor suffer, and are therefore denied equal protection under the law.

The Supreme Court disagreed, and a majority (in *San Antonio Independent School District* v. *Rodriguez*, 411 US1, 1973) declined to find such a differential as a violation of the Fourteenth Amendment. Writing for the majority of five, Justice Powell found that the poor were not a suspect classification in this case, and that education was not a fundamental right protected by the Constitution. The policy did not discriminate against the poor as a class, he argued, because not all of the poor lived in the low-spending districts. In any case

> at least where wealth is involved, the Equal Protection Clause does not require absolute equality or precisely equal advantages. (p. 37)

All were being provided with an education, and there was no evidence that the level in any school district fell below any necessary minimum provision.

A further reason for not finding the system discriminatory was that the State of Texas had recognized the problems of differential property assessments and provided funds to ameliorate the position in the poorer districts. Thus in Edgewood, of the $356 spent per pupil only $26 was raised in local taxes; $222 came from State funds and $108 from federal sources. In Alamo Heights, the respective figures were $333, $225 and $36. Thus the State was providing some equalization and the Court would not recognize that the disparities were "the product of a system that is so irrational as to be individually discriminatory" (p. 55). And if change were to be brought about, it was not for the Court to impose it. Continuing their respect for local state autonomy, the strict constructionalist majority of the Burger Court wrote that

> The persistence of attachment to government at the lowest level where education is concerned reflects the depth of commitment of its supporters. In part, local control means . . . the freedom to devote more money to the education of one's children . . . . Each locality is free to tailor local programs to local needs. (p. 52)

Education is provided in Texas by local school districts because that is what the population wants. If change is desired then the ultimate solution must come from the lawmakers and from the democratic pressures of those who elect them. (p. 58)

The minority (Justices Brennan, Douglas, Marshall and White) provided three dissenting opinions. Brennan wondered whether the Equal Protection Clause protected only those rights explicitly or implicitly guaranteed by the Constitution, and Marshall (with Douglas concurring) argued that

the right of every American to an equal start in life, so far as the provision of a state service as important as education is concerned, is far too vital to permit state discrimination. (p. 65)

And Justice White (with Brennan and Douglas) tackled the issue of local control. This is excellent as an abstract ideal, but

it provides a meaningful option to Alamo Heights and like school districts but almost none to Edgewood . . . (where) the Texan system utterly fails to extend a realistic choice to parents because the property tax, which is the only revenue-raising mechanism extended to school districts, is practically and logically unavailable. (p. 61)

Alamo Heights residents can tax themselves less than their Edgewood neighbours, and still raise more money for their children's schools. This to the Court majority is not unconstitutional, and can only be changed through the ballot box.

California says yes

The California Supreme Court disagreed with the US Supreme Court, however. In a case similar to *San Antonio*, it decided in 1971 (in *Serrano* v. *Priest*, 487 P2d 1241, 1971) that

this funding scheme invidiously discriminates against the poor because it makes the quality of a child's education a function of the wealth of his parents and neighbors. Recognizing as we must that the right to an education in our public schools is a fundamental interest which cannot be conditioned on wealth, we can discern no compelling state purpose necessitating the present method of financing. We have concluded, therefore, that such a system cannot withstand constitutional challenge and must fall before the equal protection clause. (p. 1224)

The Court noted that in the past wealth classifications had not been found suspect. However, it argued that in those cases discrimination by wealth was not intentional (e.g. *James*, p. 86) whereas in the financing of education by local property taxes it was. Furthermore, it ruled that the discrimination related to education, which is "so important that the state has made it compulsory" (p. 1259). The Californian Supreme Court thus referred the case back to the lower court, requiring the State government to come up with a non-discriminatory system.

The scheme introduced by the State government did not satisfy the original plaintiffs, who returned to the courts. Again, the Californian Supreme Court ruled that greater equity in inter-district financing of schools was needed. It was also asked to reconsider its 1971 decision following the Supreme Court's 1973 ruling on *San Antonio*. Although one judge believed that the California courts should defer to the federal Supreme Court (another dissented because absolute equality was impossible and because taking from the rich to give to the poor was itself in violation of the equal protection clause), the majority upheld the previous finding. They noted (*Serrano* v. *Priest*, 557 P2d 929, 1977) that the system was

> in violation of state and federal constitutional provisions guaranteeing the equal protection of the laws (p. 390) . . . [and that] . . . the fact that a majority of the United States Supreme Court have now chosen to contract the area of active and critical analysis under the strict scrutiny test for federal constitutional purpose can have no effect upon the existing construction and application accorded our own constitutional provision. (p. 951)

The text of the 1971 opinion had focused on the Equal Protection Clause of the United States Constitution, but one footnote had indicated that in addition the financing system violated the California State Constitution. At that time this included the statement (Article I, Section 11) that "all laws of a general nature shall have a uniform operation", and a further clause (Section 21), that "A citizen or class of citizens may not be granted privileges or immunities not granted on the same terms to all citizens". Later in the Constitution (Article IX, Section 1) education is defined as a fundamental right:

> A general diffusion of knowledge and intelligence being essential to the preservation of the rights and liberties of the people, the Legislature shall encourage by all suitable means the promotion of intellectual, scientific, moral, and agricultural improvement.

These provide the context for the Californian courts deciding that, despite the *San Antonio* decision, the inter-district disparities in school financing are unconstitutional. (Note that in 1974 an Amendment to the Californian Constitution introduced the clause – Section 24 – that "Rights guaranteed by this Constitution are not dependent on those guaranteed by the United States Constitution". This was extended in 1981 by a favourable vote on a referendum requiring Californian courts to reflect federal decisions relating to education and busing. The constitutionality of this was upheld by the California Supreme Court, and it became an amendment to the State Constitution. The US Supreme Court affirmed that decision in 1982. The Los Angeles School District has now, as a consequence, ended its mandatory busing programme: Clark, 1984.)

Success in the *Serrano* case, despite the problems of implementing a remedy, encouraged attempts to equalize inter-district financing in other States. Some have followed California's lead, in most cases because the State constitution specifically requires the provision of an educational system. (Full summaries of the situation in the States are given in Stiefel and Berne, 1981; Lawyers' Committee for Civil Rights under Law, 1980: for details of the New York and Washington cases see Andersen, 1979.) In a recent review, Andersen (1982) notes that

> Where the concern is that wealth differences merely result in unequal levels of education, the courts have not been hospitable.

Complaints of unfairness have been more sympathetically received, however, in the context of the relevant State's equal protection clause or its equivalent. Nevertheless, Andersen (1982) shows that some State courts

> have found in the need to preserve local control of funding levels an acceptable justification for a system with the tax and educational consequences there shown. (p. 590)

(Yet another example of judicial respect for local state autonomy.) Only in a few cases, especially those related to need variations between districts (Gaeta, 1982), have courts been prepared to intervene.

Even where courts have intervened, implementation has not been rapid. In most States it involves either or both of replacement of regressive (i.e. property) by progressive (i.e. income) taxes for school financing and State-wide redistribution of revenues to achieve spending equity (see Knickman and Reschovsky, 1980; Odden and Augenblick, 1980). But the principle has been established and some of the fiscal (if not the social and racial) advantages of the tight little suburban islands have been removed. The situation varies between the States, however, for, as Stengel (1980) makes clear, in almost every case based on the Fourteenth Amendment of the United States Constitution the State courts have followed the *San Antonio* decision and have declined to find inter-district disparities unconstitutional. In other States, the nature of the local Constitution is not such that judges are prepared to require fiscal reform. In Pennsylvania, for example, the State Constitution requires that (Article III, Paragraph 14):

> The General Assembly shall provide for the maintenance and support of a thorough and efficient system of public education .

This does not require equity of provision, however, and the State Supreme Court was prepared to leave the definition of "thorough and efficient" to the individual school districts. Furthermore, in the case considered (*Danson* v. *Casey*, 339 A2d 360, 1979), the district concerned, Philadelphia, was spending more than the minimum specified by the State Legislature, so could not be found guilty of failing to provide a "thorough and efficient" education. Not surprisingly perhaps, Stengel (1980) notes that in Pennsylvania full reform of disparities will only be achieved through legislative action. The same is probably true of many other States, despite the gains indicated by *Serrano* and a few other cases, so that there is far from general erosion of this aspect of local autonomy. Victory may be a long time coming, even when it does, as indicated by the prolonged litigation in the New Jersey case (*Robinson* v. *Cahill*, final opinion 360 A2d 400, 1976).

With regard to inter-district disparities in school finance, therefore, the

Supreme Court has declined to intervene. So have a number of State Courts. Only in a few States – California, New Jersey, New York, Pennsylvania, Washington, for example – has litigation been encouraged by the judicial response. Despite this, Andersen (1982) concludes that a decade of such litigation has achieved much:

> Most state systems today are more sensitive to wealth related inequities.... Issues of tax equity are seen more clearly today.... We know much more ... about the measurement of fiscal capacity, alternative funding sources, measurement of educational costs and outcomes, needs of special students, tax burdens and the measurement of effort levels and the variety of equalizing techniques used in various states. (pp. 600–601)

All this has come about, he claims (as does Gambitta, 1981), because the courts have been used to place critical issues on the public agenda. The Supreme Court may have declined to intervene in *San Antonio*, but by hearing the case it has ensured public attention to it and has stimulated debate and – perhaps, eventually – legislative actions.

CONCLUSIONS

One basic change has occurred in educational policy as a result of Supreme Court decisions in the last 40 years – explicit segregation of races in schools is unconstitutional. Since the unanimous decision on this in 1954, and despite much opposition from the general population, State governments, and the federal executive and legislature in the 1950s and the 1970s, the Supreme Court has remained adamant on this point. Whenever it has been clear that racial segregation has been intentionally practised, it has ruled – usually unanimously – that this must end. Furthermore, it has insisted on remedies that ensure racially integrated schools. Thus *de jure* segregation in the dual or "separate but equal" systems of the Southern States has been comprehensively attacked and removed, as has *de facto* segregation in northern school systems wherever the courts, following the precedents set by the Supreme Court, have been sure that there has been intent to separate the races. And in both, busing of children (often in very substantial numbers) has been identified as a proper means of achieving racial balance in schools, overriding the neighbourhood school principle which in most situations would ensure racial segregation because of residential separation.

This unyielding stance has been constrained, however, especially since the Nixon appointees joined the Burger Court, by an unwillingness of the Supreme Court to interfere in the autonomy of the local state where explicit segregation has not been practised. Thus, although the Court would not allow new school districts to be created to avoid integration, it was not prepared to recognize that one of the *raisons d'être* for residence in suburban districts, and the white flight to those districts in recent years, has always been educational provision and the nature of the school environment. As illustrated here, the minority of four on the Court in the early 1970s argued very strongly against this, as they did in the school finance cases. Thus on the three ways of promoting racial segregation in schools (p. 116), only one has been countered fully by Court decisions.

On educational issues, as with those relating to zoning, the Supreme Court has refrained from major interference that would undermine the rationale for the administrative fragmentation of suburban areas. The school districts and municipalities there are properly constituted under State legislation, and as long as they do not explicitly discriminate against racial groups they are not acting in violation of the Fourteenth Amendment: even where they are, the Court has ruled that it is the individual districts that are guilty and must meet the imposed remedy, not the States that created them – or allowed them to be created and so to generate discrimination (Tyler, 1979).

The issues of residential separation by zoning in suburban municipalities and of racial separation because of separate suburban school districts are closely linked, as several authors have recognized (Hains, 1977; Orfield, 1978; Redwine, 1981; Regal, 1976). The Courts have not been prepared to link them in most cases, however – though see the discussion in Chapter 8. Indeed, the links are not easily forged within the constraints of the Fourteenth Amendment, producing Read's (1977, p. 49) conclusion that "it is at least arguable that the limits have been reached in using the Constitution alone as a means for attaining school desegregation". The arena must be shifted, therefore, a subject discussed in Chapter 8.

SEVEN

The distribution of public goods

As indicated in Chapter 1, although land-use and land-user characteristics are the major influences on a neighbourhood's desirability, the provision of public goods to neighbourhoods also affects their perceived quality. And since, as discussed in Chapter 2, most public goods are provided by the local state and are either impure or potentially impurely distributed, then the geography of public goods is determined by the local state and those who control it. It may be, therefore, that the policy adopted by municipal and other governments is unconstitutional because it favours some areas and groups over others. In general, the evidence regarding this is far from conclusive (see Lineberry, 1977, who claims that "municipal governments more often than not achieve a rough equivalence of service among their neighbourhoods" (p. 181), and that where rough equivalence is not achieved the allocation suggests an "unpatterned inequality" (p. 183): see also, however, Boyle and Jacobs, 1982). Nevertheless, cases have been brought challenging the distributions of public goods, largely on the grounds of racial discrimination. This chapter reviews the trend of the decisions – few of which have been made in the Supreme Court.

IMPURE PUBLIC GOODS

Most impure public goods are those that are available at certain locations only, so that consumers may be disadvantaged because they have poor access to the provided services. Given the Court decision that wealth is not a suspect classification, it is unlikely that any challenge on other than racial grounds would be successful. Since, however, the decisions that overthrew "separate but equal" policies covered a wide range of services in addition to education (Witt, 1979, p. 583ff.), it is possible that such challenges could be successful on a variety of issues. But most of the cases have been decided since the inception of the Burger Court, with its strict constructionist majority and its requirement, laid down in *Washington* v. *Davis*, of explicit proof of racially discriminatory intent.

Racial discrimination and non-provision

In *Evans* v. *Abney* (396 US 435, 1970) the impact of the Burger Court majority was illustrated in a 5 : 3 majority decision (Justice Marshall taking no part) regarding an urban park. The land had been willed to Macon City to be used as a park, and it had been made clear that it was to be managed by whites, for whites. In 1966 (in *Evans* v. *Newton*, 382 US 296) the County Council was ordered to desegregate the park. To try and circumvent this, the public trustees were replaced by private ones, but it was ruled that this still involved state activity resulting in racial discrimination. And so, rather than integrate the park the council closed it, and the land reverted to the original heirs. Was this an unconstitutional action?

Writing for the majority (in *Evans* v. *Abney*, 396 US 435, 1970) Justice Black observed that

> when a city park is destroyed because the Constitution requires it to be integrated, there is reason for everyone to be disheartened. (p. 643)

Nevertheless, he interpreted the will as "embodying a preference for terminating the park rather than its integration" (p. 643) and argued, in line with the strict constructionist theory, that

> The responsibility of this Court ... is to construe and enforce the Constitution and laws of the land as they are and not to legislate social policy on the basis of our own personal inclination. (p. 645)

Closing the park treated both races equally, and unfortunate though this may be, it was not unconstitutional.

In a somewhat similar case a year later the same five-man majority ruled that closing a swimming pool disadvantaged all races equally, and so was not a discriminatory act. In 1962 the city of Jackson, Mississippi, operated five swimming pools on a racially segregated basis, four for whites only and one for blacks. The courts ruled that this was racial discrimination and ordered that the pools should be open to members of all races. Instead of complying, however, the City Council closed four of the pools and reverted the lease of the other to the YMCA, which operated it for whites only. In claiming that this was discriminatory, the plaintiffs cited the *Prince Edward County* ruling (see p. 112) that a school district could not close its public schools and reopen them as private schools for whites only supported by State money. But whereas that case, according to Justice Black, writing for the majority in *Palmer* v. *Thompson* (403 US 217, 1971), was concerned with "thinly disguised state discrimination" (p. 443), Jackson City Council did not close the pools and then reopen them in another guise. Nor did it apparently conspire with the YMCA to operate a segregated facility; and, in any case, swimming pools are not mentioned as a fundamental right in the Fourteenth Amendment (p. 442).

The explicit reason for closing the City Council's pools, according to the evidence presented to the Supreme Court, was

> because the city council felt they could not be operated safely and economically on an integrated basis. (p. 644)

This may not have been the real motivation, but

> No case in this Court has held that a legislative act may violate equal protection solely because of the motivations of the men who voted for it . . . it is extremely difficult for a court to ascertain the motivation, or collection of different motivations, that lie behind a legislative enactment. (p. 444)

No evidence had been presented that the City of Jackson was denying people access to publicly-financed swimming pools on the basis of their colour, so no constitutional infringement was involved (as Justice Blackman pointed out in his concurring opinion – p. 447). Chief Justice Burger agreed, arguing that

> We would do a great disservice, both to elected officials and to the public were we to require that every decision of local governments to terminate a desirable service be subjected to microscopic scrutiny for forbidden motives rendering the decision unconstitutional. (pp. 446–447)

Clearly, if a majority sector of the local population wishes to discriminate it should simply not provide the relevant services. In doing so, it may harm itself as well. This is a price it may be prepared to pay in order to avoid integrated facilities. For the relatively affluent – who can afford to pay for private services that are outside the Constitutional remit and who, in any case, are generally opposed to the provision of facilities via the public purse – this is almost certainly a desirable situation. It may generate discrimination by wealth, but this is not forbidden by the Constitution, according to the Supreme Court (p. 130).

The activist minority disagreed with this position in both cases. In *Evans* v. *Abney*, for example, Justice Douglas claimed that the decision "can only be a gesture toward a state-sactioned segregated way of life, now passé" (p. 647), and Justice Brennan argued that "under the Equal Protection Clause a State may not close down a public facility solely to avoid its duty to desegregate that facility" (pp. 648–649). Similarly, in *Palmer* v. *Thompson* Justice Douglas wrote that

> though a State may discontinue any of its municipal services . . . it may not do so for the purpose of perpetuating or installing apartheid or because it finds life in a multiracial community difficult or unpleasant. If that is its reason, the abolition of a designated public service becomes a device for perpetuating a segregated way of life. (p. 453)

Further, with regard to the pool that was not closed,

> if the State has a continuing connection with a swimming pool, it becomes a public facility and the State is under obligation to see that the operators meet all Fourteenth Amendment responsibilities. (p. 449)

Justice White (joined by Brennan and Marshall) argued that there could be no dispute either that the closures were state action or that they were motivated by the desegregation order. The sole motivation was racial:

> The fact is that closing the pool is an expression of official policy that Negroes are unfit to associate with whites (p. 454)

and the closure had a disproportionate effect on members of the minority race. Thus, to the Supreme Court minority, the actions were unconstitutional.

Throughout the 1970s, the Burger Court majority has been prepared to rule against explicit racialism by States and their agencies, upholding the precedents of the Warren Court. But it has required explicit evidence that an action was racially motivated, has refused to accept disproportionate impact as evidence of discrimination, has operated a limited definition of state action, and has accepted municipal autonomy even where this in itself reflects discrimination via "tight little islands". Thus in these two cases it has been prepared to allow discriminatory actions – Justice Black's opinion in *Evans* virtually admits this – because they do not violate its strict criteria. In the provision of impure public goods, it seems, the local state can discriminate by not providing services, or by closing those which it used to provide, in order to avoid serving a racial minority.

Excluding negative externalities

In many neighbourhoods, the introduction of certain land uses generates negative externalities (p. 6) that are likely to lead to a depreciation of the local environment. Zoning regulations, restrictive covenants and other mechanisms are employed to prevent this. Occasionally it happens, however, and recourse to the courts is seen as the means of protecting neighbourhood quality. As the restrictive covenant cases showed (p. 82), the Supreme Court was not prepared to countenance state action which supported explicit racial discrimination, and the *Belle Terre* decision indicated that the Burger Court limited this intrusion to local autonomy in line with its strict constructionist theory (p. 84). Somewhat surprisingly, therefore, the Supreme Court did not hear an appeal from a case that appeared to violate the *Belle Terre* decision, although the precedent set is probably extremely limited.

A large dwelling in the City of Mantoloking, New Jersey, had been willed to an organization which would operate it as a residential home for 10–12 handicapped pre-school children. The property was covered by a restrictive covenant stipulating that it be used for residential purposes only, and the city zoning plan designated the area for single-family dwellings. The case was that both requirements were violated. Regarding the covenant, the New Jersey Supreme Court found no evidence of a violation – the dwelling was being used as a home (although one judge in dissent claimed that it was being used as a "therapeutic institutional operation"). Regarding the zoning, the court found that the use was generating insufficient harm to the local environment, so that neighbourhood quality was not prejudiced, and that the definition of single-family used in the zoning plan (one person living alone or two or more related by blood/marriage/adoption living as a single unit, in both cases with servants) was unduly restrictive.

The majority opinion claimed that the *Belle Terre* precedent and the values it sought to protect were not being overturned but that (*Berger* v. *State of New Jersey*, 364 A2d 933, 1976)

> while municipalities are free . . . to prohibit . . . any use which threatens to erode such values or destroy the residential character of the area, all restrictions must, at the same time, satisfy the demands of due process. Substantive due process requires that zoning regulations be reasonably exercised; they may be neither unreasonable, arbitrary nor capricious. (p. 1002)

Mantoloking's regulations were "sweepingly excessive", and thus "legally unreasonable". Thus the decision places limits to the ability to protect neighbourhood character provided by *Belle Terre* (as also did the *East Cleveland* ruling: p. 85), but it in no way opens the door for widespread introduction of negative externalities to affluent residential areas.

IMPURELY DISTRIBUTED PUBLIC SERVICES

If the potential for discriminating against neighbourhoods and groups by the distribution of impure public services is substantial, and apparently constitutional, that for discrimination via impure distributions is probably greater, because the mechanisms are even less apparent. A decade or more ago, this conclusion appeared questionable, for the courts had ruled in a few cases that equitable distributions were required (Ratner, 1973). One case in particular stimulated such an opinion (*Hawkins* v. *Town of Shaw* – see below) and it was believed that it would lead to reallocation of "everything from police patrols to garbage pickups and park space" (*Time*, 1971, p. 59). But eight years later that opinion

> appears to be merely an interesting footnote in the field of urban law rather than the legal landmark that some observers had forecast. Only ten equalization suits have been initiated in the federal courts since 1971, and of this number, only two have been decided on behalf of the plaintiffs. (Rossum, 1979, p. 2)

The main reason for this, according to Rossum, was the limit imposed by the *Washington* v. *Davis* opinion of the Supreme Court (see p. 88 and Miller, 1977) requiring explicit evidence of racially-motivated state discrimination. Thus little has been achieved, as illustrated below.

Equality in service provision

The supposed landmark decision was handed down by the Court of Appeals for the Fifth Circuit regarding the case of *Hawkins* v. *Town of Shaw* (437 F2d 1286, 1971, and 461 F2d 1171, 1972). In this it was charged that in the town of Shaw, Mississippi, with a population of 2500 (1500 of them black, almost all of whom lived in an exclusively black area: Salih, 1972), the municipal council discriminated against the black residential area in seven ways:

1. 98 per cent of all the homes in Shaw fronting onto unpaved streets were occupied by blacks;
2. black residential areas had street lights with bare bulbs only, whereas all of the newly-obtained high intensity mercury vapour lights had been installed in white areas;
3. 97 per cent of all the homes not served by the municipal sewer were occupied by blacks;
4. white neighbourhoods had underground storm sewers and ditches but the black areas had a haphazard network of poorly maintained ditches only;
5. water pressure was lower in the black neighbourhoods because of smaller bore mains;
6. most fire hydrants were in white areas; and
7. most traffic control signs were in white areas.

This appeared to be a convincing catalogue of discrimination over a long period. The Town Council argued that its allocation procedures were based on objective criteria, professionally determined and not designed to discriminate against blacks. The District Court accepted the argument, but the Court of Appeal did not. It found a *prima facie* case of discriminatory impact that could not be justified as fulfilling a compelling state function (p. 1289). Criteria with regard to the level of provision were not laid down, but the Court ruled in its original opinion that

we have not been guided by a statutory set of standards or regulations clearly defining how many paved streets or what kind of sewerage system a town like Shaw should have. We have, however, been able to utilize what we consider a most reliable yardstick, namely the quality and quantity of municipal services provided in the white area of the town . . . this is an area which, for the most part, does not significantly differ in need or expectation from the black portion of town. Making a comparison between these two areas is hardly a insuperable judicial task. (p. 1292)

The case was reheard, *en banc* by the full complement of circuit judges, and the decision regarding discrimination upheld. Nevertheless, the majority made it clear that they believed they were dealing with a unique situation and were not setting a general precedent:

we do not imply or suggest that every disparity of services between citizens of a town or city creates a right of access to the federal courts for redress. We deal only with the town of Shaw, Mississippi, and the facts as developed in this record. (p. 1173)

The majority identified "neglect involving clear overtones of racial discrimination in the administration of . . . Shaw" (p. 1173); the dissenters did not – one of them writing that "Disparity is the necessary result of the limiting factors of resources and time" (p. 1180). More importantly, the dissenters believed that Shaw was not unique, but rather

> typical of thousands of towns and hundreds of cities in this nation. An examination of any urban gathering of people will highlight the inequalities among the places where they live (p. 1183)

which may be correlated with race, but may – if the analyses were undertaken – be correlated with several other variables besides. They would prefer "solution at the ballot box, rather than dangling the carrot of reform by judicial injunction" (p. 1185) and disagreed with a decision

> which establishes as a principle of law that a court is required to apply the compelling state interest test to a mere *prima facie* case of racial classification in the distribution of municipal services requiring capital expenditures. Such a principle permits the Equal Protection Clause to swallow the entire system of political democracy in state and local government on a procedural determination. (pp. 1180–1181)

In fact, as illustrated throughout this section of the book, the judiciary has not swallowed up local democracy, despite such fears.

Indeed, an earlier decision by a District Court in Alabama indicated that other courts were likely to be difficult to convince with regard to racial discrimination in the distribution of public services. Residents of Prattville had claimed discrimination against blacks in street paving, sidewalk construction, street lighting, fire hydrant, sewer line, traffic light and street sign installation, trash and garbage collection, the provision of recreational facilities, provision of police protection for children against traffic hazards, and hiring for the local police and fire departments. The Court found in favour of the plaintiffs only with regard to the operation of public parks, and ordered that they be desegregated (in *Hadnott* v. *City of Prattville*, 309 F Supp 967, 1970). On most of the other issues, the Court found either that there was no evidence of discrimination against the black residents or that any differences in provision reflected compelling state interests on other grounds. With regard to street paving, for example, it found that although only 3 per cent of the city's whites lived on unpaved streets compared to 35 per cent of blacks, this was because the city paved streets when petitioned to by more than half of the residents, who were charged according to property assessment. Thus the difference

> is due to the difference in the respective landowners' ability and willingness to pay for the property improvements. This difference . . . does not constitute racially discriminatory inequality. The equal protection clause of the Fourteenth Amendment . . . was not designed to compel uniformity in the face of difference. (p. 970)

The decision in *Hawkins* suggested that impurity in the distribution of public goods that discriminated substantially against blacks could only be sustained if it was demonstrated that it fulfilled a justifiable state purpose (i.e. goal of the municipal government), and the *Prattville* decision indicated how this might be done. These decisions were fortified by a further decision of the same Fifth Circuit Court of Appeals that heard the *Hawkins* appeal. The City of Delray Beach, Florida, refused an application to extend its water and sewer systems to a proposed new housing area beyond, but adjacent to, its boundaries; the housing was for low-income farm workers, and was to be subsidized by the federal government. The reasons given for the refusal were:

(1) The land was tentatively zoned for a park, in the recently devised plan for the area;
(2) if the land were to be used for residents, it should be at less than six dwellings per acre and not at the 14–18 per acre, as proposed; and
(3) Delray Beach only extends services to areas that agree to annexation with the municipality.

The case against Delray Beach was that it was using these arguments to prevent development of a low-income housing project that would benefit members of a minority group. In considering this, the court (in *United Farmworkers of Florida Housing Project Inc.* v. *City of Delray Beach, Florida*, 493 F2d 799, 1974) noted that the city had already allowed several deviations from its newly-promulgated Master Plan and that there were at least five exceptions to its annexation requirement. As a result

> we are convinced that the City failed to meet its burden of proving that its refusal was necessary to promote a compelling government interest, and thus that the city officials have deprived the farmworkers that equal protection of the law under the fourteenth amendment. (p. 811)

As with *Hawkins*, services could not be denied to an area where there was strong evidence of racial motives. Could this be extended to cover discrimination in the provision of municipal services on other grounds, such as wealth (Fessler and Hacer, 1971)? It seems not; certainly there is no evidence of widespread judicial preparedness to move in this direction.

Apart from a few cases – such as *Hawkins* and *Delray Beach* – the main trend in judicial decision-making on service-delivery cases has been to dismiss the complaints brought by plaintiffs. Cingranelli (1982, p. 157) suggests that this might have been different if the Warren Court had lasted beyond 1969, for it "hinted that classifications based on wealth were suspect", but there is little evidence to support his contention that the equity of service distributions will become a live judicial issue. Further, Merget and Berger (1982, p. 38) argue that at the State level "Only in the area of financing public education have courts . . . converted the norm of equity into more precise rules for the allocation and distribution of public resources" with the implication that future extension of such rules is unlikely. The judges have preferred to leave decisions about service distributions to local governments, and to locate conflicts over resource allocation in the political rather than the judicial arena (*Fasano* (p. 77) apparently does not apply in this area). Only where there is explicit evidence of racial discrimination will they intervene, it seems. Thus in a case relating to the conditions of parks in the Bronx, New York City (*Beal* v. *Lindsay*, 468 F2d 287, 1972) the Court of Appeals for the Second Circuit accepted that the park serving the black residential area was in a poorer condition than were the other three local parks. But this came about not because of less effort by the city authorities with regard to the first park but because of a greater level of vandalism there. Thus the Court rejected

> the proposition that the equal protection clause not merely prohibits less state effort on behalf of minority racial groups but demands the attainment of equal results. We very much doubt this. (p. 290)

Further, although accepting that the majority decision in *Hawkins* was correct, it was argued that "courts must not hold municipalities to standards of precision that are unattainable in the process of government" (p. 291). Relatively equal input of services is desirable – absent compelling reason otherwise – but the courts seem willing to accept that in most situations the distribution, to use Lineberry's words, is one of "unpatterned inequality".

The location of public housing

Public housing is not a public service similar to those discussed elsewhere in this chapter. Nevertheless, it is publicly provided, and its location is seen by many as an example of an impurely distributed public good. The impurity comes about when public housing is not equally distributed through a jurisdictional territory. To some this is undesirable, because they do not wish to live in "public housing ghettos". To others it is desirable, because public housing is a source of negative externalities. The latter, it seems, have had most influence on location policies for public housing in American cities, producing claims by the former that such manipulation of space is unconstitutional.

Attempts to have location policies regarding public housing altered by court remedy have followed several legal routes. Some cases have been concerned with the failure of local governments to provide public housing (p. 159); others have used relatively recent Congressional legislation (see the next chapter). One case is discussed here, however, because of its focus on public housing as an impurely distributed public good and because the District Court's decision (upheld in a summary decision by the Court of Appeals) was based in part on the decision in *Hawkins* v. *Town of Shaw*.

Public housing in the Cleveland metropolitan area at the time of the case was provided by the Cuyahoga Metropolitan Housing Authority (CMHA); its location policy was circumscribed by the zoning and building regulations of the municipalities within its jurisdiction. In the City of Cleveland, most of the blacks (*c*.96 per cent) lived east of the Cuyahoga river, and in that area nearly all of the black children attended all-black schools. The CMHA had produced schemes to develop public housing in west Cleveland. These had been agreed with the City Council, and building permits had been issued. During the 1971 election campaign, however, candidates in one group undertook to revoke those permits in any area where the majority of the residents opposed the project. They were elected, and fulfilled their campaign pledge. Blacks who had hoped to live in those west-side projects claimed that this was unconstitutional, and asked for an injunction to prevent the permits being revoked.

In its decision on this request, the District Court (in *Banks* v. *Perk*, 341 FSupp. 1175, 1972) argued that "this nation is committed to a policy of balanced and dispersed public housing" (p. 1179) and that

> Since this city is faced with such a massive segregation problem, a dispersal of housing patterns seems to be the most reasonable alternative to a massive busing program in order to eliminate the resulting segregation in the public schools. (p. 1178)

On these grounds, it reasoned that the City Council could only revoke the permits for demonstrable good cause, otherwise the racially discriminatory effect of such action would be construed as contrary to the Fourteenth Amendment. It found that

> There was no factual basis on which to revoke the permits here in question. The revocations were arbitrary, capricious and not in the furtherance of any compelling governmental interest (p. 1179) . . . [and so the defendants] . . . should be ready and willing to take such steps as are necessary to insure that they and their agents do not in any way hinder the efforts of CMHA to build public housing on the west side and to place Blacks therein. (p. 1180)

The plaintiffs also alleged that the CMHA operated a discriminatory policy in the allocation of tenants – blacks to public housing projects in already black residential areas, and whites to projects in white areas. Further, they alleged that CMHA by focusing its projects in east Cleveland was furthering segregation. The Court agreed; CMHA had been contributing to racial segregation in Cleveland and should both extend its activities in west Cleveland and halt its practice of allocating black tenants to black areas.

Following the decision in *Hawkins* v. *Town of Shaw*, the District Court disagreed with the CMHA's argument that plaintiffs should prove that they had a motive to discriminate in their public housing policies. The Court argued that

> If this standard were to be applied, it would be very difficult to prove a violation in a civil rights case. Actual intent or motive need not be proven. (p. 1183)

Thus, because of the policies of both the CMHA and the City Council elected in 1971,

> The plaintiffs and the class they represent have suffered and, even with this injunction, will continue to suffer the loss of safe, sanitary, decent and integrated housing; the loss

of achieving integrated schools without the necessity of massive busing; the loss of housing which is accessible to jobs; and the loss of being unable to escape the never-ending and seemingly unbreakable cycle of poverty . . . The mere fact of a severe infringement on the plaintiffs' Fourteenth Amendment rights has been substantially proven is proof enough of irreparable injury. (p. 1185)

The remedy, the Court decided, would need the CMHA to concentrate all its new projects in the west side. Even so, it would be a very long time before this policy of dispersal provided a spatial basis for racial integration in Cleveland.

This decision suggested, along with the earlier one in *Hawkins* and that on educational resources discussed in the next section, that the Fourteenth Amendment could be used by blacks to obtain both an equal distribution of public services and access to all residential areas. But, as with integrated schooling, white flight could allow integrated housing to be avoided by the affluent (see p. 122). Even more important, the Supreme Court decisions built on *Washington* v. *Davis* (p. 88) changed the ground rules for proving Fourteenth Amendment cases, and prevented further successful litigation built on the *Banks* v. *Perk* precedent.

Unequal schooling

Educational resources can be allocated by a School Board (the body operating a school district) in a variety of ways. Formulae can be used so that the allocation matches some agreed measure of need. Or a variety of other motives can be employed, with the result that some schools, and hence some segments of the population, are advantaged over others. Of course equality of resource provisions does not necessarily imply equality in outputs: the amount spent per pupil in a school is not always a good index of the quality of the education. Nevertheless, it is difficult to identify indices to guide allocation that do not require either equality of treatment (in expenditure per child, for example, and in staff:student ratio) or inequality that is justified on explicit criteria (such as compensatory education for deprived children).

Evidence of intra-district variations in resource provision has been provided in analyses of three Michigan school districts (Mandel, 1975). The conclusions were that intra-district variations, on such indices as average teacher's salary (a measure of teacher quality) and per pupil expenditure, were greater than inter-district variations. Analyses of these intra-district differences produced conflicting results. In Detroit, for example, expenditure per pupil increased with the socio-economic status of the school catchment area and with the percentage of its students who were white, whereas in Flint the relationship with SES was a reversed-J form. Mandel concludes that in addition to concern about inter-district variations (as expressed in the *Rodriguez* and *Serrano* cases) concern about equalizing educational resources must address itself . . . to inequality between schools within the same district and classes within the same school. (pp. 88–89)

Expressing that concern in litigation has not been undertaken substantially. In part, Hornby and Holmes (1972) argue, this is because the Supreme Court has not provided sufficient precedent:

> it has referred broadly to the importance of education in American life, but never has it specifically identified education as a fundamental interest that sparks a special protection analysis. (p. 1138)

All of its decisions relating to education have referred to the impact of racial segregation on the educational process and it has nowhere indicated that education is a fundamental right that must be equally provided, irrespective of race, religion, wealth or any other factor. (This is the basis of the *Rodriguez* opinion. State Constitutions may, of course, be more explicit about education being a fundamental right.)

The issue has been tackled in one case only. It was built on the basis of racially-motivated discrimination, and was not appealed to the Supreme Court. The District of Columbia's "separate but equal" school system was dismantled in 1954 – following the decision, delivered with *Brown I*, in *Bolling* v. *Sharpe*, 347 US 497, 1954. It was replaced by a neighbourhood school system which meant that, because of the extreme segregation of blacks from whites in the federal capital, most of the elementary schools were either more than 90 per cent white or more than 90 per cent black (Horowitz, 1977; Baratz, 1975a). Optional zones were introduced in mixed neighbourhoods (see p. 116), allowing whites in those areas to transfer their children to all-white schools. (There was no busing, so blacks could not afford this option and send their children to any alternative under-enrolled school.) And in all schools a "tracking" system was used whereby students were allocated to a track according to ability. Most remained in their initial classification, which tended to increase segregation.

Attempts to get changes to the system via political pressure failed , and in 1966 the first of a series of cases (*Hobson* v. *Hansen*) was filed by a civil rights activist against the DC Board of Education. The District Court found in his favour, ruling that there had been racial discrimination in the disbursement of funds, and that (in *Hobson* v. *Hansen* 269 F2d 401, 1967):

> If whites and Negroes or rich and poor are to be consigned to separate schools in the District of Columbia . . . the minimum the Constitution will require and guarantee is that for their objectively measurable aspects the schools should be run on a basis of real equality, at least unless any inequalities are adequately justified. (p. 496)

For a remedy, the Court realized that because of the overwhelming majority (93 per cent) of black students in the capital, integration via busing would not be feasible. Thus it laid down a six-point remedy (outlined in detail in Baratz, 1975b) which required the School Board to produce a plan to remove racial and economic discrimination and to report annually on its compliance with the remedy.

The School Board decided not to appeal, so the Superintendent resigned. An individual Board member did appeal, but the Court of Appeals did not overturn (see Horowitz, 1977). And so the Board set out to comply with the District Court's remedy. In 1969 Hobson, by then an elected member of the Board, went back to the District Court claiming that "compliance" with the remedy was not equalizing per-pupil expenditure and asking for a new remedy that would require expenditure per pupil in all schools to be within 5 per cent of the DC mean, for all elementary schools.

The Court agreed with the claim, noting (in *Hobson* v. *Hansen*, 372 F2d 843, 1971) that

> the best data now available to this court indicates that there is still a substantial differential in per pupil expenditures, which favors elementary schools West of the Park [i.e. the white residential areas] and that a *prima facie* case of violation of the 1967 decree seems to have been made out. (p. 846)

The Judge invited the Board to indicate why it could not equalize expenditures to within 5 per cent of the mean. The Board's response (see Baratz, 1975b, p. 55) was that it was not discriminating, that any pattern of expenditures was "completely random", and that per-pupil expenditure was in any case a poor measure of educational opportunity. The Court found against the Board, requiring a 5 per cent maximum deviation in expenditures, except in certain allowed circumstances (Baratz, 1975b, pp. 57–58), and an annual report on each school providing 18 different pieces of information. The Board voted to comply, and did not appeal.

The case of *Hobson* v. *Hansen* created a considerable amount of academic interest, not least for Judge Wright's complaints about the elaborate statistical analyses presented by social science expert witnesses at the second hearing, which seemed to

> lose sight of the disadvantaged youngster . . . in an overgrown garden of numbers and charts and jargon like standard deviation of the variable, statistically significant and Pearson product moment correlations. (p. 859)

(On this broader issue, see Horowitz, 1977.) Although it achieved greater equalization of resources within the District of Columbia (but to little effect with regard to racial discrimination, for by 1975 the DC school enrolment was 97 per cent black; Baratz, 1975a) it had little impact outside. The reason, according to Horowitz, was that subsequent Supreme Court decisions invalidated much of the *Hobson* decision. In 1972, a ruling on a case relating to discriminatory effect in welfare programmes – some programmes were less well funded than others and minority groups tended to suffer accordingly – the Court found that the formulae were not irrational, so that the differential impact was not unconstitutional (the case was *Jefferson* v. *Hackney*, 406 US

535, 1972). Welfare programmes provide privileges to the recipients, however, whereas education might be considered a right. But in the *Rodriguez* decision (p. 130), the Supreme Court ruled that, at least under the federal Constitution, no right to education is conferred. As a result, according to Horowitz, by 1973 the constitutional basis of the *Hobson* decision and remedy had been undermined; if the School Board had appealed, it may well have had the decision overturned.

CONCLUSIONS

Many public services must, by their nature, be impure in their distribution; most others are readily impurely distributed. Thus there is great potential for local governments to manipulate distributions to benefit certain areas, and hence groups living there, and to disadvantage others. There can be little doubt that this happens. In some cases, it represents the outcome of explicit discrimination against certain groups – defined by race and by wealth in particular. Only the first of these is a suspect classification according to judicial interpretations of the Fourteenth Amendment. Where it has been proven, courts have been willing to insist on an equalization remedy. But apparent discrimination by race (or by wealth) can in many cases be readily accounted for on other criteria, so that evidence supporting a viable Fourteenth Amendment case is hard to establish and support. As a result, there would appear to be little hope that inequalities in the provision of public services will be rendered impossible by judicial decree. This element of the conflict over neighbourhood characteristics is not readily accorded the treatment given aspects of educational and land-use policy.

EIGHT

Removing municipal autonomy?
Civil rights v. the suburban majority

The discussion in the previous three chapters has indicated that with one major exception – racial discrimination in schools – the Supreme Court has handed down no decisions that substantially erode the autonomy of local governments with regard to land-use planning, fiscal independence, and the allocation of services. It still requires that there be no explicit racial motivation to municipal policies, but in general it has declined to impose the sorts of constraints to municipal autonomy that various groups – including the activist minority still on the Court – would wish. Some State courts have been a little more compliant with these demands, notably in recognizing education as a fundamental right under local Constitutions and in finding discrimination by wealth in the provision of education unacceptable. But other State court decisions, especially those on land-use planning, have proved to be at best hollow victories for the proponents of "opening up the suburbs".

In summary, therefore, several decades of conflict in the Courts have failed to undermine the rationale for separate municipalities in the suburban aureole of American metropolitan areas. Exclusionary zoning is still widely practised. The separate school districts are almost all dominated by white students. Suburban residents can provide a high quality education for their children in most States at relatively low cost to themselves, and without substantially contributing to the costs of educating those living elsewhere. And local decision-making on the allocation of services within a territory can discriminate against areas – as long as there is no racial motive that is explicit and undefendable on other grounds. The Courts have very largely acted as protectors of suburban separateness.

How, then, can this be changed? Given the failure of the "conflict via the courts" strategy, what can be done to open up the suburbs? Two major avenues are open. One is to use the State governments to remove the privileges of the suburban municipalities and to impose forms of local government which deny to small groups the potential for opting-out. The other is to use the federal system. The pitfalls of both are outlined here, with especial attention in the last part of the chapter to a series of decisions by the Warren Court that has diminished the chances of success with either.

STATE ACTION

All local governments in America – municipalities, school districts, special districts, townships etc. – obtain their powers and authority from their relevant State governments. Thus these could be revoked or altered by legislative action (see Danielson, 1976, p. 278). Why, in general, have they not?

State restrictions on local action

In 1969, the Legislature of the State of Massachusetts passed a *Zoning Appeals Law* (widely known as the Anti-Snob Zoning Law: Danielson, 1976, pp. 300ff.; Krefetz, 1979) providing "for the construction of low or moderate income housing in cities and towns in which local restrictions hamper such construction". This was passed despite considerable opposition from legislators representing suburban areas, especially around Boston where exclusionary zoning is common. The law provided an appeals procedure whereby developers baulked by exclusionary zoning might apply to a Housing Appeals Committee which could override the local decision. In addition, a quota was set which specified that each local government would have met its need to provide for subsidized housing if low cost housing either constituted at least 10 per cent of all dwelling units there or occupied at least $1 \cdot 5$ per cent of all developed land; an annual construction rate of $0 \cdot 3$ per cent of the municipality's area (or ten acres in municipalities of less than $0 \cdot 5$ square miles) indicated satisfactory progress towards meeting these norms.

The effect of the law has been relatively slight, and alone it will undoubtedly not lead to an "opening up of the suburbs". Its main success has been in encouraging the construction of low-cost housing for the elderly in the suburbs:

> Suburban officials apparently do not object to the idea of creating housing opportunities in their communities for Senior Citizens on fixed incomes. This is probably because the elderly are seen as both "deserving" and "unthreatening". As one observer has snidely remarked: "Old people as a rule are not dangerous. They do not, as a rule, produce children. (Krefetz, 1979, p. 291)

One reason why it has had little effect apart from this is that it is a passive piece of legislation that leaves the control of zoning in local hands, relies on developers proposing low- and medium-income housing projects with no positive obligation on the local community (which retains oversight of building standards), and sets very modest quotas. All of this resulted from political compromise designed to get the measure passed (the bill went through 15 drafts in subcommittee: Krefetz, 1979, p. 297).

The political compromise was necessary because of the concentration of legislative power in suburban areas, as Danielson (1976) makes clear. In other States, attempts to open up the suburbs have been less successful than those undertaken in Massachusetts: Danielson (1976, p. 289) cites failure to pass measures seeking to control exclusionary zoning in the legislatures of Illinois, New York, Pennsylvania and Wisconsin, and he outlines in some detail the failure of New Jersey proposals where:

> For most members of the legislature, the message came through loud and clear, particularly in an election year in which few wanted to campaign with the burden of having opposed home rule and having favored low-income housing in the suburbs. (p. 297)

Reorganization of local government

Instead of changing the legislative context within which local governments act, State governments could change the local government structure itself. This would presumably involve removing the incorporation facility for new municipalities and creating new local government units covering entire built-up areas, thereby denying any local autonomy *within* suburbia.

The case for metropolitan government has been put very frequently by academic observers. Gorham and Glazer (1976), for example, claim that

> If planning has values for an urban area, then clearly it must be metropolitan planning, because the entire metropolis forms a single market at least for jobs, for transportation, for recreation and culture, and usually a single environment for air, water, and waste. Such planning would best be done within common political institutions. (p. 8)

At the same time, efficiency in providing services would be achieved through scale economies (and spatial economies; see Barlow, 1981, for some interesting Canadian examples), and there would be greater fiscal equity between central city and suburbs.

Since local governments are created by (or allowed to be created by) State legislatures, it is for those bodies to take the initiative and to dissolve the fragmented system. But in almost every State, despite efforts by some legislators, no such major initiatives have been taken. In many States, the legislature plays a passive role in that it will allow metropolitan governmental units to be formed, if the local population desire it, and express that desire in a referendum. But few have been approved by the voters, in general because metropolitan government is not in the interests of most suburban residents, who tend to be both the more active politically (relative to central city residents) and most likely to vote on the issue. (On this, see *inter alia*, Hallman, 1977, and Honey, 1976.) And where metropolitan government has been voted for, it has in almost every case been for a restricted range of services only (as in Indianapolis' Uni-Gov, p. 126, which excluded education); the suburbs have retained their control over crucial functions, such as land-use planning and education, and have not yielded their power over the purse. (In Minnesota, legislation allocates increases in tax yields – the result of property-value inflation – to municipalities and other units on a per capita basis: Weaver, 1972.)

This failure to provide for comprehensive metropolitan government and planning reflects on the entrenched interests of local groups which benefit from the present situation. This consists mainly, but not entirely, of the suburban residents. In some central cities, the black voters now control the local government, but they would be in a minority in a metropolitan government (Bryce and Martin, 1976). The only widely-applied concession to metropolitan government has been in response to federal initiatives. Increasingly, in recent decades, local governments have been recipients of federal aid for the amelioration of urban problems (much of this money has been channelled through State governments). A number of the federal programmes require certain local conditions to be met, including some form of regional government. Honey (1976) lists several such programmes, including: the Federal Aid to Highways Act, 1962, which provides funds for highway construction; the Housing Act, 1965, which requires regional plans; the Demonstration Cities and Metropolitan Development Act, 1966 (known as the "Model Cities" Act) which allocated money to designated regional planning agencies; the Intergovernmental Cooperation Act, 1968, which required regional agencies to process local applications for federal funds; and the Housing and Urban Development Act, 1968, which included a requirement for comprehensive metropolitan land-use plans. The usual response to these requirements has been the creation of a metropolitan Council of Governments, or similar body. These are voluntary bodies, whose members are the various local governments of the metropolitan area concerned. Their number increased very rapidly in the late 1960s (nearly 100 were created in 1968 alone) in response to the federal initiatives. Most lack either substantial fiscal resources or powers to enforce particular plans on members. They are advisory only, providing meeting places for local politicians and bureaucrats and acting as intermediaries with State and federal governments. They have in no way overridden the local autonomy of the constituent municipalities, counties, school and special districts. In effect, they are special districts, created largely to obtain federal aid (which is now being provided in block grants rather than through special programmes for which application was needed). Thus, they are

> a useful development because they advance interlocal cooperation and help adapt local government to the conditions of metropolitan areas. They have created a forum for local elected officials to meet, share information, exchange ideas, bargain, and come up with cooperative solutions to common problems ... (But) As planning vehicles most of them are failures ... (and they) only have a modest potential for dealing with unplanned growth as long as they lack authority over implementation measures. (Hallman, 1977, pp. 77–78)

Metropolitan Councils of Government (COGs) are not likely to be the catalysts of major changes in metropolitan government, therefore. Indeed, as presently constituted, most of them are biased in favour of the suburbs and municipal fragmentation, because representation is of units of government not population (Danielson *et al.*, 1977, p. 73). In general, the cause of suburban autonomy is promoted, leading to the conclusions that

> In the larger, more politically fragmented, and highly differentiated metropolitan areas, area wide government is an idea whose time has passed. Attachment to the existing decentralized political system is deep in both city and suburb (Danielson *et al.*, 1977, p. 76) . . . [and] Short of a compelling state interest to change the governance of metropolitan areas − and it is hard to imagine how that would arise − widespread movement toward metropolitan-wide government is unlikely. (Gorham and Glazer, 1976, p. 8)

FEDERAL INTERVENTION

The United States' Constitution severely constrains the ability of the federal government to become involved in the activities of local governments, and thus in the planning and organization of metropolitan areas. These are functions reserved to the States by the Tenth Amendment, which could only be altered by Constitutional amendment re-allocating powers to Washington. Since such an amendment must be ratified by the legislatures of at least three-quarters of the States (Article V), the inbuilt protection of States' rights is seen to be almost unbreachable.

All that the federal government can do with regard to metropolitan land use, planning, and governmental issues is to stimulate (as in the example of GOGs, discussed above). It can attempt this because of its financial power within the federal structure (and also its ability, according to Reagan (1972) through the Commerce Clause, to control the development of the capitalist space-economy: see also G. L. Clark, 1981). Thus

> Congress cannot outlaw billboards on highways, because billboard regulation is not among the enumerated powers of Congress in the U.S. Constitution. But the federal government, through its power to tax and spend, can provide financial assistance to the states to build highways and then pass a law threatening to withdraw financial aid, if the states do not outlaw billboards themselves. (Dye, 1969, p. 45)

The more aid that is offered, and the more that the State and local governments are unable to refuse it, the more control the federal government obtains − as does the State government which both channels federal funds and allocates its own (Clark and Dear, 1981).

The federal executive can also become directly involved in court cases, in which it is not one of the original parties. The system of *amicus curiae* (friend of the court) briefs allows interested parties, with the court's approval, to participate in a case that raises fundamental issues, and the "friend" may even take over the detailed pleading. Since such activity is voluntary, its use depends on the attitude of the Executive (especially the President and the Attorney-General) to particular types of case. Finally, Federal legislation can require judicial intervention by the executive on behalf of individuals claiming injury under federal law.

The Federal Government and suburban exclusion

Many federal policies have promoted suburban development and the residential segregation that has accompanied it (Harvey, 1975b), most of them inadvertantly. A few policies have been designed to change that, and to open up the suburbs, not merely by eliminating all discriminatory practices associated with federal loans (especially for housing) but also by seeking to ensure a more balanced provision of housing types throughout suburbia (of the type suggested by the New Jersey court decisions: p. 94).

The key element in this opening-up process has been provided by what is known as "fair housing", or "open housing". In this federal action lagged behind State and local initiatives (though these were not all popular, and some, as in Berkeley, were defeated in referenda: Casstevens, 1965). Dayton, Ohio, developed a fairshare regional housing plan, for example (see Danielson, 1976, p. 250ff.), as did Chicago (see Berry, 1979). But in order for such plans to be effective, strong federal support, including finance, was needed.

The federal government realized the need to provide better housing for lower-income people in its Housing Act of 1937, which provided subsidies to local governments operating approved schemes. It could not require such schemes, however, as a federal court made clear in 1974. Five suburbs of Cleveland, Ohio (including the City of Euclid; see p. 74), had decided not to cooperate with the Department of Housing and Urban Development in the development of lower-income housing projects within their territories. They were sued by individuals who claimed that as a consequence their right to live in those municipalities, as defined under the Fourteenth Amendment, was violated. The Court disagreed. Referenda had been held in the municipalities (see the *Valtierra* decision, p. 86), and under the 1937 Act (*Mahaley* v. *Cuyahoga Metropolitan Housing Authority*, 500 F2d 1087, 1974):

> the federal legislation does not purport to require that local governments accept this (aid) or to outlaw local referendums on whether the aid should be accepted. (p. 1091)

Following the general doctrine of municipal autonomy, and lacking any proof of racially discriminatory intent (which a dissenting judge claimed was there; p. 1099), the Act implies

> that it is for the municipalities to decide whether they need low-rent housing and whether they desire to sign cooperation agreements. There is no basis to infer discrimi-

nation upon the part of a municipality from doing what it has a lawful right to do. (p. 1092)

Fair housing

Clearly a stronger federal initiative than the 1932 Act was needed if the suburbs were to be prised open. Two events in 1968 apparently provided the catalyst for such an initiative and, more importantly, the backing for its successful implementation.

The first of these events was the passing of the Civil Rights legislation, which included, as Title VIII, what has become known as the Fair Housing Act (U.S. Public Law 90–284). The preamble to this states that

> It is the policy of the United States to provide, within constitutional limitations, for fair housing throughout the United States.

Discrimination in the provision of housing, including the financing of housing, was to be forbidden. Any aggrieved party could file a complaint with the Secretary of the Federal Department of Housing and Urban Development (HUD) charging discrimination and if, after 30 days, compliance had not been obtained, the party could go to court. Specifically defined as discrimination in the Act were:

(1) a refusal to sell or rent a property, after receipt of a *bona fide* offer, or to negotiate a sale or rental because of race, colour, religion or national origin (RCRNO);

(2) to vary the terms of sale or rental because of RCRNO;

(3) to publish anything that suggests discrimination on the grounds of RCRNO;

(4) to deny that a property is available, when it is, because of RCRNO; and

(5) to induce an owner to sell or rent a property with regard to potential entry on the grounds of RCRNO.

The second event was the decision of the Supreme Court in the case of *Jones* v. *Alfred H. Mayer Co.* (392 US 409, 1968). In this, a black complained that he had been discriminated against, under the 1866 Civil Rights Act, on the grounds that he had been refused the right to buy a house in St. Louis because of his race. The Court upheld his complaint (with two dissenters – Harlan and White), arguing that the 1866 Act was intended, as indicated by a review of the Congressional debates then, to prohibit all discrimination on the grounds of race. The Act aimed at removing the "badges of slavery" including the right to buy and lease property, whether the discrimination was state-backed or private (the dissenters believed it applied only to state-backed discrimination). The Court majority found that the Act was properly passed under the Thirteenth Amendment, and that in effect all racial discrimination in housing markets was unconstitutional (it was not, however, a comprehensive fair housing act: p. 1193). Note, however, that in a later decision (*Lindsey* v. *Normet*, 405 US 56, 1972) the Court did not extend this right to one of equality in standard of housing. Writing for a majority of five (only seven Justices participated in the case) on an issue relating to the payment of rents, Justice White remarked that:

> We do not denigrate the importance of decent, safe, and sanitary housing. But the Constitution does not provide judicial remedies for every social and economic ill. We are unable to perceive in that document any constitutional guarantee of access to dwellings of a particular quality . . . . Absent constitutional mandate, the assurance of adequate housing and the definition of landlord–tenant relationships are legislative, not judicial, functions. (pp. 50–51)

Together, the Fair Housing Act and the *Jones* decision should ensure the absence of discriminatory practices. Berry (1979, Ch. 3) reviews the use of the *Jones* precedent in Chicago, and shows that it was generally successful. And the Courts have backed up the Fair Housing Act. In *Trafficante* v. *Metropolitan Life Insurance Co.* (409 US 205, 1972) the Supreme Court ruled unanimously in favour of residents of an apartment block in San Francisco who claimed that discrimination by their landlord injured them in that:

> (1) they had lost the social benefits of living in an integrated community; (2) they had missed business and professional advantage which would have accrued if they had lived with members of minority groups; (3) they had suffered embarassment and economic damage in social, business and professional activities from being "stigmatised" as residents of a "white ghetto". (p. 418)

(This ruling was given despite doubts regarding the standing of the complainants; they were already residents of the block and were not individually discriminated against.) And in 1979 the Court found in favour of complainants against the actions of a real estate company which "steered" black potential buyers away from certain areas and so prevented their development as integrated communities (*Gladstone Realtors* v. *Village of Bellwood*, 441 US 91, 1979). (Again, there was an issue of standing, because the "potential black buyers" were "testers" employed for the case and were not *bona fide* clients of the realtors. For this reason, Justices Rehnquist and Stewart dissented.) Another unanimous decision (with Justice Rehnquist not participating), found that a local ordinance banning "For Sale" and "Sold" notices was unconstitutional, under the First Amendment which provides for freedom of speech. The ordinance was introduced because it was believed that the number of signs suggested a very high level of property turnover and stimulated a "white flight" panic. Justice Marshall (in *Linmark Associates and William Millman* v. *Township of Willingborough and Gerald Daly*, 431 US 85, 1977) noted that the purpose of the ordinance was "promoting stable, racially integrated housing", but found that respondents had

> failed to establish that this ordinance is needed to insure that Willingborough remains an integrated community. (p. 163)

Thus no compelling state purpose was identified that allowed suppression of free speech and the presentation of information about the community. In an earlier case, a Court of Appeals had come to a contrary opinion, ruling (*Barrick Realty Incorporated* v. *City of Gary, Indiana*, 491 F2d 161, 1974) that the absence of signs did not frustrate prospective buyers and did not differentially affect blacks.

More significant with regard to the Act, perhaps, is whether discriminatory intent must be proved in order to indicate a violation or whether a differential impact is sufficient (for Fourteenth Amendment cases, as indicated above, discriminatory intent must be shown; the key precedent is *Washington* v. *Davis* – see p. 88). Several cases heard in the Courts – but not successfully appealed to the Supreme Court – have led to the conclusion that differential impact is sufficient:

> Action which results in a predictable, disproportionate racial effect, such as the exclusion of minorities from a white neighbourhood, establishes a *prima facie* case of illegal discrimination. (Jorgensen, 1981, p. 213)

Note that in the *Arlington Heights* case, the Supreme Court ruled only on the Fourteenth Amendment challenge, and returned the issue to the District Court for a decision relating to the Fair Housing Act. On appeal (in *Metropolitan Housing Development Corporation* v. *Village of Arlington Heights*, 558 F2d 1283, 1977) it was decided that

> defendant has a statutory obligation to refrain from zoning policies that effectively foreclose the construction of any low-cost housing within its corporate boundaries (p. 1285) . . . [and the Court could not] . . . agree that the Congress in enacting the Fair Housing Act intended to permit municipalities to systematically deprive minorities of housing opportunities simply because those municipalities act discreetly. (p. 1290)

Other decisions uphold this interpretation. The Mayor of Philadelphia resisted the development of subsidized public housing there, which it was claimed was racially motivated and was discriminatory under the Act; the Court found against him (*Resident Advisory Board* v. *Rizzo*, 564 F2d 126, 1977) and the Supreme Court denied the application for a writ of *certiorari*. (This action by the Supreme Court appears to uphold the differential impact interpretation. More importantly, so does a labour case, brought under Title VII of the Civil Rights act which deals with equality of employment opportunity. In *Griggs* v. *Dike Power Company* (401 US 424, 1971; see also *Albemarle Paper Company* v. *Moody*, 422 US 405, 1975) Chief Justice Burger wrote for a unanimous Court that pre-employment tests, such as possession of a diploma and a general intelligence test, that disproportionately affected black employment prospects and were not necessary to identify ability to undertake the job applied for, were discriminatory. *Washington* v. *Davis* might have produced a different conclusion had it been fought on these grounds.)

Together, the Fair Housing Act, the Court decisions relating to it, plus

Court decisions under the 1866 Civil Rights Act, support the goal of integrated housing throughout the metropolitan area by prohibiting racial discriminatory policies and impacts. Not all judgements went in that direction, however. Plans for low-income housing on a former USAF base in Nassau County, New York, were abandoned, except for the provision for senior citizens (most of which is occupied by whites). Such abandonment of plans discriminated against blacks hoping to move to the area, it was claimed, especially as white senior citizens were not similarly affected. But the Court of Appeals ruled that the municipality was not required to construct low-income housing (in *Acevedo* v. *Nassau County, New York*, 500 F2d 1078, 1974): "This is clearly not required by any provision of the Constitution" (p. 1081). Note, however, the earlier decision – preceding the 1968 Fair Housing Act – favouring a group of minority residents of a city who claimed they could no longer live there because the redevelopment programme did not adequately meet the needs of low-income residents: *Norwalk CORE* v. *Norwalk Redevelopment Agency* (395 F2d 920, 1968).

Although the 1968 Act and the Court decisions did much to outlaw discriminatory practices, they did relatively little to promote any "opening up of the suburbs". If blacks cannot afford suburban housing then there will be no overt discrimination. Only if positive action is taken to provide low-income housing in the suburbs will integration be achieved.

This issue was clarified by a Supreme Court decision relating to the operation of the Chicago Housing Authority (CHA) in its construction of low-income homes, using HUD financial backing. It was claimed that CHA/HUD were responsible for *de jure* racial segregation because of both the site selection process for public housing and the tenant allocation procedure. There was extended litigation over this, beginning in 1966 (see Berry *et al.*, 1976; Mercer and Hultquist, 1976). It was finally settled in the Court of Appeals in 1974 (in *Gautreaux* v. *Chicago Housing Authority*, 503 F2d 930, 1974) when ex-Supreme Court Justice Clark noted that a reader of the case history

> quickly discovers a callousness on the part of the appellees towards the rights of the black, underprivileged citizens of Chicago that is beyond comprehension. (p. 932)

HUD had apparently decided that it was better to fund a segregated public housing system than no system, but the Court of Appeal ruled for

> the adoption of a comprehensive metropolitan area plan that will not only disestablish the segregated public housing system in the City of Chicago which has resulted from CHA's and HUD's unconstitutional site selection and tenant assignment procedures but will increase the supply of dwelling units as rapidly as possible. (p. 939)

This opinion was handed down after the *Milliken* decision (p. 124), but the Court majority held that *Milliken* did not forbid a metropolitan-wide remedy in this case because there was no long tradition of local control of public housing, and there was both a pervasive pattern of federal involvement and clear segregation throughout the metropolitan area. (A similar remedy was handed down for metropolitan Cleveland in *Banks* v. *Perk* – 341 F Supp 1175, 1972.)

HUD appealed, not because it denied the "crime" of which it had been convicted, but because it was unsure whether it could properly take remedial action outside the City of Chicago. Such a remedy, it was felt, required HUD to ignore local autonomy and political processes. A unanimous Supreme Court (with Justice Stevens not participating) disagreed – *Hills* v. *Gautreaux*, 425 US 284, 1976. Justice Stewart wrote that

> a judicial order directing relief beyond the boundary line of Chicago will not necessarily entail coercion of uninvolved government units (p. 804) . . . [and that it] . . . need not abrogate the role of local governmental units in the federal housing-assistance programs. Under the major housing program in existence . . . local housing authorities and municipal governments had to make application for funds or approve the use of funds in the locality before HUD could make housing assistance money available (pp. 806–807)

so local autonomy was protected.

The situation appears to have been created, therefore, where on the one hand zoning and other practices aimed at excluding the low-income were unconstitutional and/or illegal because they had a disproportionate effect on blacks but local autonomy in the oversight of low-income developments in the suburbs was to be retained. In effect, the Act was not broad enough in scope, and judicial relief was insufficient, since it did not require regional housing plans. This was recognized in the passage of the Housing and Community Development Act of 1974 (Public Law 93–383) which replaced a variety of federal programmes, most of which provided funding for capital infrastructure projects, by a block grant system. To qualify for a grant (a Community Development Block Grant, CDBG) municipalities must submit, and have approved by HUD, a Housing Assistance Plan (HAP) which assesses local needs for lower income housing and which acts as an entitlement for HUD housing subsidies (only local governments with population exceeding 50 000 are covered by this legislation). As T. A. Clark (1982a) points out, this legislation requires municipalities to balance the advantages of a CDBG against the disadvantages of the zoning requirements in the HAP; small, affluent municipalities may decide to forego federal aid. This may not prevent the construction of low-income housing there, since HUD is able, under the Act, to deal directly with local developers. Nevertheless, it is likely to reduce the likelihood of subsidized housing projects.

Some of the implications of the CDBG system were tested in a case referring to Hartford, Connecticut. The City of Hartford sought to prevent HUD allocating funds to certain suburban municipalities because their estimates of the needs for low-income housing (under the HAP) were either unrealistic or improperly derived. Allocating money to them would impact unfairly on the City, which housed 90 per cent of the metropolitan area's poor. The case *City of Hartford* v. *Towns of Glastonbury* (561 F2d 1032, 1976) involved complicated issues relating to standing and to how suburban municipalities should estimate needs. Initially, the Court accepted the City's arguments, in a judgement that might have meant that suburban municipalities could only receive CDBG money if they made substantial efforts to provide housing for lower-income people. After a rehearing, however (and the Supreme Court's denial of a writ of *certiorari*), the Court of Appeals reversed its decision. They were unable to trace the alleged injury to Hartford back to any unlawful action on the part of the defendant municipalities, argued that Hartford had insufficient interest in planning procedures of independent municipalities to bring a case, and found that Hartford had failed to demonstrate that relief would help. Thus the autonomy of the suburban municipalities was preserved, and the courts were unwilling to accede to wide-ranging remedies. (Under both the Act and the Equal Protection Clause, however, the courts agreed to hear a case regarding discriminatory intent against blacks by the Town of Manchester – another Hartford suburb – which decided in a referendum to withdraw its application for CDBG funds after four years: *Angell* v. *Zinsser*, 473 F Supp 488, 1979).

With regard to wide judicial relief, the Supreme Court gave little encouragement in *Hills* v. *Gautreaux*. It noted that under the 1974 Act, HUD does not need to get local government approval for projects but can deal directly with private developers. Nevertheless, Justice Stewart wrote that

> the local governmental units retain the right to comment on specific assistance proposals, to reject certain proposals that are inconsistent with the approved housing-assistance plans, and to require that zoning and other land use restrictions be adhered to by builders. (p. 808)

That Court's defence of local autonomy, until such time as State legislatures removed it, was apparently being maintained. But a District Court has recently imposed a wide-ranging remedy to proven discrimination (see T. A. Clark, 1982a, b). In *United States* v. *City of Parma* (494 F Supp 1049, 1980) HUD claimed, under the Fair Housing Act, that the City of Parma, the largest municipality in suburban Cleveland, had a long history of racial discrimination in its housing and planning policies. Five specific violations were cited: (1) the city council's failure to pass a resolution welcoming "all persons of good will" as residents; (2) persistent opposition to all public and low-income housing; (3) rejection of federally-subsidized low-income development; (4) refusal to submit an adequate HAP in the application for CDBG funds; and (5) the passage of density and building size ordinances intended to restrict low-income housing opportunities. The court ruled that policies could be found in violation of the Act" if there is a showing of a racially discriminatory effect, even absent of a racially discriminatory motive" (p. 1053). Further, the evidence of intent did not need to be blatant:

> a finding of intent cannot be limited to instances where decision-makers articulate

overtly bigoted opinions. Such would reward subtlety and camouflage . . . . Even though the overt public expression of bigotry has become unfashionable . . . racial intent can still be shown by a series of decisions *all* of which have had a segregative effect.

In the event, the Court was provided with extensive evidence of intent to exclude blacks from Parma, notably statements by the Mayor. In its defence, the City claimed that the absence of blacks from Parma reflected choice on behalf of blacks, who preferred to live elsewhere in the metropolitan area. The Court rejected the evidence of Parma's "academic expert" on this, writing in disbelief that

Parma would have this Court believe that blacks prefer the life of the ghetto with its attendant filth, degradation, and crime to the life of suburbia because they do not wish to live in white or integrated neighbourhoods. (p. 1061)

Instead it found that

The evidence shows that Parma's virtually all-white composition was created by pervasive acts of purposeful discrimination . . . . Every time Parma was confronted with a choice between decisions that would have an integrative or segregative effect, Parma chose the latter. The City of Parma consistently has made decisions which have perpetuated and reinforced its image as a city where blacks are not welcome. This is the very essence of a pattern and practice of racial discrimination. (p. 1097)

A remedy was required involving the construction of 133 low-income housing units each year (following a HUD opinion that the local need was for 2669 such units); an ex-judge was appointed to oversee implementation of the remedy. (An appeal to the Supreme Court was denied *certiorari* in May, 1982.)

The Parma decision is an important one with regard to the impact of local zoning and housing policies – especially if it is upheld at later appeals. It is also very important in its apparent outlawing – by a federal, not a State, court – of exclusionary zoning ordinances. For example, one of its ordinances requires 2·5 parking spaces per dwelling unit in apartment buildings. This inhibits the development of low-income housing. In addition, in November 1974 an ordinance was enacted – by the voters at a referendum – requiring voter approval at a referendum before any land-use ordinance (e.g. a zoning plan) can be changed. Again, this inhibits the development of low-income housing (for which there was currently no allowance in the zoning plan), because the developer has to gain voter approval for a zoning change. Finally, there is a specific requirement in the ordinances for a referendum on any proposal for subsidized low-income housing. The District Court found that all such ordinances formed part of the programme of racial exclusion practised by Parma:

The City of Parma cannot choose to make decisions on the basis of racial considerations. Actions which are typically lawful, such as a mandatory referendum on housing and zoning matters, a locality's decision not to apply for federal assistance in housing, and a community's refusal to promote low-income housing, lose that character when they are undertaken for a discriminatory purpose. (p. 1099)

Whether this indicates wholesale rejection of the defence of local autonomy
– as laid out in *James* v. *Valtierra* (p. 86), *Hills* v. *Gautreaux* (p. 161), *City
of Eastlake* v. *Forest City Enterprises* (p.86), *Acevedo* v. *Nassau County*
(p. 160), and *Village of Belle Terre* v. *Boraas* (p. 84) – is doubtful, because
of the clear evidence relating to racial intent in Parma. Only further judicial
interpretations will tell. Nevertheless, the *Parma* decision may stimulate a
new round of litigation (not necessarily, as in that case, led by the federal
government) seeking to break down the exclusive barriers of the "tight little
islands".

Although the *Parma, Gautreaux* and other opinions make clear the
requirement of local governments and their agencies to promote racial
integration, successful pursuit of this federally-required goal may not
necessarily act in favour of members of minority groups. In New York, the
City Housing Authority was redeveloping a district with a fairly equal
white:non-white racial balance. Its regulations required it to give first
priority in the selection of tenants for homes in the renewal project to those
who had been displaced. The result was that, because non-whites took up
the offers in greater proportions than whites, an integrated neighbourhood
was being replaced by a black ghetto, with a 4:1 balance of non-whites to
whites.

A case was brought that application of the Authority's regulations was
creating a segregated neighbourhood and thus violated the statutory duty –
under the 1968 Act – to foster racial integration. The Court of Appeals
agreed, thereby overturning a contrary decision by a District Court. The
latter had found that

> the affirmative duty to integrate public housing should not be given effect where it
> would deprive such (minority) groups of available and desirable housing.

But the Court of Appeals disagreed in *Otero* v. *New York City Housing
Authority*, 484 F2d 1122, 1973):

> Such a rule of thumb gives too little weight to Congress' desire to prevent segregated
> housing patterns and the ills which attend them. To allow housing officials to make
> decisions having the long range effect of increasing or maintaining racially segregated
> housing patterns merely because minority groups will gain an immediate benefit would
> render such persons willing, and perhaps unwitting, partners in the trend toward the
> ghettoization of our urban centers.... The purpose of racial integration is to benefit the
> community as a whole, not just certain of its members. (p. 1134)

And yet, until the *Parma* decision, the judicial respect for municipal
autonomy in the suburbs ensured that this last statement could not be put
into practice.

The impact of federal housing legislation

This recent activity suggests that both the federal government and the
Courts were only half-heartedly prepared to promote integration in the

suburbs and to enact remedies that would ensure it; only the Parma decision indicates a strong commitment, in the face of blatant racialism. However, not all commentators are convinced that even this is particularly effective, or that it will be pursued by later administrations. Certainly the 1974 Act extended the range of intervention, but Danielson points out the HUD's main sanctions related to grant programmes (for subsidized housing, urban renewal, etc.) that were of little interest to suburban governments. As he expressed it:

> Denying federal aid for what a community did not want was unlikely to produce changes in local policies. In suburban Baltimore County, for example, fear of blacks moving into federally-funded projects in white neighbourhoods led to the abolition of the local urban-renewal agency in a 1965 referendum. HUD responded by cutting off funds for urban renewal and subsidized housing, a move which was welcomed by those who wanted the county to have nothing to do with low-cost housing. (Danielson, 1976, p. 220)

And with regard to more recent activities, Lake and Winslow (1982) conclude that suburban integration is likely to come about in a small number of communities only (see also Lake, 1981).

A fully effective policy for opening-up the suburbs requires strong executive backing, Congressional support, and a substantial budget. In recent years, there has been little evidence of all three being used to make a concerted attack on the problem. Lamb (1978) argues that "responsibility for eliminating discrimination in housing ultimately rests with the President and the powerful enforcement bureaucracy at his disposal" (p. 630). He finds that recent Presidents have not been prepared to unleash that powerful bureaucracy. Nixon, for example, made contradictory statements on fair housing, among which was one supporting the Supreme Court's respect for local municipal autonomy (Lamb, 1978, p. 635), and he significantly reduced the funds available to HUD as part of his anti-inflation measures (see also Danielson, 1976, Ch. 8). During Ford's Presidency, the Housing and Community Development Act, 1974, the Home Mortgage Disclosure Act, 1975, and the Equal Credit Opportunity Act, 1974, became law, but little active pursuit of integration was undertaken. And in his election campaign, Carter made no clear indication of an intention to alter the Nixon-Ford policies, claiming that whereas discrimination in neighbourhood choice should be prevented so should racial integration forced by government action (Lamb, 1978, p. 649). And there is no evidence of a strong commitment by Reagan.

An important reason for the reluctance of the federal government to pursue integrated housing in the suburbs is, as with the State governments, the electoral issue. As Danielson (1976, pp. 200–201) points out:

> The insulation of federal officials from local pressures is relative rather than absolute; and few can afford to ignore local opposition which is widespread and vocal. By making grass-roots support essential for nomination and election, the decentralized American

party system insures the sensitivity of elected officials in the nation's capital to local concerns . . . federal officials are likely . . . to be cautious in instances where the majority is able to associate its interests with such traditional virtues as grass-roots democracy, local autonomy, and the protection of property values.

And these interests are likely to influence selection of nominees for the nation's senior judicial positions.

The federal government, school desegregation, and school district finance

With regard to school desegregation, the basic requirement of the federal government was not that it take the initiative in an area that the Supreme Court was unprepared to enter but rather that it provide the needed backing to ensure that the Court's remedies were complied with. As indicated in Chapter 5, during the Eisenhower Administration such backing was very largely absent. The Kennedy Administration fought to introduce Civil Rights legislation, and its agencies filed *amicus curiae** briefs supporting certain desegregation cases, but it was only under Johnson that the Civil Rights Act of 1964 was passed (Harvey, 1973). This outlawed racial discrimination in public places and facilities, thereby giving legislative support to the Supreme Court judgements. Title IV required school desegregation, provided federal assistance to school districts involved in the implementation of integration plans, and allowed the Attorney-General to sue in order to ensure desegregation if private persons could not do this effectively. The Act did not require busing in order to achieve racial balance in schools.

It was the sanctions laid out in the Civil Rights Act that gave the federal government its power to ensure compliance with the desegregation requirement. Under Title VI, discrimination on the grounds of race, colour and national origin was outlawed under any federal programme, and federal agencies were empowered to withdraw funds, as a last resort, from State and local agencies which failed to comply with this requirement. The Department of Health Education and Welfare (HEW) announced school desegregation guidelines in 1965 for all school districts wishing to receive federal financial assistance (see Wasby *et al.*, 1977), and these were upheld when challenged in the courts – *Singleton* v. *Jackson Municipal Separate School District*, 348 F2d 729, 1975, and *Price* v. *Davison Independent School District Board of Education*, 348 F2d 1010, 1975. In this way, the federal administration was able to speed-up desegregation, and by early 1966, 97 per cent of districts had complied with the guidelines, although by then only 16 per cent of black students were enrolled at the same schools as whites (Harvey, 1973, p. 175). The southern States tried to prevaricate, but the Courts accepted the HEW guidelines as the best means of achieving desegregation (in *United States* v. *Jefferson County Board of Education*, 372 F2d 836, 1966).

* An *amicus cureae* – friend of the court – is an individual (such as the Attorney-General) not directly involved in a case who files a brief, or is invited to, with the court in order to influence its decision.

Further backing to the HEW guidelines was given by the injection of major federal funding programmes under the Elementary and Secondary Education Act of 1965. This

> brought massive allotments and the possibility of a real "carrot" to bring about desegregation: if you want the money, desegregate, was the message. (Wasby *et al.*, 1977, p. 212)

Thus the incentive to desegregate was stimulated by the offer, to many relatively poor school districts especially, of large federal grants. The federal contribution to the school budget was only 8·8 per cent of total expenditure in 1979, however, compared to 7·4 per cent in 1969 (Ogden and Augenblick, 1980). The main shift has been the increase of State support – from 39·9 to 47·4 per cent of total expenditure, so it is State criteria that are much more important to local school boards.

On the issue of desegregation, the federal government and the Supreme Court were pursuing the same goals from the early 1960s on. With regard to school finance, they diverged somewhat, however, following the Court's decision in *San Antonio* v. *Rodriguez* (p. 130) and its own disagreement with the decisions in several State courts. The Elementary and Secondary Education Act (passed in 1965 and reauthorized in 1978) sought to reduce differentials – not simply to produce equality of opportunity but rather to prevent its funds being used to achieve it, by "levelling up" (Kirp, 1980). Title I of the Act provides for substantial aid to schools serving the "educationally disadvantaged". To be eligible for such aid, however, school districts must ensure that the potential recipient schools are comparable (i.e. spend as much per pupil) as non-recipient schools. Thus intra-district disparities are being removed and the recipient schools benefit from federal funds. The substantial differences are inter-district, however.

REFORM, SUBURBAN POWER AND THE SUPREME COURT'S IMPACT

In several places in this chapter, it has been pointed out that reform of many aspects of suburbia – especially the autonomy of its local governments – is unlikely to be achieved because it is politically unacceptable. The reason for this is quite simple – electoral arithmetic. The United States is increasingly a suburban nation. According to the 1980 Census, 40 per cent of the population lived in the suburbs of the 277 Standard Metropolitan Statistical Areas; 28 per cent lived in the inner cities, 2 per cent on the metropolitan fringes, and 30 per cent in non-metropolitan areas. Not all of these suburbanites – some 89 million – are necessarily opponents of local government reform for suburbia, but most almost certainly are, especially when the likely impact of reform on their tax bills is pointed out. Tax-cutting measures, such as California's Proposition 13 (see also Palaich *et al.*, 1980) get much of their support from the suburbs, and fiscal motives are central to the support for suburban fragmentation among its residents (Miller, 1981). Thus any representative of a suburban district, whether in the State or the federal legislature, will be wary of supporting a measure that threatens constituency interests. (Patterson (1976, p. 190) reports that legislators identify their constituencies as the main influence on their actions.)

The strength of the suburban lobby is bolstered by much business support. As indicated in Chapter 1, drawing on the work of scholars such as Harvey (1975a), the continued expansion of American suburbia is necessary to guarantee the success of a very wide range of businesses whose prosperity is tied up with providing either the physical infrastructure or the consumer durables on which suburban living is based – not to mention the many financial institutions whose solvency and speculative gains are derived from the success of these firms. Suburban expansion is not necessary to capitalist success, but once it has been established, the investment in it is such that any major diversion could require a substantial restructuring of the American economy and would probably generate a major medium-term dislocation of employment prospects. Thus the pro-suburban business lobby is a substantial one; it requires continued confidence in both support for suburban expansion and the desirability of suburbia in the market-place. Major changes in the social and economic morphology of suburbia could seriously jolt that confidence, so the business lobby works on State and federal legislatures to ensure that no such jolts take place.

The combination of electoral arithmetic and business interests is probably sufficient to ensure legislator reluctance to interfere with the economic, social and political structure of suburbia. But in recent decades the first of these factors has been bolstered by a series of Supreme Court decisions. These comprise what is widely known as the "reapportionment revolution" and probably rank second behind the desegregation decisions as the major extensions of the meaning of Equal Protection achieved by the Warren Court. Warren himself is quoted in several places as claiming it as the major achievement of his Court.

In the early 1960s, urban and suburban votes were devalued, whereas there was a bias towards rural votes. Elliott (1974, p. 101) reports that although each vote should have a weight of $1 \cdot 0$, in voting for the House of Representatives in 1964 urban votes had a value of $0 \cdot 95$, and suburban votes only $0 \cdot 83$, whereas the average value of a rural vote was $1 \cdot 08$. As a consequence – exacerbated by the greater electoral safety of rural seats (Johnston, 1980b) – the distribution of power in the House very much favoured the Representatives of rural areas: 14 of the 20 major committees were chaired by (Democrat) members for rural constituencies, and 16 of the ranking minority (Republican) members of those committees came from similar backgrounds. The same pattern held in most State Legislatures.

The reason for this pro-rural bias was malapportionment: constituencies in rural areas on average had fewer electors than did those in urban areas, which in turn were smaller than their counterparts in the rapidly growing suburban areas. In some cases, especially with regard to State Legislatures, this resulted from relatively benign neglect. Constituencies were infrequently redrawn, and population shifts away from the rural areas created the major differentials. But in most cases it was the result of political action (or intentional inaction) arranged to protect rural legislative power from the flow of population to other constituencies. In most States, redistricting was a political task undertaken by the Legislature (this included redistricting for the federal House). By creating smaller districts (in terms of electors) in the rural areas, the rural minority could maintain legislative majority. The extent of this malapportionment was indexed in a variety of ways, including:

(1) simple measures of the difference between the largest and the smallest district (in Georgia, for example, the largest Congressional District had a population of 823 680 in 1963, whereas the smallest contained 272 154: in Tennessee in 1962, the smallest district for the lower house of the State Legislature contained 2340 people and the largest 42 298);

(2) a population variance ratio, which is the ratio of the largest to the smallest district (the largest ratios in 1962 for State Legislatures were, for the lower houses, 827·5 in Vermont, and, for the upper houses, 422·5 in California: these figures and others below are taken from Dixon, 1968);

(3) the electoral percentage, which is the smallest percentage of the population that can elect a legislative majority – i.e. in a State divided into 100 districts, if 20 per cent of the population only live in the 51 smallest districts, the electoral percentage is 20 (in 1962, a majority of Nevada's Senate could be elected by only 8 per cent of the population, and in Connecticut, Florida and Vermont a majority of the House could be elected by 12 per cent); and

(4) the percentage deviations from the average electorate (in 1962 the maximum positive percentage deviations were 1991 for the Vermont House and 1432 for the Californian Senate; the maximum negative deviations were 97·9 for the Rhode Island House and 99·7 for the New Hampshire Senate).

All indicated that malapportionment was widespread. Electoral percentages exceeding 40 occurred in 10 States with respect to the House and 11 for the Senate, in 1962.

The extent of the malapportionment was widely recognized by academics and voters alike. But there was little they could do about it. The entrenched political interests in the State Legislatures were not going to redistrict their power away, and it was not in the interests of the federal House to try and insist on changes in the States. It had passed a Federal Reapportionment Act in 1911, which laid down standards of compactness, contiguity and population equality for redistricting, but when this was used to contest population inequality in 1932 the Supreme Court ruled (in *Wood* v. *Brown*, 287 US 1, 1932) that the Act had expired.

The Courts seemed no more likely to aid those seeking population equality in electoral districts than were the legislatures. In 1946, the Supreme Court (in *Colegrove* v. *Green*, 328 US 549, 1946) declined to hear a challenge relating to population inequalities in Illinois' Congressional Districts (a population variance ratio of 8·15). Writing for the 4:3 majority, Justice Frankfurter noted that the case had major political and party connotations, creating a "political thicket" that the Court should not enter; in his opinion "The remedy for unfairness in districting is to secure State legislatures that will apportion properly, or to invoke the ample powers of Congress" (p. 556).

All changed in 1962, when the Warren Court not only agreed to hear a malapportionment case, but ruled in favour of the challenge. By a 6:2 majority (in *Baker* v. *Carr*, 369 US 186, 1962) the Court ruled that mal-apportionment was "arbitrary and capricious state action, offensive to the Fourteenth Amendment" (p. 207). The decision provided no remedy, but set the precedent for future challenges, settlement of which might indicate reapportionment standards. Two years later, the basis of this standard was set: in *Wesberry* v. *Sanders* (376 US 1, 1964) the Supreme Court introduced the "one man, one vote" doctrine for Congressional districts ("as nearly as is practicable, one man's vote in a congressional election is to be worth as much as another's": p. 7), and in *Reynolds* v. *Sims* (377 US 533, 1964) it extended this doctrine to both houses of State Legislatures. "How equal is equal?" was still a question to be determined. In *Kirkpatrick* v. *Preisler* (394 US 526, 1969) and *Wells* v. *Rockefeller* (394 US 542, 1969) the Warren Court disallowed maximum deviations of 3·1 and 6·6 per cent, respectively. More recently (e.g. *Gaffney* v. *Cummings*, 412 US 736, 1973, and *White* v. *Regester*, 412 US 755, 1973) the Burger Court has been prepared to allow deviations of up to 10 per cent if a compelling purpose (such as minority representation) can be proved. The redistricting in the 1980s has produced a maximum percentage deviation of 2·96 for Congressional Districts (Grofman, 1982).

Full discussion of the "reapportionment revolution" is outside the brief of this book (see Dixon, 1968, for a detailed presentation of the early cases and Witt, 1979, for an outline of the full period – a full survey is Dodge and McCauley, 1982; for critical discussion see Elliott, 1974 and Berger, 1977). The important point here concerns the consequence of reapportionment – the redistribution of political power in favour of the suburbs. In 20 years, 1950–1970, the number of members of the House of Representatives sitting for rural constituencies declined from 198 (46 per cent of the total) to 136 (31 per cent: Lehne, 1972). In 1962, within the metropolitan majority, 106 (42 per cent) represented central city districts whereas 92 (36 per cent) represented suburban areas (the remainder represented mixed districts that crossed the city-suburb boundary). Twelve years later, 109 (36 per cent) of the 305 metropolitan districts were in the central cities, compared to 132 (43 per cent) in the suburbs (Lehne, 1975). By 1980, Lehne (1972) predicted, 46 per cent of all 435 Representatives would be sitting for suburban districts, as would 60 per cent in 2000. More properly, Lehne should have referred to 1982, the date of the first Congressional elections to be fought in districts defined using 1980 census data.

Suburban representatives are not a homogeneous block in terms of voting behaviour on all issues, as Lehne (1972, 1975) has demonstrated. But on issues relating to suburbia, they now present a formidable potential coalition (in the State legislatures as well as the federal House) that will almost certainly block any attempts to "open up" the suburbs and affect the social and political milieux of their constituents (not to mention their investments in property). Thus the likelihood of any major legislative initiative, or legislative support for executive initiatives, aimed at such change is remote. The business lobby and the distribution of population almost ensure that; the consequences of the Court-based reapportionment revolution make it a virtual certainty.

CONCLUSIONS

The Courts, and especially the Supreme Court since 1970, have been un-willing to use the Fourteenth Amendment to open up the suburbs in the face of exclusionary zoning and to provide equality of opportunity in education – except where clear racially discriminatory intent is proven. They have, in large measure, upheld the autonomy of local governments, especially municipalities and school districts, to act consistently with their interpreta-tions of local desires irrespective of the impact of these actions on the rest of the metropolitan area. And where, as in New Jersey, local autonomy has been constrained somewhat by court decisions and remedies, the impact has usually been but slight. Local government units are the creations of State governments, and so long as the administrations of those units either do not explicitly contravene the constitution or are not created so as to achieve unconstitutional ends, the Courts are not prepared to interfere with their activities. Thus, despite all the litigation of the past few decades, the pro-cesses of distancing via the creation of separate political territories, as described in Chapters 1 and 2, have continued largely unabated.

If the litigation has failed, then for those seeking to alter the morphology of suburbia alternative means must be found. The main one available – and the one to which activists have frequently been directed by the Courts – is legislative change, at both State and federal level. Initiatives have been taken, by representatives of deprived (usually urban) constituencies and by executive leaders (State Governors plus United States Presidents) with strong commitments to civil rights. Some of these have failed, in the face of opposition from representatives of other types of constituency, and some have been passed in modified form only, lacking the power to achieve major change. And some, when enacted, have been frustrated by the lack of administrative and legislative support, particularly in the provision of funds to support housing programmes for low- and middle-income families in the suburbs. Thus measures such as the federal Fair Housing Act and the Housing and Community Development Act, and State actions such as the Massachusetts "Anti-Snob" Law, have promised much but, as analyses of the 1980 census are now showing, have achieved little by the way of residential desegregation.

Why have these initiatives largely failed? The United States is, numerically, a suburban nation. And the residents of suburbia are in general white, middle class and affluent. These are the people who have traditionally held power, which has almost invariably been used to further their own interests. To do this, of course, may occasionally involve making concessions to other interests. Civil rights provide the best example of this, with concessions to blacks being yielded in order to maintain the legitimacy of the system as a whole, which makes the suburban affluent affluent. Suburban interests benefit from the protection of local autonomy and its use in the distancing processes. Suburban-dominated legislatures, plus others in which the suburban block is large and influential if not in the majority, are very unlikely to act against local autonomy in any meaningful way. Suburban local autonomy having been created and proved successful, it is now almost impossible to change it – because a majority of Americans are benefiting from that success, as are a large number of businesses.

Power, then, lies in the suburbs. It is bolstered by the decisions of the Supreme Court over the malapportionment cases, which have ensured that suburban representation is approximately equal to suburban population. From this, it is difficult to perceive any successful major challenge to present suburban practices. The legislatures will not act against suburban interests. Nor, it seems, will the Courts. (And, of course, the suburban majorities have control over the Courts, in the federal system indirectly through the President as nominator and the Senate, for the Supreme Court, as approver. In many of the States (see p. 69) they have control because judges are elected.) A similar situation existed with regard to reapportionment prior to 1962, of course, and it was only the readiness of a majority on the Warren Court to enter that "political thicket" that produced the major constitutional change. But will the Burger Court and its successors be prepared to enter another "political thicket", that of suburban political autonomy?

PART THREE

Conclusions

NINE

Summary

This book has been presented as a case study of the various uses of the political process in the manipulation of space for economic and social reasons. As such, the conclusions to be drawn relate to both the particular substantive issue and the more general concepts which the case study illustrates.

THE CONFLICTS THAT FAILED?

American metropolitan areas have very high levels of residential segregation. These reflect the operation of distancing processes which, it is argued, are general to capitalist societies based on the private ownership of property and the goal of individual accumulation of wealth. Institutions are deeply implicated in those processes, and are crucial to the creation and reproduction of spatial structures which both reflect and help to maintain socio-economic inequality (on this general theme of the role of institutions, see Flowerdew, 1982). The state is one of those institutions, and the guarantor of many others. In the United States, it has been used to assist in the creation and maintenance of residential segregation via the fragmented system of local governments in suburbia. Control of land use, of elementary and secondary education, and of the property-taxing power, has allowed the affluent to use political boundaries in the distancing process. The poor have been excluded from much of suburbia, whose governmental structure involves a series of "tight little islands with very strict immigration controls".

Most political processes generate conflicts, because they produce winners and losers; the latter seek to alter the situation, perhaps by changing the "rules of the game", whereas the former seek to preserve it. Arbitration is required and it is invariably provided by the state. The nature of the conflict is determined by the substantive issues. Its detailed course is predicated in the juridical context, the legal and institutional environment within which the conflict is pursued.

The conflicts over residential areas in American suburbia and the political element therein involve the search by the losers – those excluded from suburbia – for a way in, countered by the defence of those already firmly established there. The aim has been to "open up" the suburbs, ostensibly for all but in particular for the blacks who are underprivileged as a class within American society and whose access to the more desirable and pleasanter residential districts has been substantially restricted. Such a conflict is not a local one, for it involves general principles. Thus although local issues have, of necessity because of the juridical context, been the foci of the conflicts, these have been raised in those fora – the State and federal courts – where decisions on particular issues set precedents for all others of the same type. Thus representatives of distinct national groups (notably the NAACP) have been involved in promoting the litigation on behalf of all those they seek to represent, and they have used the United States Constitution, with its guarantee of certain, ill-specified, individual rights and freedoms as the document supporting most of their representations.

What, then, of that conflict? Have the original losers succeeded in removing the barriers erected by the political manipulation of space? Basically, the answer is that they have not, despite success in certain areas. If the basis of the conflict is taken as that of racial inequality, then even that success has to be doubted. Sitkoff (1981) notes that although the percentage of black students in the South attending desegregated schools increased from two in 1964 to 58 in 1970 – when President Nixon sought to restrain federal involvement in the integration process – in the cities of the country as a whole in 1980 over two-thirds of black students attended schools that were at least 90 per cent black. Certainly, the general quality of education for blacks has increased and the output is greater (in terms of years of schooling completed and qualifications obtained) but, on what to many of the protagonists was the crucial issue, "More black students attended segregated schools in 1980 than at the time of *Brown*" (p. 231).

The success with regard to school desegregation was achieved in the South, especially the rural South, and related to a particular educational system – the dual "separate but equal" schools. Elsewhere, the success was very limited. The gerrymandering of school catchment areas *within* school districts to promote racial segregation was outlawed, but the remedies proposed and their enforcement were insufficient to promote integration, and busing generated much hostility. As Sitkoff (1981, p. 208) argues:

> The success of the struggle for racial equality in the South accelerated aspirations but did nothing to improve the day-to-day lot of ghetto blacks. The panoply of court decisions, congressional acts, and executive orders failed to affect the subordinate status of blacks in the North. None of the . . . peaceful protest abolished filthy dope-ridden streets or inferior segregated schools . . . the more urban blacks sought change, the more apprehensive and resentful Northern whites became . . . when they felt their neighbourhood school or lily-white union threatened by the presence of blacks. The white backlash grew harsh. Resistance to open housing flared in every Northern city, as did opposition to funding the War on Poverty, to ending de facto school segregation.

Furthermore, the blacks lost the support of, and thus their confidence in, the Supreme Court following its restructuring with the Nixon appointments of 1969, 1970 and 1971. Under Chief Justice Warren, the decisions regarding "separate but equal" schools and voting rights had given the black population hope that what they saw as fundamental, Constitutionally-guaranteed rights would be upheld. But the Court had changed before the key issue, that of residential segregation, had been tackled. Thus, Sitkoff (1981, p. 233) claims:

> Despite court rulings and legislation outlawing racial discrimination in housing, such discrimination persisted. The index of residential segregation (for blacks) rose in nearly every American city between 1960 and 1980. Whites of every class continued to resist housing integration if it involved anything other than token numbers of blacks.

The reason for this key failure has been the lack of any ruling by the Supreme Court that overrides municipal autonomy in the control of land use, except where racial motives have been made explicit and no other compelling reason has been established. In general, the State Courts have followed this lead, and the federal and State Legislatures have been unwilling to invade the interests of the majority of their constituents – the white residents of suburbia. Thus even when federal laws have been enacted that seek to "open up the suburbs" – indirectly, via financial carrots, since the federal government cannot interfere directly with local government – these have generally been underfinanced, have lacked executive support since 1968, and have been emasculated by the decisions not only of the strict constructionist Supreme Court under Chief Justice Burger but also by many State Courts (whose judges are responding to the ideology of the, mainly suburban, constituents who elected them; see Clark, 1983, on a Californian judge who lost his elected position after a busing case).

Of course, not every suburb houses extremely affluent people only and not every urban black lives in the inner cities. In 1970, 3·6 million blacks lived in the suburbs of the defined SMSAs, and this figure had increased, largely through inmigration, to 4·6 million in 1978 (T. A. Clark, 1979, pp. 54–55). Some of those blacks who have moved to the suburbs have been enabled to do so because of increased prosperity. But many more are no better-off than their counterparts in the central cities. The suburbs that they occupy are old and low-income, either developed initially for the poor or filtered down as the housing depreciates. Such black suburbanites, according to T. A. Clark (1979, p. 57), are suburban by "statistical quirk" only; some are there because those are the places where subsidized housing accessible to blacks has been provided. The ghetto is expanding across the city-suburban boundary, therefore. Relatively few suburban municipalities are involved in this. In a study of New Jersey using 1970 Census data, Lake (1981; see also Lake and Cutter, 1980) found that only 93 of the 440 units in the suburbs there (mainly of either New York or Philadelphia) qualified as black concentrations, exceeding the State means of 11·4 per cent of the population who are black and 16·9 per cent of the public school enrolment who are black. These 93 were classified into six types:

(1) central-city spillover,
(2) dormitory,
(3) metropolitan rural,
(4) outer industrial,
(5) subsidized – concentrations of publicly-subsidized housing, and
(6) mixed.

Twenty-eight of the 93 were in type (3) and a further 32 in types (1) and (2). During the period 1971–1976, the most rapid growth in black school enrolment was in the central-city spillover suburbs (27·2 per cent, involving 51·2 per cent of the total increase of black students in the suburbs). The stereotype dormitory suburbs' enrolment grew by 14·2 per cent – at the same time experiencing a 20·4 per cent decline in their white school enrolments. In general, then, black suburbanization is merely the extension of the ghetto and the related invasion-succession processes across the central city border into the inner cities; it represents neither residential/school integration nor an "opening up of the suburbs".

Why did they fail?

The simple answer to this question is that the challengers in the various Court cases did not have the law and the Constitution on their side. Laws and Constitutions are usually imprecise documents, however, enunciating general principles that must be interpreted in particular situations. In many cases, the context in which they were enacted no longer exists; social and economic changes have created new environments, calling for new interpretations.

Laws and Constitutions are *texts*, therefore, to be interpreted by relevant individuals. In the present context the key text is the United States Constitution, especially the Fourteenth Amendment (the equal protection/due process clause). And the key individuals are the Justices of the Supreme Court, the final arbiters of the meaning of the Constitution and of federal legislation. Thus, the determinants of the outcome of the conflicts rest strongly on those key actors, the *higher managers*, on how they perceive their role in society, how they read the texts, and how they are influenced by the evidence and arguments presented to them. (The terminology of this paragraph is taken from Johnston (1983) where the argument is extended and exemplified further.)

As outlined in Chapter 4, there are two main theories of how the Supreme Court Justices should interpret their role. One argues that they should be activists, extending the meaning and use of the extant texts so as to fit the demands of the contemporary environment. The other argues a much more conservative position, that the texts should be interpreted only in the ways that were intended when they were written. Anything else involves the Justices rewriting the law, which is the proper task of the legislature, directly accountable to the electorate.

In the 1960s, it was the first of these theories that prevailed among the majority of the Justices then on the Court, producing the decisions relating to school desegregation and electoral reapportionment. Increasingly, however, the Justices' decisions were inconsistent with popular opinion and there was strong political pressure to revert to the more conservative, strict constructionist theory, withdrawing the Supreme Court from its active role in social policy-making. This was achieved in the early 1970s, when several vacancies in the Court allowed a President (Nixon) who supported the strict constructionist theory to appoint four Justices in tune with that ideology, thereby ensuring a majority in favour of judicial restraint rather than activism.

Apart from a brief interlude of a decade-and-a-half, therefore, the Supreme Court has been dominated by a theory of judicial action that favours restraint and by an ideology that both promotes the interests of private property owners and glorifies local democracy. With regard to many of the issues considered in this book, this ideology supports the concept of land-use planning that permits the retention and accumulation of wealth via the resources inherent in, and invested in, land (see Kirk, 1980). Involving the law in this makes it what McAuslan (1980, p. 270) describes as "a partisan participator in the struggle for control over power and resources and not a neutral referee policing the struggle".

Thus the failure has occurred because, at the time when the key elements of the conflict were brought before the Courts, the Justices were unsympathetic to the goal of residential desegregation and "opening up the suburbs". This implies that if the cases had been heard a decade earlier the decisions may have been different. Perhaps so, but, as the history of school desegregation shows, judicial attempts at major social change need strong executive and legislative support if they are to succeed. This may have been forthcoming before 1969, but after that — as the impact of various items of civil rights legislation shows — it is almost certain that judicial attempts to force spatial restructuring of metropolitan areas would have been frustrated. For the basic ideology relating to land, property, and their use in the United States has not changed. The Supreme Court may be a useful catalyst for change in that context, but this is doubtful. In any case, the composition of the Supreme Court at present and its likely composition for at least the next decade makes the prospect of any judicial challenge to the reigning ideology extremely unlikely. Nor are the State courts, especially those whose Judges are elected (by suburban majorities in most States with regard to the key courts — Appeals and Supreme), likely to oppose the ideology of the suburban majority.

And so the challenge has very largely failed. Suburbia remains the preserve of the middle-classes and above, except in its older and dilapidated portions. As local governments act to promote the social, economic, educational and fiscal interests of local residents and to frustrate the aspirations of would-be poorer immigrants, the State and federal legislatures have been unwilling to interefere with this situation. (In 1974, the United States Commission on Civil Rights recommended that no federal aid be allocated to metropolitan areas lacking a Metropolitan Housing Agency with "power to override various local and State laws and regulations, such as large-lot zoning ordnances" – p. 69. All other attempts at ensuring racial residential segregation had failed, according to the Commission. Perhaps not surprisingly, its solution has not been tried.)

The black strategy of using the Courts rather than the ballot box to stimulate change has failed. Of course, it is not only blacks who would like to live in the suburbs but cannot afford to. Poor whites would like to move there as well. But their hopes of ending exclusion have been even more frustrated by the Courts. Some small victories have been won by blacks, when they have been able to prove racial discrimination, but the Supreme Court has been entirely unwilling to accept that discrimination by wealth is unconstitutional (even when it has been shown that this is, in effect, discrimination by race too, which violates certain federal statutes, but not the Constitution). Some State Courts have required equality in terms of wealth, but only with respect to inter-district disparities in the financing of education (see, however, the argument of Scheingold, 1974, and Gambitta, 1981, that litigation, even though unsuccessful, places an issue on the legislative agenda). Desegregation by income is no closer than desegregation by race in the residential areas of American suburbs. Breaking down the exclusionary barriers because they are racially motivated might have promoted both. The failure to achieve racial entry on a large scale has removed most of the hope of achieving it for the poor.

THE QUESTION OF THE LOCAL STATE

Much of the discussion in Chapters 5–8 revolved around the functioning and decisions of local governments in the organization and government of suburbia. Most of the relevant Supreme Court decisions respected the autonomy of the local state, as a properly-constituted element of State government, and the Justices were unprepared to impose policies on local governments if neither they, nor the State legislatures which created them and to which they are responsible, were sympathetic to such policies. (The caveat, of course, was that the Justices would not sustain local government policies explicitly motivated with regard to race.) These findings have some relevance to the debate on the local state among geographers.

To some writers (e.g. Cockburn, 1977) the local state is indistinguishable from the central state; it has been created to further the goals of the latter and has no independence of action. Others provide less restrictive views, arguing that although the central state has ultimate control over the local state, the latter in effect has some freedom of action (see, for example, Short, 1982; Kirby, 1982). In the American context, both G. L. Clark (1981b) and Dear (1981) have argued that although the functional operation of the local state gives the impression of autonomy and response to local democratic pressure, in fact:

> the organizational and ideological contraints imposed upon the local state tend to minimize the impact that democratic politics could have on the local and national capitalist system . . . . The local state, the original basis for democracy, has become disenfranchised in the development of capitalism . . . its own legitimacy is dependent upon the national state . . . (and its) functions, although important in the reproduction of capital, are predetermined at the centre. (G. L. Clark, 1981b, pp. 126–128)

This conclusion clearly suggests that little can be gained from studying local states as independent entities. Dear (1981), however, notes that whereas the nature of the local state cannot be separated from that of the central state

> the local state has a distinctive spatial and functional constitution. In spatial terms, two aspects are worth particular research attention: urban and regional planning policies and outcomes; and the limits and functions of electoral politics. (p. 198)

Both of these aspects are central to the analyses of the case study reported here.

As Dear suggests, the relationship between local and central state has two components. The first relates to the independence of action allowed by the local state, given its existence. On this, Dear and Clark (1981) have postulated that local state autonomy is limited by the financial constraints imposed by the central state, so that local state autonomy is invariant within the territory of each central state. They tested these propositions against data from the State of Massachusetts, with particular reference to the City of Cambridge, and concluded that the fiscal controls – as operated through categorical grant programmes – give the central state a tight grip on local action.

From the materials presented here, this would appear to be an over-statement. Certainly some local governments are so dependent on financial allocations from State and federal authorities that they gear their operations towards maximizing income from those sources. But others, notably the most affluent, are not so tied. Some may decide to decline the proffered aid, so that they can retain freedom of action without strings. And others have been created in order to promote autonomy (as Miller's, 1981, work on California shows). In general, their rights to act in these ways have been upheld by the Courts.

The second component refers to the origins of those rights. Dear and Clark (1981, p. 1283) postulated that local state autonomy is severely constrained by constitutional and legislative arrangements, and demonstrated this with a comprehensive review of the sources of local authority. Their conclusion that "the local state has no inherent legal authority of power" (p. 1286) is clearly correct. Local states may be abolished or reformed by State legislatures (the central states in this context) with no right of appeal or redress. Nevertheless, given that they currently exist, the autonomy vested in them by the central state is substantial (even if constrained fiscally), and, as illustrated in this book, it has been upheld by the Courts. Indeed, to some commentators the Courts have extended that autonomy – notably in the decision on *Milliken* v. *Bradley* (p. 124) when a majority of the Supreme Court ruled that individual school districts could not be held responsible for the pattern of school segregation in the Detroit metropolitan area, despite the arguments of the minority that the State of Michigan, by its creation of those districts, was responsible. By this decision the Supreme Court extended the autonomy of existing local states, therefore, although other decisions, such as those in *Gomillion* (p. 100), *Emporia* and *Scotland Neck* (p. 113), did not allow the unrestricted creation of new local state units in order to gain autonomy in a particular sphere of action.

The local state has no independent existence, therefore. It can have powers revoked by superior bodies and its actions can be pruned drastically. Nevertheless, it is deeply engrained in American democratic ideology, and can be used to advance the interests of particular groups within society without much fear of interference from above. While this ideology prevails, and informs the theory of the local state employed by the judiciary, some independence of action is likely, especially if it is involved in advancing the interests of powerful groups in society. Small, suburban local states fulfil the wishes – democratically expressed – of local affluent populations with regard to both land-use planning and educational provision. Their ideological bulwark is a useful tool for those who seek to promote class interests in suburbia.

THE STATE AND THE POLITICAL MANIPULATION OF SPACE

All societies are dominated by their economic systems, the ways in which the processes of production and reproduction are organized. Associated with the economic system are social and political systems, and together all three are involved in the organization of space. Thus the geography of a society reflects its economic system, as mediated through the social and political systems and influenced by its physical environment. The operations of the economic system are, in turn, affected by its social and political manifestations.

Many societies in the contemporary world are classified as capitalist. These are characterized by a particular form of economic organization dominated by private property ownership, the accumulation of wealth by individuals, and the treatment of human labour as a commodity to be bought and sold in the market place. This economic system leads to a social system dominated by conflict between groups differentially located with regard to the labour market and the ownership of property and wealth, and a political system which operates to maintain those economic and social structures. Details of all three vary among societies, however, in part because of differences in the physical environment, in part because of the cultural context inherited from pre-capitalist economic systems, and in part because of different interpretations of how economy, society, policy and physical environment should be managed. Thus there are international variations in the nature of capitalism as a reality, but these are all built on the same base.

The geography of capitalist societies therefore reflects the way in which space has been organized in a particular cultural and physical context by local social and political institutions; understanding that geography involves combining an appreciation of the general processes or forces that operate in all capitalist societies with an analysis of their interpretation in the local context; each capitalist society has created a geography that is consistent with its operation within the world-economy of capitalism (Taylor, 1982); that geography then acts as a constraint on future actions, including the future organization of space. Just as societies are continually reproducing their social and political institutions, so they are continually reproducing their geographies. Each generation is slightly different from its predecessor, but continuity is a major element in change; significant alterations are strongly resisted, because they are likely to be against the vested interests of many members, especially the more powerful.

The study of suburbia in America must be set in this context. The United States is a capitalist society. Its social structure is predicted on class inequalities and its political institutions are dedicated to the protection of the status quo. With regard to its spatial organization of residential districts the extensive land area plus the strong ideology of individualism and private ownership of land developed during the colonial era have contributed to the construction of wide-flung, segregated suburbia as both desirable living arrangements and a profitable form of capital investment. Further, an early strong belief in local administration and a fear of centralization stimulated the creation of a local state system with relatively few constraints. This local state system, as illustrated here, has been used in the creation of a particular geography of suburban America. (Throughout the book, it has been argued that distancing and residential segregation are inevitable elements of a capitalist society. This is probably not so. In certain circumstances, perhaps reflecting difficult physical environments, social distancing may not be accompanied by physical distancing.)

As with the other institutions and creations of capitalist society, once a particular geography has been created there are strong forces for its preservation. On the other hand, there are usually forces for change too. In the present context, those forces for change have been led by the black population, a group whose racial characteristics (and stereotypes about them) have been used to create an under-privileged class. Social conflict is general in capitalist societies, but each has its own reflecting its particular structures and institutions. Mediation in such conflict is invariably undertaken by the state, part of the political environment, created in order to protect the economic system. In general, therefore, the mediation favours the status quo, although occasional reforms may be allowed in order to maintain social cohesion (and thus preserve the core elements of the status quo).

Much of the present book has been concerned with one particular form of mediation in the United States – that undertaken by the courts in the context of the Constitution. Overall it is clear that the decisions taken have favoured the status quo. This is not because the decision-makers – the Supreme Court Justices and the judges of the various other courts – have analysed each case in the terms outlined here. Rather, it comes about because the ideology within which they operate, into which they have been socialized, and which they demonstrated to their patrons/constituents, strongly favours the status quo. The justices have been put there, and the texts that they have to interpret have been written, to provide stability, to mediate conflicts in such a way that the strength of the system is enhanced.

The Justices have some freedom in their decision-making, as indicated by the cases discussed here. They may promote certain changes, in the belief that these are both right and in the long-term interests of the society. Thus they may assist in the generation of new structures, new institutions, and new geographies as society reproduces itself. But the conservative forces are strong, and the innovations usually only minor. As demonstrated here, despite a great deal of litigation, and even more academic analysis, the geography of suburban America has not been fundamentally altered in recent decades as a result of judicial decisions.

The conflicts discussed here are integral elements of capitalist society, in which the major issues concern the allocation of society's "goods" and "bads" – which in spatial terms are expressed as positive and negative externalities. These conflicts do not threaten, nor even approach, the nature of capitalism itself. The protaganists are seeking to improve their relative status within the capitalist system whereas the defenders are working to maintain relatively privileged positions. However, the conflicts are resolved, the solutions are likely to have at most a minimal influence on the path of American capitalism (though not necessarily on the allocation of success and failure as that path is followed). All capitalist societies are characterized

by inequalities in the allocation of rewards and by conflicts over that allocation. In most such societies, space is manipulated to protect the positions of
those who have benefited from the allocation. As a result, there is conflict
over the manipulation of space, resolution of which stimulates further
manipulation. All the while the capitalist system continues to function –
with some sectors gaining ground and others losing, with some individuals
winning more rewards, and so on. Its geography is being recreated continually, in ways peculiar to its institutional structure erected to maintain that
capitalist system.

IN SUMMARY

This book has contributed to the literature of human geography in two ways.
First, the details of its case study illustrate how conflict over aspects of
residential segregation has been organized and mediated in the United
States. It is a contribution to the human geography of that country.
Secondly, interpretation of the case study material has aided in the understanding of the general forces that operate in contemporary capitalist
societies, and which have been realized in a particular form in the United
States. All the world is not the United States of America, and geographers
are becoming increasingly wary – much more so than in the recent past –
about generalizing from the American experience. Generalizations can be
drawn, or at least suggested, not based on the empirical details of the
geography of the United States but about the general processes that buttress
the particulars of that geography. Progress in geographical understanding
must first separate, and then reintegrate, the immanently local from the
configurational general.

Finally, this book has illustrated the thesis advanced by several authors
that one cannot have an autonomous discipline of human geography (see
Eyles and Lee, 1982; Eliot Hurst, 1980). One can take a geographical
viewpoint within the social sciences, emphasizing the study of particular –
usually spatial – aspects of a society. But that geographical viewpoint cannot
be isolated, for a full understanding of spatial organization requires investigation of many aspects of economic, social and political organization. Thus
integration of human geography with the social sciences may involve
studies with a geographical focus considering work from viewpoints rarely
covered by geographers. One of these is law (see Teitz, 1978), the study of
which is integral to the understanding of the organization of a class-based
society (Collins, 1982), including the residential mosaic of its suburbs.
Thus this case study not only illuminates the understanding of American
suburbia through an exploration of the interrelationships between
immanent and configurational forces in capitalist society, it also introduces
human geographers to an important, unfortunately ignored, subject matter.

References

Adams, J. S. and Brown, K. M. (1976). Public school goals and parochial school attendance in twenty American cities. *In* "Urban Policymaking and Metropolitan Dynamics" (J. S. Adams, ed.), pp. 219–256. Ballinger, Cambridge, Mass.

Andersen, W. R. (1979). School finance litigation – the styles of judicial intervention. *Washington Law Review* **55**, 137–173.

Andersen, W. R. (1982). State school finance litigation. *The Urban Lawyer* **14**, 583–601.

Anon (1978). Developments in the law-zoning. *Harvard Law Review* **91**, 1427–1708.

Ashton, P. J. (1978). The political economy of suburban development. *In* "Marxism and the Metropolis" (W. K. Tabb and L. Sawers, eds), pp. 64–89. Oxford University Press, New York.

Babcock, R. F. and Bosselman, F. P. (1973). "Exclusionary Zoning, Land Use Regulation and Housing in the 1970s". Praeger, New York.

Baratz, J. C. (1975a). Court decisions and educational change: a case history of the DC public schools. *Journal of Law and Education* **4**, 63–80.

Baratz, J. C. (1975b). "A Quest for Equal Educational Opportunity in a Major Urban School District: The Case of Washington, D.C." Education Policy Research Institute, Washington D.C.

Barlow, M. H. (1981). "Spatial Dimensions of Urban Government". John Wiley, Chichester.

Bass, J. (1981). "Unlikely Heroes". Simon and Schuster, New York.

Baum, L. (1981). "The Supreme Court". Congressional Quarterly Press, Washington D.C.

Bell, C. and Newby, H. (1976). Community, communication, class and community action: the social sources of the new urban politics. *In* "Social Areas in Cities" (D. T. Herbert and R. J. Johnston, eds), Vol. 2, pp. 189–208. John Wiley, Chichester.

Bennett, R. J. (1980). "The Geography of Public Finance". Methuen, London.

Berger, R. (1977). "Government by Judiciary". Harvard University Press, Cambridge, Mass.

Berry, B. J. L. (1979). "The Open Housing Question". Ballinger, Cambridge, Mass.

Berry, B. J. L. *et al.* (1976). "Chicago: Transformations of an Urban System". Ballinger, Cambridge, Mass.

Bigger, R. and Kitchin, J. D. (1952). "Metropolitan Los Angeles: A Study of Integration". The Haynes Foundation, Los Angeles.

Bisgaier, C. (1977). Notes on implementation *In* "After Mount Laurel: The New Suburban Zoning" (J. G. Rose and R. E. Rothman, eds) pp. 139–149. Center for Urban Policy Research, Rutgers University, New Brunswick, NJ.

Boal, F. W. (1976). Ethnic residential segregation. *In* "Social Areas in Cities" (D. T. Herbert and R. J. Johnston, eds), Vol. 1, pp. 41–80. John Wiley, Chichester.

Bossert, S. T. (1978). Education in urban society. *In* "Handbook of Contemporary Urban Life" (D. Street and Associates), pp. 288–318. Jossey-Bass, San Francisco.

Boyle, J. and Jacobs, D. (1982). The intracity distribution of services: a multivariate analysis. *American Political Science Review* **76**, 371–379.

Bryce, H. J. and Martin, E. (1976). The quality of cities with black mayors *In* "Urban Governance and Minorities" (H. J. Bryce, ed.), pp. 30–54. Praeger, New York.

Burnett, A. D. (1981). The distribution of local political outputs and outcomes in British and North American cities. *In* "Political Studies from Spatial Perspectives" (A. D. Burnett and P. J. Taylor, eds) pp. 201–236. John Wiley, Chichester.

Campbell, A. K. and Dollenmayer, J. A. (1975). Governance in a metropolitan society. *In* "Metropolitan America in Contemporary Perspective" (A. H. Hawley and V. P. Rock, eds), pp. 355–396. Halsted Press, New York.

Carroll, P. N. and Noble, D. W. (1977). "The Free and the Unfree". Penguin, New York.

Casstevens, T. W. (1965). "Politics, Housing and Race Relations: The Defeat of Berkeley's Fair Housing Ordinance". Institute of Governmental Studies, University of California, Berkeley.

Castells, M. (1977). "The Urban Question". Edward Arnold, London.

Checkoway, B. (1980). Large builders, federal housing programmes and postwar suburbanization. *International Journal of Urban and Regional Research* **4**, 21–45.

Cingranelli, D. L. (1982). The costs of service equalization: standards of service equity and their impacts on municipal budgets. *In* "The Politics of Urban Services" (R. C. Rich, ed.), pp. 157–170. D. C. Heath, Lexington.

Clark, G. L. (1981a). Law, the state, and the spatial integration of the United States *Environment and Planning A* **13**, 1197–1227.

Clark, G. L. (1981b). Democracy and the capitalist state: towards a critique of the Tiebout hypothesis. *In* "Political Studies from Spatial Perspectives" (A. D. Burnett and P. J. Taylor, eds), pp. 111–129. John Wiley, Chichester.

Clark, T. A. (1979). "Blacks in Suburbs: A National Perspective". Center for Urban Policy Research, Rutgers University, New Brunswick, NJ.

Clark, T. A. (1982a). Federal initiatives promoting the dispersal of low-income housing in suburbs: a commentary on recent legislation and litigation. *The Professional Geographer* **34**, 136–146.

Clark, T. A. (1982b). Race, class, and suburban housing discrimination: alternative judicial standards of proof and relief. *Urban Geography* **2**, 327–338.

Clark, W. A. V. (1980). Residential mobility and neighborhood change: some implications for racial residential segregation. *Urban Geography* **1**, 95–117.

Clark, W. A. V. (1981a). The social scientist as expert witness. *Environment and Planning A* **13**, 1468–1471.

Clark, W. A. V. (1982). Judicial intervention as policy: impacts on population distribution and redistribution in urban areas in the United States. *Population Research and Policy Review* **1**, 79–100.

Clark, W. A. V. (1984). Judicial intervention, busing and local residential change. *In* "Geography and the Urban Environment" (D. T. Herbert and R. J. Johnston, eds), Vol. 7. John Wiley, Chichester.

Clotfelter, C. T. (1975a). Spatial rearrangement and the Tiebout hypothesis: the case of school desegregation. *Southern Economic Journal* **42**, 263–271.

Clotfelter, C. T. (1975b). The effect of school desegregation in housing prices. *Review of Economics and Statistics* **57**, 446–451.

Clotfelter, C. T. (1978). The implications of "resegregation" for judicially imposed school desegregation remedies. *Vanderbilt Law Review* **31**, 829–854.

Cockburn, C. (1977). "The Local State". Pluto Press, London.

Collins, H. (1982). "Marxism and Law". Oxford University Press, Oxford.

Collison, P. (1963). "The Cutteslowe Walls". Faber and Faber, London.

Cox, A. (1976). "The Role of the Supreme Court in American Government". Oxford University Press. Oxford.

Cox, K. R. (1973). "Conflict, Power and Politics in the City". McGraw Hill, New York.

Cox, K. R. (1978). Local interests and urban political processes in market societies. *In* "Urbanization and Conflict in Market Societies" (K. R. Cox, ed.), pp. 94–108. Maaroufa Press, Chicago.

Cox, K. R. (1979). "Location and Public Problems". Blackwell, Oxford.

Cox, K. R. (1981). Capitalism and conflict around the communal living space. *In* "Urbanization and Urban Planning in Capitalist Society" (M. Dear and A. Scott, eds), pp. 431–456. Methuen, London.

Cox, K. R. (1983). Residential mobility, neighbourhood activism, and neighbourhood problems. *Political Geography Quarterly* 2, 99–118.

Cox, K. R. and Johnston, R. J. (eds) (1982). "Conflict, Politics and the Urban Scene". Longman, London.

Cox, K. R. and McCarthy, J. J. (1980). Neighborhood activism in the American city: behavioral relationships and evaluation. *Urban Geography* 1, 22–38.

Cox, K. R. and McCarthy, J. J. (1982). Neighborhood activism as a politics of turf: a critical evaluation. *In* "Conflict, Politics and the Urban Scene" (K. R. Cox and R. J. Johnston, eds), pp. 196–219. Longman, London.

Cox, K. R. and Nartowicz, F. Z. (1980). Jurisdictional fragmentation in the American metropolis: alternative perspectives. *International Journal of Urban and Regional Research* 4, 196–211.

Daly, M. T. (1982). "Sydney Boom Sydney Bust". George Allen and Unwin, Sydney.

Danielson, M. N. (1976). "The Politics of Exclusion". Columbia University Press, New York.

Danielson, M. N., Hersey A. M. and Bayne, J. M. (1977). "One Nation, So Many Governments". D. C. Heath, Lexington.

Dear, M. J. (1981). A theory of the local state *In* "Political Studies from Spatial Perspectives" (A. D. Burnett and P. J. Taylor, eds), pp. 183–200. John Wiley, Chichester.

Dear, M. J. and Clark, G. L. (1981). Dimensions of local state autonomy. *Environment and Planning A* 13, 1277–1294.

Dear, M. and Long, J. (1978). Community strategies in locational conflict. *In* "Urbanization and Conflict in Market Societies" (K. R. Cox, ed.), pp. 113–127. Maaroufa Press, Chicago.

Delafons, J. (1969). "Land Use Controls in the U.S.A." The M.I.T. Press, Cambridge, Mass.

Dentler, R. A. and Scott, M. B. (1980). "Schools on Trial". Abt. Associates, Cambridge, Mass.

Dixon, R. G. (1968). "Democratic Representation: Reapportionment in Law and Politics". Oxford University Press, New York.

Dodge, J. F. and McCauley, P. B. (1982). Reapportionment: a survey of the practicality of voting equality. *University of Pittsburg Law Review* 43, 527–599.

Dolbeare, K. N. (1969). Who uses the State trial courts? *In* "The Politics of Local Justice" (J. R. Klonoski and R. L. Mendelsohn, eds). Little, Brown, Boston.

Doucet, M. J. (1982). Urban land development in nineteenth century North America. *Journal of Urban History* 8, 399–342.

Dunleavy, P. (1980). "Urban Political Analysis". Macmillan, London.

Dye, T. R. (1969). "Politics in States and Communities". Prentice-Hall, Englewood Cliffs, NJ.

Edelman, S. (1980). The segregative impact of changing demographics upon school districts subject to court-ordered desegregation. *George Washington Law Review* 49, 100–122.

Eliot Hurst, M. E. (1980). Geography, social science and society: towards a de-definition. *Australian Geographical Studies* 18, 3–21.

Elliott, W. E.Y. (1974). "The Rise of Guardian Democracy". Harvard University Press, Cambridge, Mass.

Ely, J. H. (1980). "Democracy and Distrust". Harvard University Press, Cambridge.

Exline, C. H. (1978). "Impacts of Growth Control Legislation on Two Suburban Counties: Marin and Sonoma Counties". PhD Thesis, University of California, Berkeley.

Eyles, J. D. (1974). Social theory and social geography. In "Progress in Geography 6" (C. Board *et al.*, eds), pp. 27–88. Edward Arnold, London.

Eyles, J. D. and Lee, R. (1982). Human geography in explanation. *Transactions, Institute of British Geographers* NS 7, 117–122.

Fessler, D. W. and Haar, C. M. (1971). Beyond the wrong side of the tracks: municipal services in the interstices of procedure. *Harvard Civil Rights – Civil Liberties Law Review* 6, 442–465.

Flowerdew, R. T. N. (ed.) (1982). "Institutions and Geographical Patterns". Croom Helm, London.

Fox, C. A. (1981). A tentative guide to the American Law Institute's proposed model land development code. *In* "The Land Use Awakening" (R. H. Freilich and E. O. Stuhler, eds), pp. 81–102. American Bar Association, Chicago.

Fox, K. (1977). "Better City Government". Temple University Press, Philadelphia.

Freilich, R. H. (1981). Fasano v. Board of County Commissioners of Washington County: is rezoning an administrative or legislative function? *In* "The Land Use Awakening" (R. H. Freilich and E. O. Stuhler, eds), pp. 75–80. American Bar Association, Chicago.

Frey, W. H. (1979a). White flight and central-city loss. *Environment and Planning A* 11, 129–147.

Frey, W. H. (1979b). Central city white flight: racial and nonracial causes. *American Sociological Review* 44, 425–448.

Gaeta, N. M. (1982). Solutions to the school finance inequities posed by the *Levittown* decision. *The Urban Lawyer* 14, 603–617.

Gambitta, R. A. L. (1981). Litigation, judicial deference, and policy change. *In* "Governing Through Courts" (R. A. L. Gambitta *et al.*, eds), pp. 259–282. Sage Publications, Beverly Hills.

Gambitta, R. A. L., May, M. L. and Foster, J. C. (eds) (1981). "Governing Through Courts". Sage Publications, Beverly Hills.

Gordon, D. M. (1978). Capitalist development and the history of American cities. *In* "Marxism and the Metropolis" (W. K. Tabb and L. Sawers, eds), pp. 25–63. Oxford University Press, New York.

Gorham, W. and Glazer, N. (1976). Introduction and overview. *In* "The Urban Predicament" (W. Gorham and N. Glazer, eds), pp. 1–34. The Urban Institute, Washington, D.C.

Grofman, B. (1982). Reformers, politicians and the courts. *Political Geography Quarterly* 1, 303–316.

Hall, F. W. (1977a). An orientation to Mount Laurel. *In* "After Mount Laurel: The New Suburban Zoning" (J. G. Rose and R. E. Rothman, eds), pp. 3–13. Center for Urban Policy Research, Rutgers University, New Brunswick, NJ.

Hall, F. W. (1977b). A review of the Mount Laurel decision. *In* "After Mount Laurel: The New Suburban Zoning" (J. G. Rose and R. E. Rothman, eds), pp. 39–45. Center for Urban Policy Research, Rutgers University, New Brunswick, NJ.

Hallman, H. W. (1977). "Small and Large Together: Governing the Metropolis". Sage Publications, Beverly Hills.

Halpern, S. C. and Lamb, C. M. (eds) (1982). "Supreme Court Activism and Restraint". D. C. Heath, Lexington, Mass.

Harrison, R. S. (1982). The effects of exclusionary zoning and residential segregation on urban-service distributors. *In* "The Politics of Urban Public Services" (R. C. Rich, ed.), pp. 83–99. D. C. Heath, Lexington, Mass.

Hartshorn, T. A. (1980). "Interpreting the City". Harper and Row, New York.

Harvey, D. (1975a). Class structure in a capitalist society and the theory of residential differentiation. *In* "Processes in Physical and Human Geography: Bristol Essays" (R.

Peel, M. Chisholm, and P. Haggett, eds), pp. 354–369. Heinemann, London.

Harvey, D. (1975b). The political economy of urbanization in advance capitalist societies. *In* "The Social Economy of Cities" pp. 119–163. Sage Publications, Beverley Hills.

Harvey, D. (1978a). The urban process under capitalism: A framework for analysis. *International Journal of Urban and Regional Research* **2**, 101–132.

Harvey, D. (1978b). Labor, capital, and class struggle around the built environment in advanced capitalist societies. *In* "Urbanization and Conflict in Market Societies" (K. R. Cox, ed.), pp. 9–37. Maaroufa Press, Chicago.

Harvey, J. C. (1973). "Black Civil Rights During the Johnson Administration". University and College Press of Mississippi, Jackson.

Hawley, W. D. (ed.) (1981). "Effective School Desegregation". Sage Publications, Beverly Hills.

Heck, E. V. (1981). Civil liberties voting patterns in the Burger Court, 1975–78. *Western Political Quarterly* **34**, 193–202.

Heins, M. (1977). Housing remedies in school desegregation cases: the view from Indianapolis. *Harvard Civil Rights – Civil Liberties Law Review* **12**, 649–691.

Herr, J. P. (1982). Metropolitan political fragmentation and conflict in the location of commercial facilities. *In* "Conflict, Politics and the Urban Scene" (K. R. Cox and R. J. Johnston, eds), pp. 28–44. Longman, London.

Hill, R. E. (1974). Separate and unequal: governmental inequality in the metropolis. *American Political Science Review* **68**, 1557–1568.

Hirsch, F. (1977). "The Social Limits to Growth". Routledge and Kegan Paul, London.

Hirschman, A. O. (1970). "Exit, Voice and Loyalty". Harvard University Press, Cambridge.

Hirschman, A. O. (1980). Exit, Voice, and Loyalty: further reflections and a survey of recent contributions. *Milbank Memorial Fund Quarterly* **58**, 431–453.

Hodder-Williams, R. (1980). "The Politics of the Supreme Court". George Allen and Unwin, London.

Honey, R. D. (1976). Metropolitan governance. *In* "Urban Policymaking and Metropolitan Dynamics", (J. S. Adams, ed.) pp. 425–462. Ballinger, Cambridge Mass.

Hooker, C. P. (1978). Issues in school desegregation litigation. *In* "The Courts and Education" (C. P. Hooker, ed.), pp. 84–115. University of Chicago Press, Chicago.

Hornby, D. B. and Holmes, G. W. (1972). Equalization of resources within school districts. *Virginia Law Review* **58**, 1119–1156.

Horowitz, D. L. (1977). "The Courts and Social Policy". The Brookings Institution, Washington D.C.

Hulbary, W. E. and Walker, T. G. (1980). The Supreme Court selection process: Presidential motivations and judicial performance. *Western Political Quarterly* **33**, 185–196.

Jackson, H. E. (1971). Discrimination and busing: the Denver School Board Election of May 1969. *Rocky Mountain Social Science Journal* **8**, 101–108.

James, F. J. and Hughes, J. W. (1973). "Modelling State Growth: New Jersey 1980". Center for Urban Policy Research, Rutgers University, Brunswick NJ.

James F. J. and Windsor, O. D. (1976). Fiscal zoning, fiscal reforms, and exclusionary land use controls. *Journal, American Institute of Planners* **42**, 130–141.

Janelle, D. G. and Millward, H. A. (1970). Locational conflict patterns and urban ecological structure. *Tijdschrift voor Economische en Sociale Geografie* **67**, 102–113.

Jenkins, M. A. and Shepherd, J. W. (1972). Decentralizing high school administration in Detroit: an evaluation of alternative strategies of control. *Economic Geography* **48**, 95–106.

Jessop, B. (1978). Capitalism and democracy: the best possible shell. *In* "Power and the State" (G. Littlejohn, B. Smart, J. Wakeford and N. Yuvel-Davis, eds), pp. 10–51. Croom Helm, London.

Jessop, B. (1982). "The Capitalist State". Martin Robertson, Oxford.

Johnston, R. J. (1971). "Urban Residential Patterns". G. Bell and Sons, London.

Johnston, R. J. (1980a). "City and Society". Penguin, London.

Johnston, R. J. (1980b). "The Geography of Federal Spending in the United States" John Wiley, London.

Johnston, R. J. (1981). The state and the study of social geography. *In* "Social Interaction and Ethnic Segregation" (P. Jackson and S. J. Smith, eds), pp. 205–222. Academic Press, London.

Johnston, R. J. (1982a). "Geography and the State". Macmillan, London.

Johnston, R. J. (1982b). "The American Urban System". St. Martin's Press, New York.

Johnston, R. J. (1982c). Voice as a strategy in locational conflict. *In* "Conflict, Politics and the Urban Scene" (K. R. Cox and R. J. Johnston, eds), pp. 111–126. Longman, London.

Johnston, R. J. (1983). Texts and higher managers: judges, bureaucrats and the political organization of space. *Political Geography Quarterly* 2, 3–20.

Jorgensen, P. V. (1981). Tearing down the walls: the federal challenge to exclusionary land use laws. *The Urban Lawyer* 13, 201–231.

Jud, G. D. (1980). The effects of zoning on single-family residential property values: Charlotte, North Carolina. *Land Economics* 56, 142–154.

Judd, D. R. (1979). "The Politics of American Cities". Little, Brown and Co., Boston.

Kantrowicz, N. (1981). Ethnic segregation: social reality and academic myth. *In* "Ethnic Segregation in Cities" (C. Peach, V. Robinson and S. Smith, eds), pp. 43–60. Croom Helm, London.

Kay, R. S. (1981). The Equal Protection Clause in the Supreme Court 1873–1903. *Buffalo Land Review* 29, 667–725.

Kellogg, C. V. (1967). "N.A.A.C.P." Johns Hopkins University Press, Baltimore.

Kirby, A. M. (1982). The external relations of the local state in Britain: some empirical examples. *In* "Conflict, Politics and the Urban Scene" (K. R. Cox and R. J. Johnston, eds), pp. 88–106. Longman, London.

Kirk, G. (1980). "Urban Planning in a Capitalist Society". Croom Helm, London.

Kirp, D. L. (1980). Law, politics, and equal educational opportunity: the limits of judicial reform. *In* "Education Finance and Organization Research Perspectives for the Future" (C. S. Benson *et al.*, eds), pp. 13–34. National Institute of Education, Washington D.C.

Kluger, R. (1976). "Simple Justice". Alfred A. Knopf, New York.

King, P. E. (1979). Exclusionary zoning and open housing: a brief judicial history. *Geographical Review* 69, 459–469.

Knickman, J. R. and Reschovsky, A. (1980). The implementation of school finance reform. *Policy Sciences* 12, 301–315.

Knox, P. L. (1982). Residential structure, facility location and patterns of accessibility. *In* "Conflict, Politics, and the Urban Scene" (K. R. Cox and R. J. Johnston, eds), pp. 62–87. Longman, London.

Knox, P. L. and Cullen, J. (1981). Planners as urban managers: an exploration of the attitudes and self-images of senior British planners. *Environment and Planning A* 13, 885–898.

Krefetz, S. P. (1979). Low- and moderate-income housing in the suburbs: the Massachusetts "anti-snob zoning" law experience. *Policy Studies Journal* 8, 288–299.

Lake, R. W. (1981). "The New Suburbanites: Race and Housing in the Suburbs". Centre for Urban Policy Research, Rutgers University, New Brunswick, NJ.

Lake, R. W. and Cutter, S. C. (1980). A typology of black suburbanization in New Jersey since 1970. *Geographical Review* 70, 167–181.

Lake, R. W. and Winslow, J. (1982). Integration management: municipal constraints on residential mobility. *Urban Geography* 2, 311–326.

Lamb, C. M. (1978). Presidential fair housing policies: political and legal trends. *Cumberland Law Review* 8, 619–660.

Lamb, C. M. and Lustig, M. S. (1979). The Burger Court, exclusionary zoning, and the activist-restraint debate. *University of Pittsburgh Law Journal* **40**, 169–226.

Lawyer's Committee for Civil Rights Under Law (1980). "Update on State-wide School Finance Cases". The Committee, Washington D.C.

Lehne, R. (1972). Population change and Congressional representation. *In* "Governance and Population: The Governmental Implications of Population Change" (A. E. Keir Nash, ed.), pp. 83–98. Commission on Population Growth and the American Future: Research Report IV, Washington D.C.

Lehne, R. (1975). Suburban foundations of the new Congress. *Annals, American Academy of Political and Social Science* **422**, 141–151.

Ley, D. (1974). "The Black Inner City as Frontier Outpost". Association of American Geographers, Washington D.C.

Ley, D. and Mercer, J. H. (1980). Locational conflict and the politics of consumption. *Economic Geography* **56**, 89–109.

Lineberry, R. L. (1977). "Equality and Urban Policy". Sage Publications, Beverly Hills.

Listokin, D., Kerlach, L. and Cybiner, B. (1974). "Zoning – Exclusionary Zoning: A Selected Bibliography". Council of Planning Librarians, Exchange Bibliography 684, Monticello, Illinois.

Lord, J. D. (1975). School busing and white abandonment of public schools. *Southeastern Geographer* **15**, 81–92.

Lord, J. D. (1977). "Spatial Perspectives on School Desegregation and Busing". Commission on College Geography, Association of American Geographers, Washington D.C.

Lord, J. D. and Catau, J. C. (1976). School desegregation, busing and suburban migration. *Urban Education* **11**, 275–294.

Lord, J. D. and Catau, J. C. (1977). School desegregation policy and intra-school district migration. *Social Science Quarterly* **57**, 784–796.

Lord, J. D. and Catau, J. C. (1981). The school desegregation–resegregation scenario. *Urban Affairs Quarterly* **16**, 369–376.

Lupu, I. C. (1979). Untangling the strands of the Fourteenth Amendment. *Michigan Law Review* **77**, 981–1077.

McAuslan, P. (1980). "The Ideologies of Planning Law". Pergamon, Oxford.

McCarthy, J. J. (1981). Research on neighbourhood activism: review, critique and alternatives. *South African Geographical Journal* **63**, 107–131.

Macmanus, S. A. (1978). "Revenue Patterns in U.S. Cities and Suburbs". Praeger, New York.

Mandel, A. S. (1975). "Resource Distribution Inside School Districts". Lexington Books, Lexington.

Mandelker, D. R. (1977). Racial discrimination and exclusionary zoning: a perspective on Arlington Heights. *Texas Law Review* **55**, 1217–1253.

Manley, R. E. (1978). Litigation and metropolitan integration. *The Urban Lawyer* **10**, 73–118.

Mann, M. S. (1976). "The Right to Housing". Praeger, New York.

Marans, R. W. and Rodgers, W. (1975). Toward an understanding of community satisfaction. *In* "Metropolitan America in Contemporary Perspective" (A. H. Hawley and V. P. Bock, eds), pp. 299–352. Halsted Press, New York.

Marchand, B. (1982). Dialectical analysis of value: the example of Los Angeles. *In* "A Search for Common Ground" (P. Gould and G. Olsson, eds), pp. 232–251. Pion, London.

Markusen, A. R. (1978). Class and urban social expenditure: a marxist theory of metropolitan government. *In* "Marxism and the Metropolis" (W. K. Tabb and L. Sawers, eds), pp. 90–112. Oxford University Press, New York.

Marshall, T. (1968). The continuing challenge of the Fourteenth Amendment. *Georgia Law Review* **3**, 1–10.

Mendelson, W. (1972). From Warren to Burger: the rise and decline of substantive equal protection. *American Political Science Review* **66**, 1226–1233.

Mercer, J. H. and Hultquist, J. (1976). National progress toward housing and urban renewal goals. *In* "Urban Policymaking and Metropolitan Dynamics" (J. S. Adams, ed.), pp. 101–162. Ballinger, Cambridge, Mass.

Merget, A. E. and Berger, R. A. (1982). Equity as a decision rule in local services. *In* "Analyzing Urban-Service Distributions" (R. C. Rich, ed.), pp. 21–44. D. C. Heath, Lexington.

Miller, B. A. (1977). Proof of racially discriminatory purpose under the Equal Protection Clause. *Harvard Civil Rights-Civil Liberties Law Review* **12**, 725–770.

Miller, G. J. (1981). "Cities by Contract: The Politics of Municipal Incorporation" The M.I.T. Press, Cambridge, Mass.

Moskowitz, D. H. (1977). "Exclusionary Zoning Litigation". Ballinger, Cambridge, Mass.

Muller, P. O. (1981). "Contemporary Suburban America". Prentice-Hall, Englewood Cliffs.

Neenan, W. B. (1972). "Political Economy of Urban Areas". Markham, Chicago.

Nelson, H. J. (1952). The Vernon area, California: a study of the political factor in urban geography. *Annals, Association of American Geographers* **42**, 171–191.

Ogden, A. and Augenblick, J. (1980). "School Finance Reform in the States: 1980". Education Commission of the States, Denver.

O'Donnell, D. E. (1980). The inequitable burden of school desegregation remedies: the effect of shifts in Supreme Court decisions in the Buffalo school desegregation case. *Buffalo Law Review* **29**, 729–758.

Orbell, J. M. and Uno, T. (1972). A theory of neighborhood problem-solving: political action vs residential mobility. *American Political Science Review* **66**, 471–489.

Orfield, G. (1978). If wishes were houses then busing could stop. *The Urban Review* **10**, 108–124.

Palm, R. (1981). "The Geography of American Cities". Oxford University Press, New York.

Patterson, S. C. (1976). American State Legislatures and public policy. *In* "Politics in the American States" (H. Jacob and K. N. Vines, eds), third edition, pp. 135–195. Little Brown and Co., Boston.

Pearlman, K. (1978). The closing door: the Supreme Court and residential segregation. *American Institute of Planners' Journal* **45**, 158–169.

Peltason, J. (1971). "Fifty-Eight Lonely Men". University of Illinois Press, Urbana.

Peterson, G. E. (1976). Finance. *In* "The Urban Predicament" (W. Gorham and N. Glazer, eds), pp. 35–118. The Urban Institute, Washington

Polyviou, P. G. (1980). "The Equal Protection of the Laws". Duckworth, London.

Poole, M. A. and Boal, F. W. (1973). Religious residential segregation in Belfast in mid-1969. *In* "Social Patterns in Cities" (B. D. Clark and M. B. Gleave, eds), pp. 1–40. Institute of British Geographers, London.

Popper, F. J. (1981). "The Politics of Land-Use Reform". University of Wisconsin Press, Madison.

Radford, J. P. (1981). The social geography of the nineteenth century US city. *In* "Geography and the Urban Environment" (D. T. Herbert and R. J. Johnston, eds), Vol. 4, pp. 257–294. John Wiley, Chichester.

Raffel, J. A. (1977). Political dilemmas of busing. *Urban Education* **11**, 375–395.

Ratner, G. M. (1973). Inter-neighbourhood denials of equal protection in the provision of municipal services. *Harvard Civil Rights-Civil Liberties Law Review* **4**, 1–63.

Read, F. T. (1977). Judicial evolution of the law of school integration since *Brown v. Board of Education*. *In* "The Courts, Social Science and School Desegregation" (B. Levin and W. D. Hawley, eds), pp. 7–49. Transaction Books, New Brunswick, NJ.

Reagan, M. (1972). "The New Federalism". Oxford University Press, New York.

Redwine, S. (1981). Busing across district lines: the ambiguous legacy of *Milliken v. Bradley*. *Houston Law Review* **18**, 585–609.

Rees, P. H. (1979). "Residential Patterns in American Cities 1960". Department of Geography Research Paper 189, University of Chicago, Chicago.

Regal, D. W. (1976). Metropolitan desegregation: buttressing the barrier of *Milliken* v. *Bradley. Brooklyn Law Review* **43**, 507–522.

Reynolds, D. R. (1976). Progress towards achieving efficient and responsive spatial-political systems in urban America. *In* "Urban Policymaking and Metropolitan Dynamics" (J. S. Adams, ed.), pp. 463–538. Ballinger, Cambridge, Mass.

Rice, B R. (1977). "Progressive Cities". University of Texas Press, Austin.

Rice, R. L. (1968). Residential segregation by law, 1910–1917. *Journal of Southern History* **34**, 179–199.

Rich, R. C. (ed.) (1982a). "The Politics of Urban Public Services". D. C. Heath, Lexington, Mass.

Rich, R. C. (ed.) (1982b). "Analyzing Urban-Service Distributions. D. C. Heath, Lexington, Mass.

Robson, B. T. (1969). "Urban Analysis". Cambridge University Press, Cambridge.

Robson, B. T. (1982). The Bodley barricade. *In* "Conflict, Politics and the Urban Scene" (K. R. Cox and R. J. Johnston, eds), pp. 45–61. Longman, London.

Rose, H. M. (1971). "The Black Ghetto". McGraw Hill, New York.

Rose, J. G. (1977a). *Oakwood at Madison*: a tactical retreat by the New Jersey Supreme Court to preserve the *Mount Laurel* principle. *In* "After Mount Laurel: The New Suburban Zoning" (J. G. Rose, and R. E. Rothman, eds), pp. 222–229. Center for Urban Policy Research, Rutgers University, New Brunswick, NJ.

Rose, J. G. (1977b). After the recent New Jersey Supreme Court decisions: what is the status of suburban zoning? *In* "After Mount Laurel: The New Suburban Zoning" (J. G. Rose and R. E. Rothman, eds), pp. 241–253. Center for Urban Policy Research, Rutgers University, New Brunswick, NJ.

Rose, J. G. (1979). Myths and misconceptions of exclusionary zoning litigation. *Real Estate Law Journal* **8**, 99–124.

Ros, J. G. and Levin, M. R. (1977). What is a "developing municipality"? *In* "After Mount Laurel: The New Suburban Zoning" (J. G. Rose and R. E. Rothman, eds), pp. 46–71. Center for Urban Policy Research, Rutgers University, New Brunswick.

Rose, J. G. and Rothman, R. E. (eds) (1977). "After Mount Laurel: The New Suburban Zoning". Center for Urban Policy Research, Rutgers University, New Brunswick, NJ.

Rosen, P. L. (1972). "The Supreme Court and Social Science". University of Illinois Press, Urbana.

Rossum, R. A. (1979). The rise and fall of equalization litigation. *State Government.*

Sagalyn, L. B. and Sternleib, G. (1973). "Zoning and Housing Costs." Centre for Urban Policy Research, Rutgers University, New Brunswick, NJ.

Sager, L. G. (1969). Tight little islands: exclusionary zoning, equal protection, and the indigent. *Stanford Law Review* **21**, 767–800.

Sager, L. G. (1978). Insular majorities unabated. *Harvard Law Review* **91**, 1373–1475.

Salih, K. (1972). "Judicial Relief and Differential Provision of Public Goods". Discussion Paper 20, Research on Conflict in Locational Decisions, Department of Regional Science, University of Pennsylvania, Philadelphia.

Saunders, P. (1980). "Urban Politics". Penguin, London.

Scheingold, S. A. (1974). "The Politics of Rights". Yale University Press, New Haven, Conn.

Schwartz, S. I. *et al.* (1979). "The Effect of Growth Management on New Housing Prices: Petaluma, California. Institute of Governmental Affairs, University of California. Davis.

Sennett, R. (1973). "The Uses of Disorder". Penguin Books, London.

Shlay, A. B. and Rossi, P. H. (1981a). Keeping up the neighborhood: estimating net effects of zoning. *American Sociological Review* **46**, 703–719.

Shlay, A. B. and Rossi, P. H. (1981b). Putting politics into urban ecology: estimating net effects of zoning. *In* "Urban Policy Analysis" (T. N. Clark, ed.), pp. 256–286. Sage Publications, Beverly Hills.

Short, J. R. (1982). "An Introduction to Political Geography". Routledge and Kegan Paul, London.

Simmie, J. M. (1981). "Power, Property and Corporation". Macmillan, London.

Simon, J. F. (1973). "In His Own Image: The Supreme Court v. Richard Nixon's America". D. McKay, New York.

Sinclair, R. and Thompson, B. (1976). "Detroit". Ballinger, Cambridge, Mass.

Sitkoff, H. (1981). "The Struggle for Black Equality 1954–1980". Hill and Wang, New York.

Slonim, M. and Lowe, J. H. (1979). Judicial review of laws enacted by popular vote. *Washington Law Review* **55**, 175–209.

Smith, C. J. (1980). Neighbourhood effects on mental health. *In* "Geography and the Urban Environment" (D. T. Herbert and R. J. Johnston, eds), Vol. 5, pp. 363–416. John Wiley, Chichester.

Spaeth, H. J. (1979). "Supreme Court Policy Making". W. H. Freeman, San Francisco.

Spaeth, H. J. and Teger, S. H. (1982). Activism and restraint: a cloak for the Justices' policy preferences. *In* "Supreme Court Activism and Restraint" (S. C. Halpern and C. M. Lamb, eds), pp. 277–302. D. C. Heath, Lexington, Mass.

Spain, D. (1979). "Reasons for Intrametropolitan Mobility: Are Schools a Key Issue?" Population Division, U.S. Bureau of the Census.

Stengel, L. F. (1980). School finance in Pennsylvania: judicial response, legislative responsibility. *University of Pittsburgh Law Review* **41**, 715–734.

Stetzer, D. G. (1975). "Special Districts in Cook County". Research Paper 169, Department of Geography, University of Chicago, Chicago.

Stiefel, L. and Berne, R. (1981). The equity effects of State school finance reforms. *Policy Sciences* **13**, 75–98.

Strong, A. L. (1981). Land as a public good: an idea whose time has come again. *In* "The Land Use Policy Debate in the United States" (J. I. de Neufville, ed.), pp. 217–232. Plenum Press, New York.

Suttles, G. D. (1967). "The Social Order of the Slum". University of Chicago Press, Chicago.

Suttles, G. D. (1972). "The Social Construction of Communities". University of Chicago Press, Chicago.

Taeuber, K. E. (1968). The effect of income redistribution on racial residential segregation. *Urban Affairs Quarterly* **3**, 5–14.

Taeuber, K. E. *et al.* (1981). A demographic perspective on school desegregation in the U.S.A. *In* "Ethnic Segregation in Cities" (C. Peach, V. Robinson and S. Smith eds), pp. 83–108. Croom Helm, London.

Taper, B. (1962). "Gomillion versus Lightfoot". McGraw Hill, New York.

Tate, C. N. (1981). Personal attribute models of the voting behaviour of U.S. Supreme Court Justices: liberalism in civil liberties and economics decisions, 1946–1978. *American Political Science Review* **75**, 355–367.

Taylor, P. J. (1978). Political geography. *Progress in Human Geography* **1**, 130–135.

Taylor, P. J. (1982). A materialist framework for political geography. *Transactions, Institute of British Geographers* NS **7**, 15–34.

Teaford, J. C. (1979). "City and Suburb: The Political Fragmentation of Metropolitan America, 1850–1970". Johns Hopkins University Press, Baltimore.

Teitz, M. B. (1978). Law as a variable in urban and regional analysis. *Papers, Regional Science Association* **41**, 29–42.

Tiebout, C. M. (1956). A pure theory of local expenditure. *Journal of Political Economy* **64**, 416–424.

Timms, D. W. G. (1971). "The Urban Mosaic". Cambridge University Press, Cambridge.

Tull, S. I. (1969). "Zoned America". Grossman, New York.

Tyler, R. S. (1979). School desegregation litigation in the Supreme Court. *Emory Law Journal* **28**, 985–1032.

Vines, K. N. and Jacob, H. (1976). State courts and public policy. *In* "Politics in the American States" (H. Jacob and K. N. Vines, eds), third edition, pp. 242–266. Little Brown and Co., Boston.

Von der Heyde, A. C. (1977). Constitutional law-zoning: proof of intent required to establish discrimination. *Rutgers Law Review* **30**, 1283–1317.

Vose, C. E. (1959). "Caucasians Only". University of California Press, Berkeley and Los Angeles.

Walker, R. A. (1978). The transformation of urban structure in the nineteenth century and the beginnings of suburbanization. *In* "Urbanization and Conflict in Market Societies" (K. R. Cox, ed.), pp. 165–211. Maaroufa, Chicago.

Walker, R. A. (1981). A theory of suburbanization: capitalism and the construction of urban space in the United States. *In* "Urbanization and Urban Planning in Capitalist Society" (M. J. Dear and A. J. Scott, eds), pp. 383–430 Methuen, London.

Walsh, C. M. (1976). Alternatives to *Warth* v. *Seldin*: the potential resident challenges of an exclusionary zoning scheme. *Urban Law Annual* **11**, 223, 256.

Ward, D. (1971). "Cities and Immigrants". Oxford University Press, New York.

Wasby, S. L., D'Amato, A. A. and Metrailer, R. (1977). "Desegregation from Brown to Alexander". Southern Illinois University Press, Carbondale.

Weaver, C. R. (1972). The Minnesota approach to solving urban fiscal disparity. *State Government* **45**, 100–105.

White, M. J. (1975). Fiscal zoning in fragmented metropolitan areas. *In* "Fiscal Zoning and Land Use Controls" (E. S. Mills and W. S. Oates, eds), pp. 31–100. DC Heath, Lexington.

Whiteman, J. (1983). Deconstructing the Tiebout hypothesis. *Environment and Planning. D: Society and Space* **1**, 339–354.

Williams, N. (1950). Racial zoning again. *The American City* **65**, (November), 137.

Williams, O. P. *et al.* (1965). "Suburban Differences and Metropolitan Policies". University of Pennsylvania Press, Philadelphia.

Windsor, D. (1979). "Fiscal Zoning in Suburban Communities". Lexington Books, Lexington.

Witt, E. (ed.) (1979). "Congressional Quarterly's Guide to the U.S. Supreme Court". Congressional Quarterly Press, Washington D.C.

Wolch, J. R. and Gabriel, S. A. (1981). Urban housing prices and land development behavior of the local state. *Environment and Planning A* **13**, 1253–1272.

Wolf, E. P. (1981). "Trial and Error". Wayne State University Press, Detroit.

Wolfson, D. K. (1977). Exclusionary zoning and timed growth: resolving the issue after Mount Laurel. *Rutgers Law Review* **30**, 1237–1259.

Woodward, B. and Armstrong, S. (1979). "The Brethren: Inside the Supreme Court". Simon and Schuster, New York.

Woodward, C. V. (1955). "The Strange Career of Jim Crow". Oxford University Press, New York.

Zech, C. E. (1980). Fiscal effects of urban zoning. *Urban Affairs Quarterly* **16**, 49–58.

Zeigler, D. J. and Brunn, S. D. (1980). Geopolitical fragmentation and the pattern of growth and need. *In* "The American Metropolitan System" (S. D. Brunn and J. A. Wheeler, eds), pp. 77–92. V. H. Winston, Washington.

Zimmerman, J. F. (1979). The metropolitan governance maze in the United States. *Urban Law and Policy* **2**, 265–284.

Subject Index

Index of Cases Cited